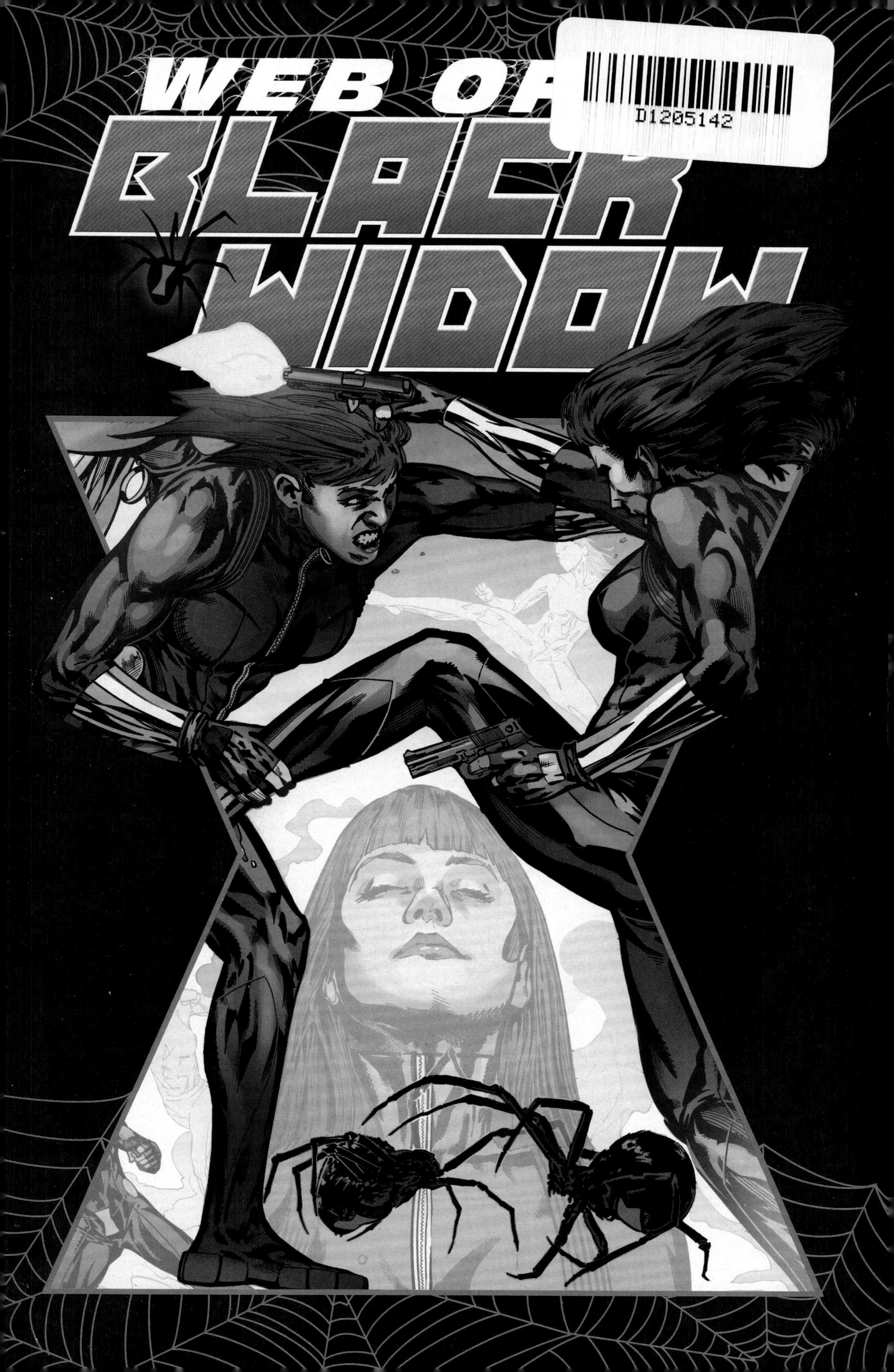
WEB O
BLACK
WIDOW

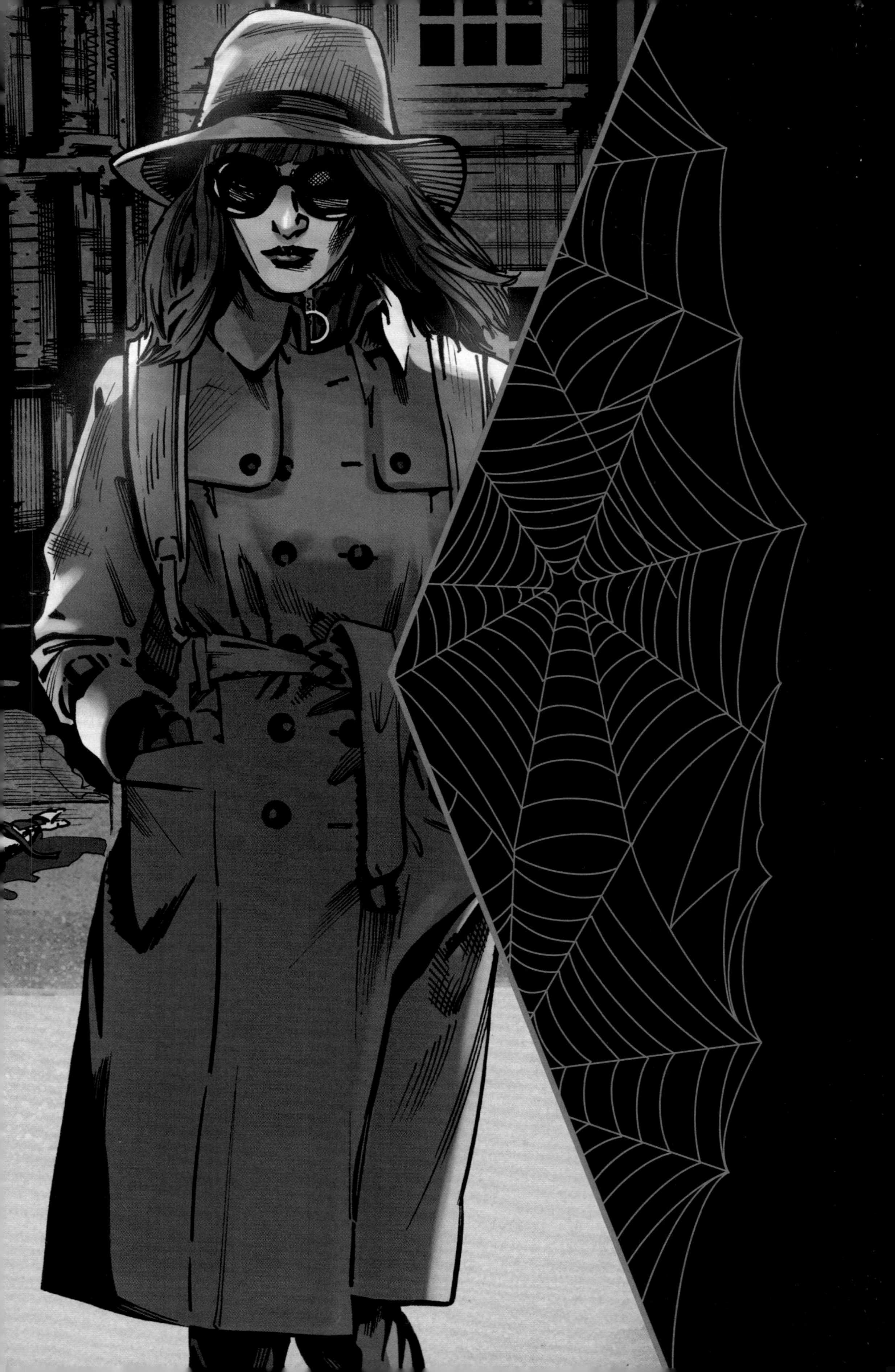

Natasha Romanoff, A.K.A. THE BLACK WIDOW, is an ex-KGB assassin trained in the notorious Red Room. She turned her back on Russia and joined the Avengers years ago, but the path to atonement is long, and there's still red in her ledger. Recently she was killed and resurrected as a clone with implanted memories. Now the past is coming back to her...and it's out for vengeance.

WEB OF BLACK WIDOW

WRITER
Jody Houser

ARTIST
Stephen Mooney

COLOR ARTIST
Tríona Farrell

LETTERER
VC's Cory Petit

COVER ART
Junggeun Yoon

EDITOR
Sarah Brunstad

EXECUTIVE EDITOR
Tom Brevoort

COLLECTION EDITOR **Jennifer Grünwald**
ASSISTANT MANAGING EDITOR **Maia Loy**
ASSISTANT EDITOR **Caitlin O'Connell**
EDITOR, SPECIAL PROJECTS **Mark D. Beazley**

VP PRODUCTION & SPECIAL PROJECTS **Jeff Youngquist**
BOOK DESIGNER **Adam Del Re**
SVP PRINT, SALES & MARKETING **David Gabriel**
EDITOR IN CHIEF **C.B. Cebulski**

THE WEB OF BLACK WIDOW. Contains material originally published in magazine form as THE WEB OF BLACK WIDOW (2019) #1-5. First printing 2019. ISBN 978-1-302-92007-4. Published by MARVEL WORLDWIDE, INC., a subsidiary of MARVEL ENTERTAINMENT, LLC. OFFICE OF PUBLICATION: 1290 Avenue of the Americas, New York, NY 10104. © 2019 MARVEL No similarity between any of the names, characters, persons, and/or institutions in this magazine with those of any living or dead person or institution is intended, and any such similarity which may exist is purely coincidental. **Printed in Canada.** KEVIN FEIGE, Chief Creative Officer; DAN BUCKLEY, President, Marvel Entertainment; JOHN NEE, Publisher; JOE QUESADA, EVP & Creative Director; TOM BREVOORT, SVP of Publishing; DAVID BOGART, Associate Publisher & SVP of Talent Affairs; Publishing & Partnership; DAVID GABRIEL, VP of Print & Digital Publishing; JEFF YOUNGQUIST, VP of Production & Special Projects; DAN CARR, Executive Director of Publishing Technology; ALEX MORALES, Director of Publishing Operations; DAN EDINGTON, Managing Editor; SUSAN CRESPI, Production Manager; STAN LEE, Chairman Emeritus. For information regarding advertising in Marvel Comics or on Marvel.com, please contact Vit DeBellis, Custom Solutions & Integrated Advertising Manager, at vdebellis@marvel.com. For Marvel subscription inquiries, please call 888-511-5480. **Manufactured between 12/27/2019 and 1/28/2020 by SOLISCO PRINTERS, SCOTT, QC, CANADA.**

10 9 8 7 6 5 4 3 2 1

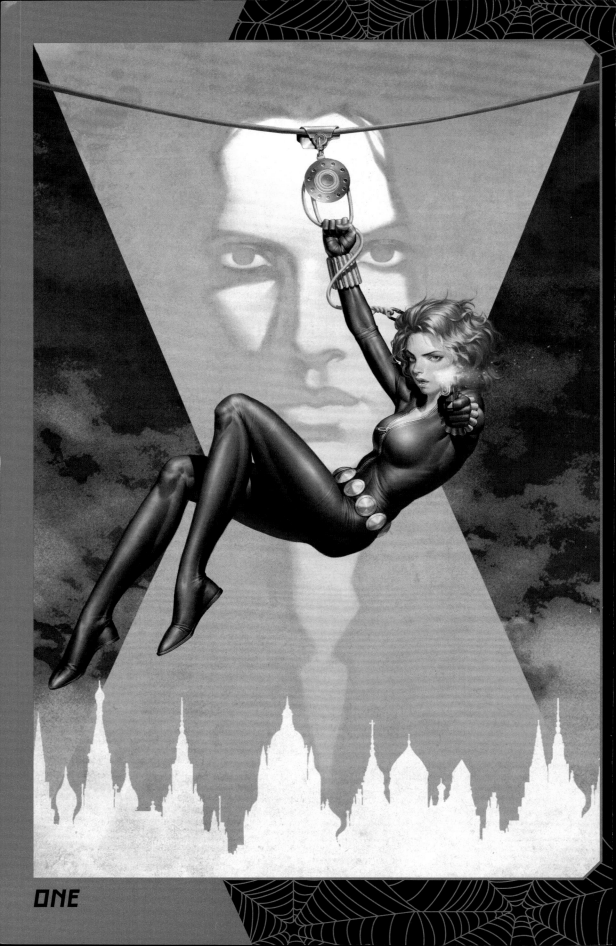

ONE

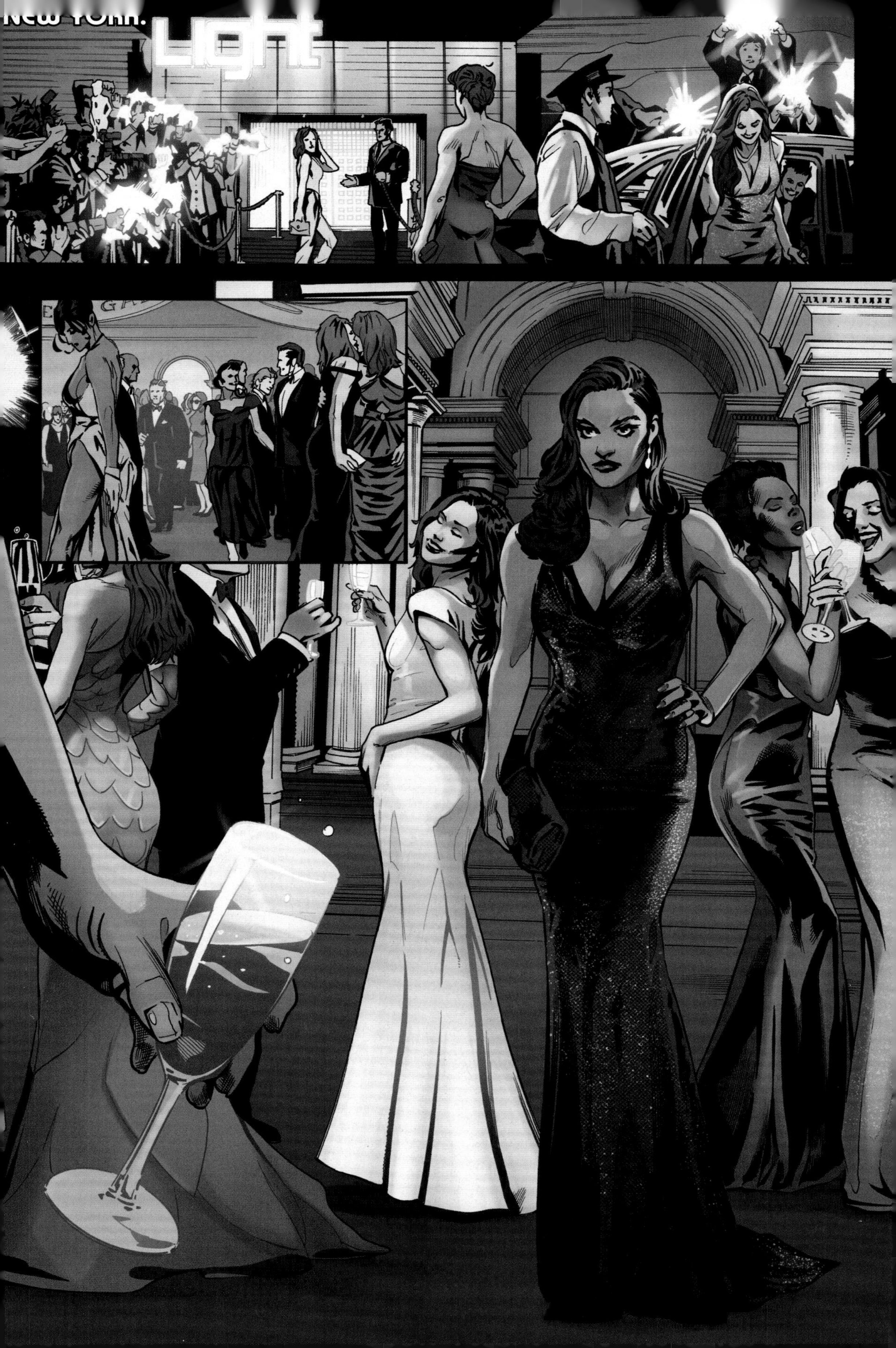
New York.
Light

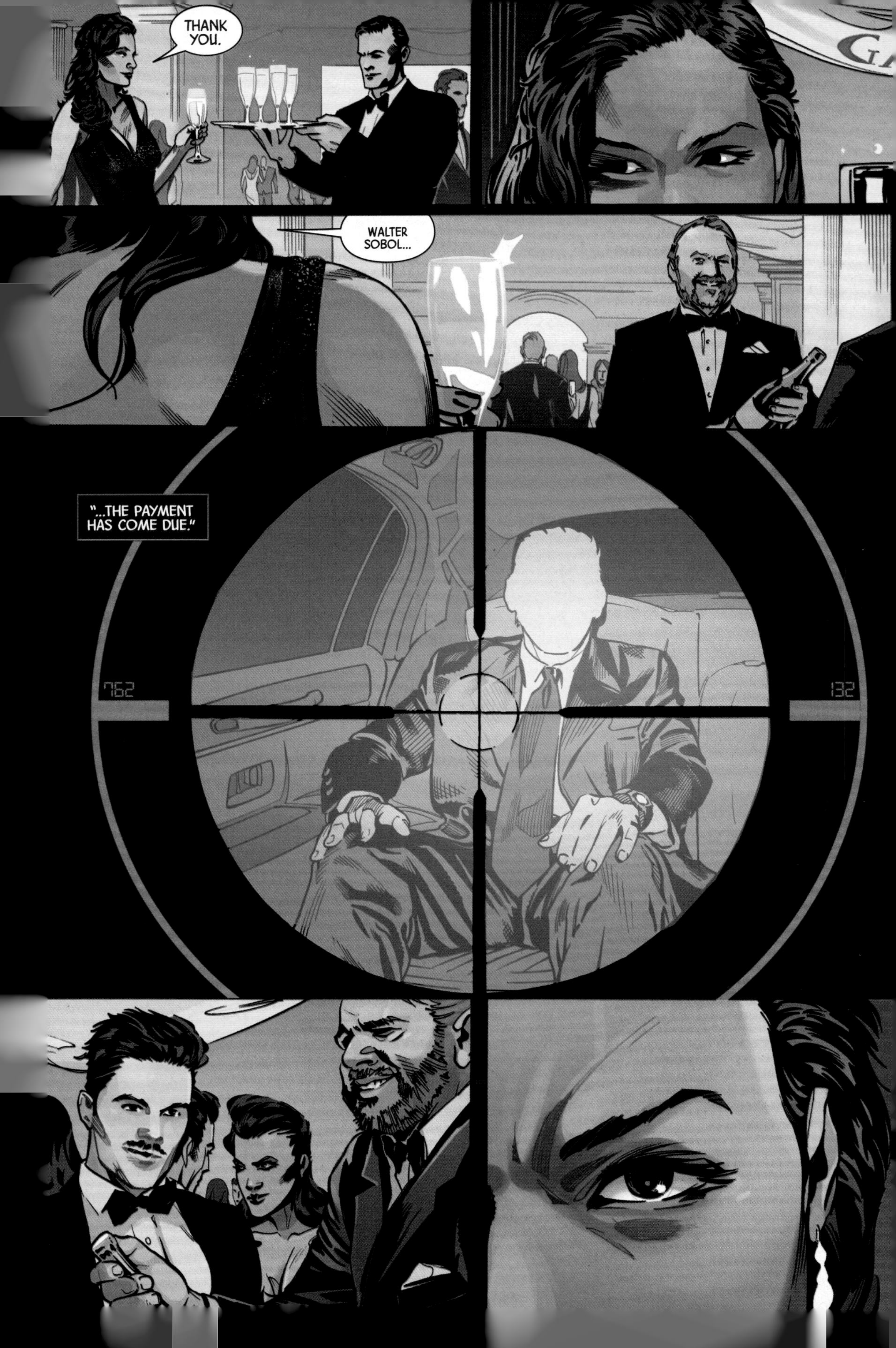
THANK YOU.
WALTER SOBOL...
"...THE PAYMENT HAS COME DUE."
762
132

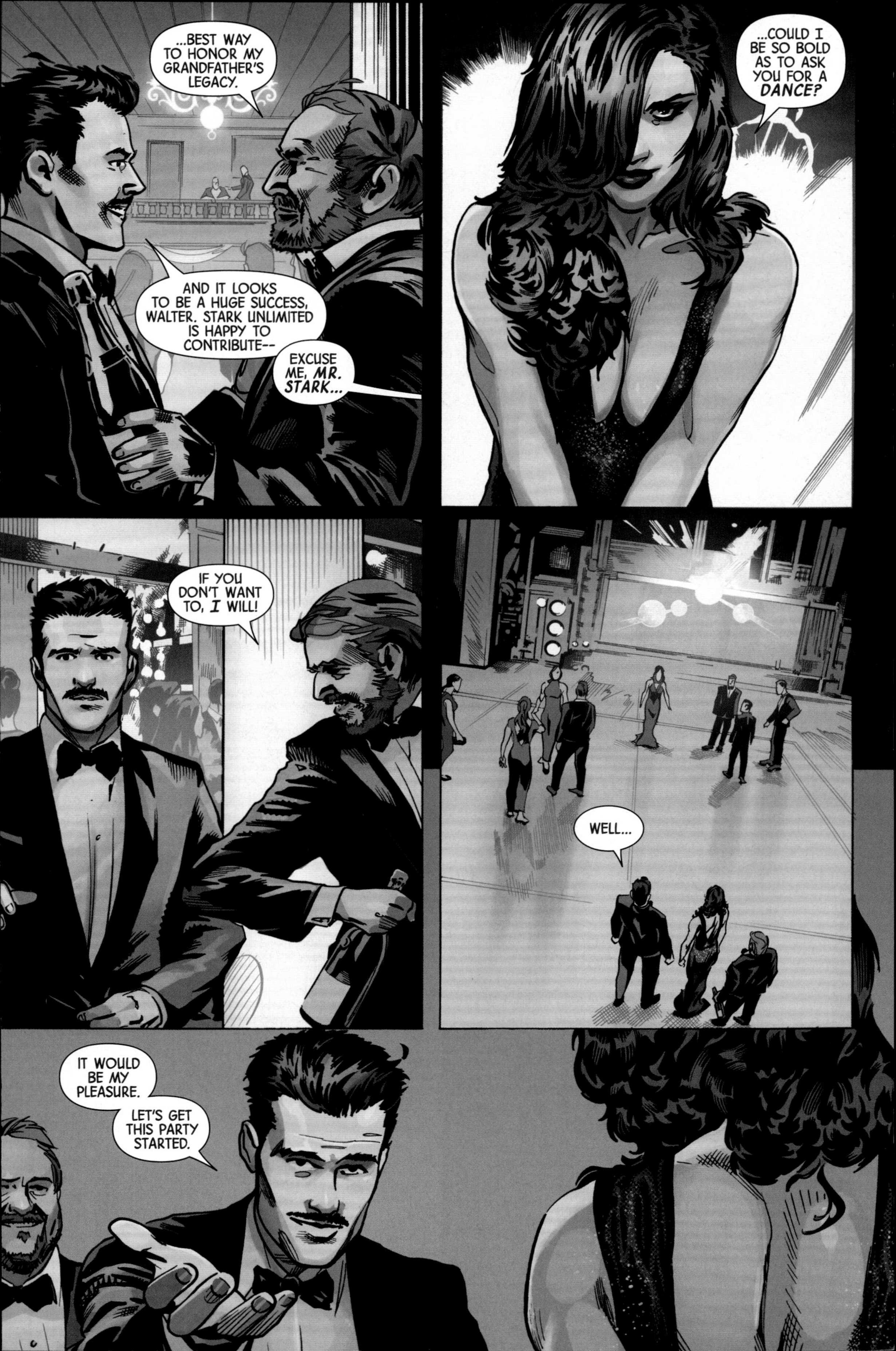
...BEST WAY TO HONOR MY GRANDFATHER'S LEGACY.
AND IT LOOKS TO BE A HUGE SUCCESS, WALTER. STARK UNLIMITED IS HAPPY TO CONTRIBUTE--
EXCUSE ME, MR. STARK...
...COULD I BE SO BOLD AS TO ASK YOU FOR A DANCE?
IF YOU DON'T WANT TO, I WILL!
WELL...
IT WOULD BE MY PLEASURE.
LET'S GET THIS PARTY STARTED.

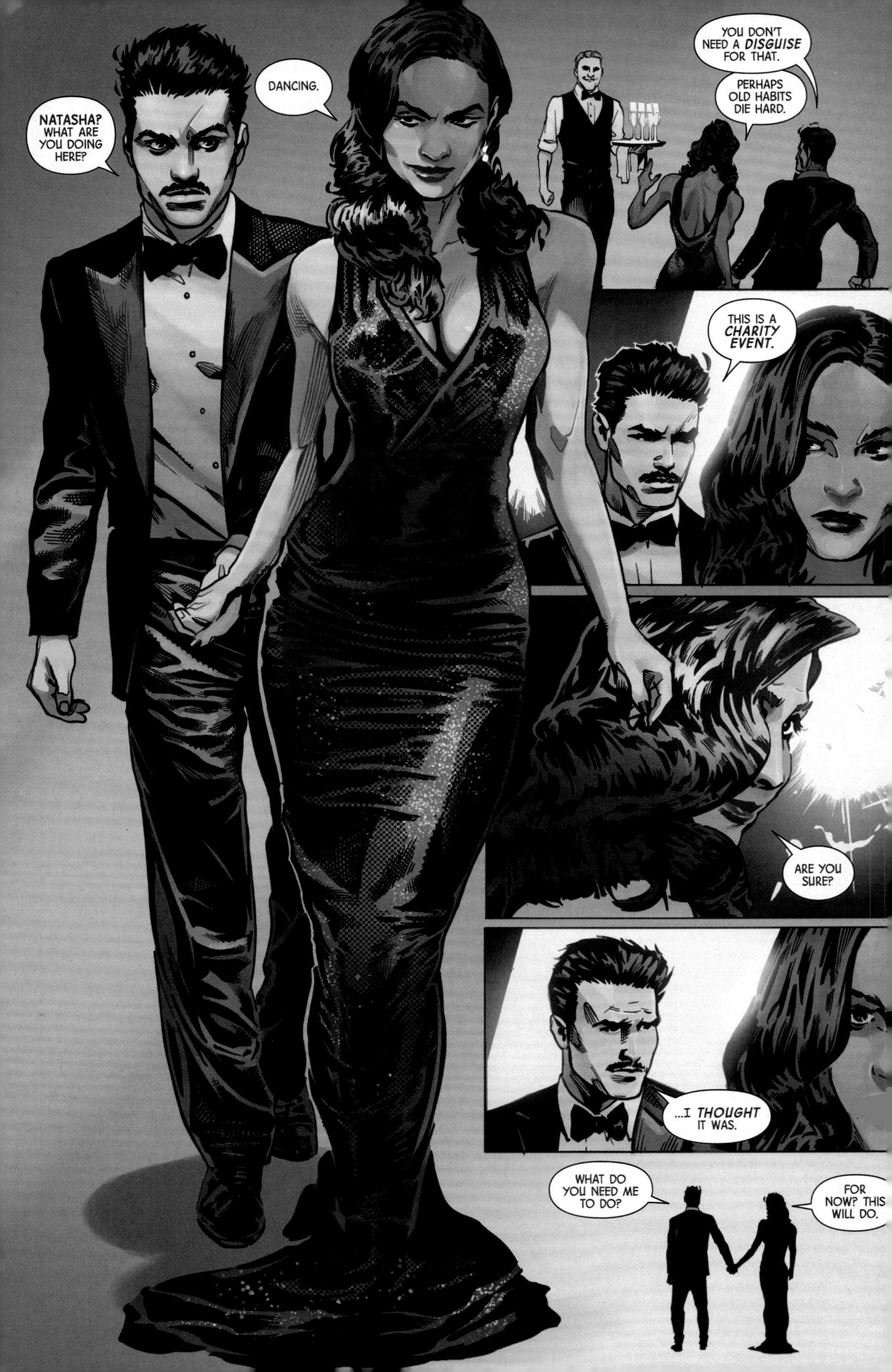
NATASHA? WHAT ARE YOU DOING HERE?
DANCING.
YOU DON'T NEED A DISGUISE FOR THAT.
PERHAPS OLD HABITS DIE HARD.
THIS IS A CHARITY EVENT.
ARE YOU SURE?
...I THOUGHT IT WAS.
WHAT DO YOU NEED ME TO DO?
FOR NOW? THIS WILL DO.

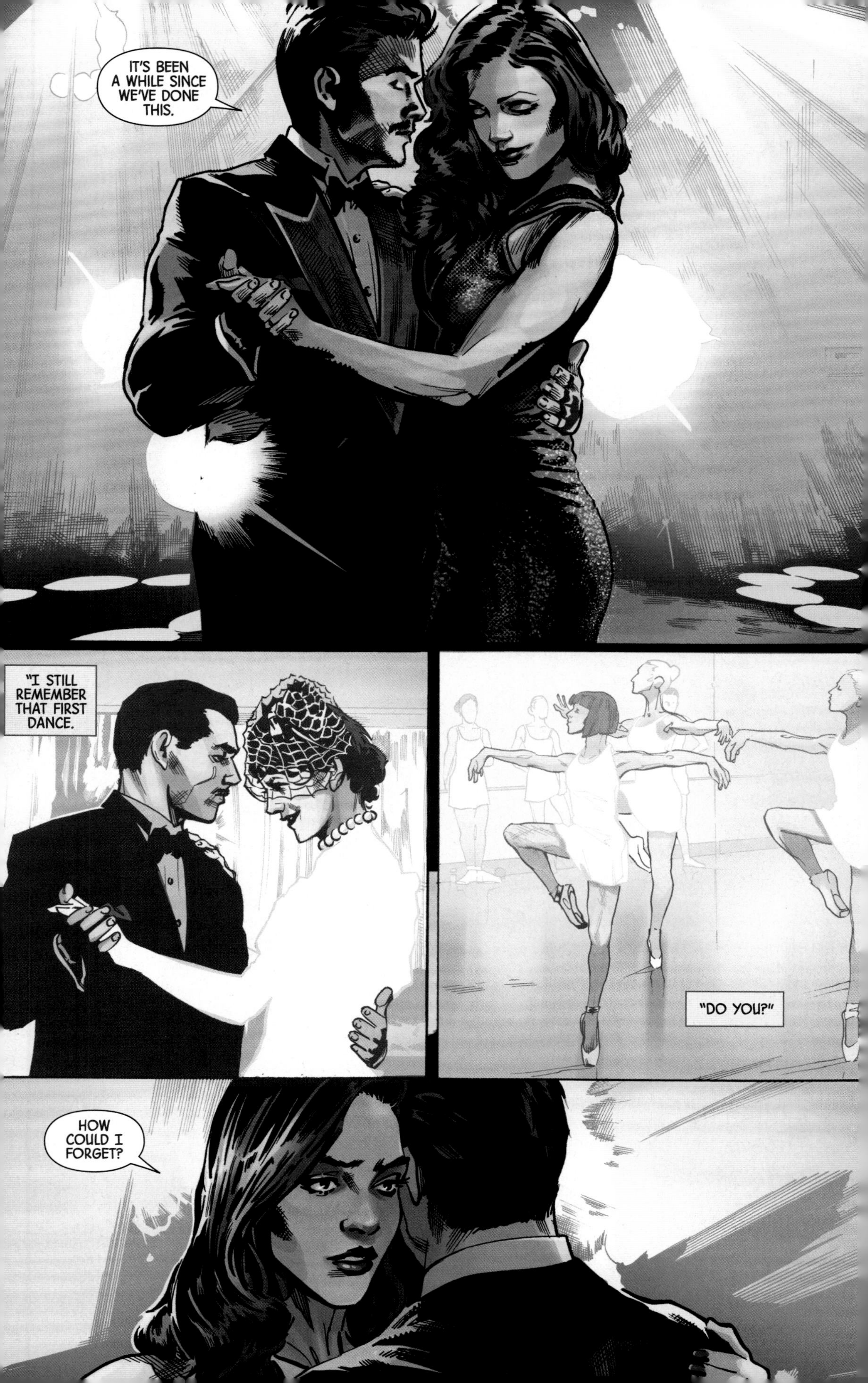
IT'S BEEN A WHILE SINCE WE'VE DONE THIS.
"I STILL REMEMBER THAT FIRST DANCE.
"DO YOU?"
HOW COULD I FORGET?

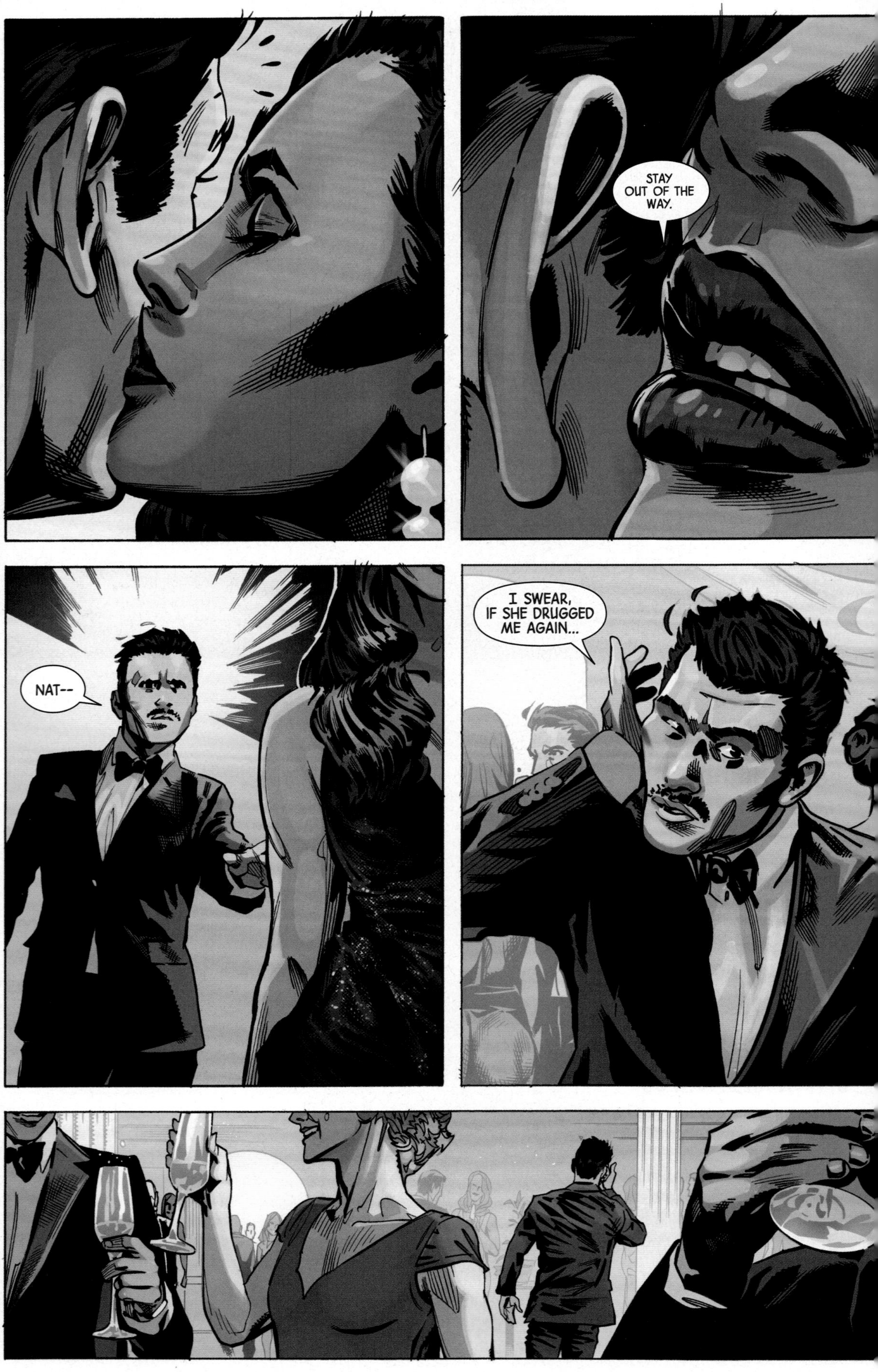
STAY OUT OF THE WAY.
NAT--
I SWEAR, IF SHE DRUGGED ME AGAIN...

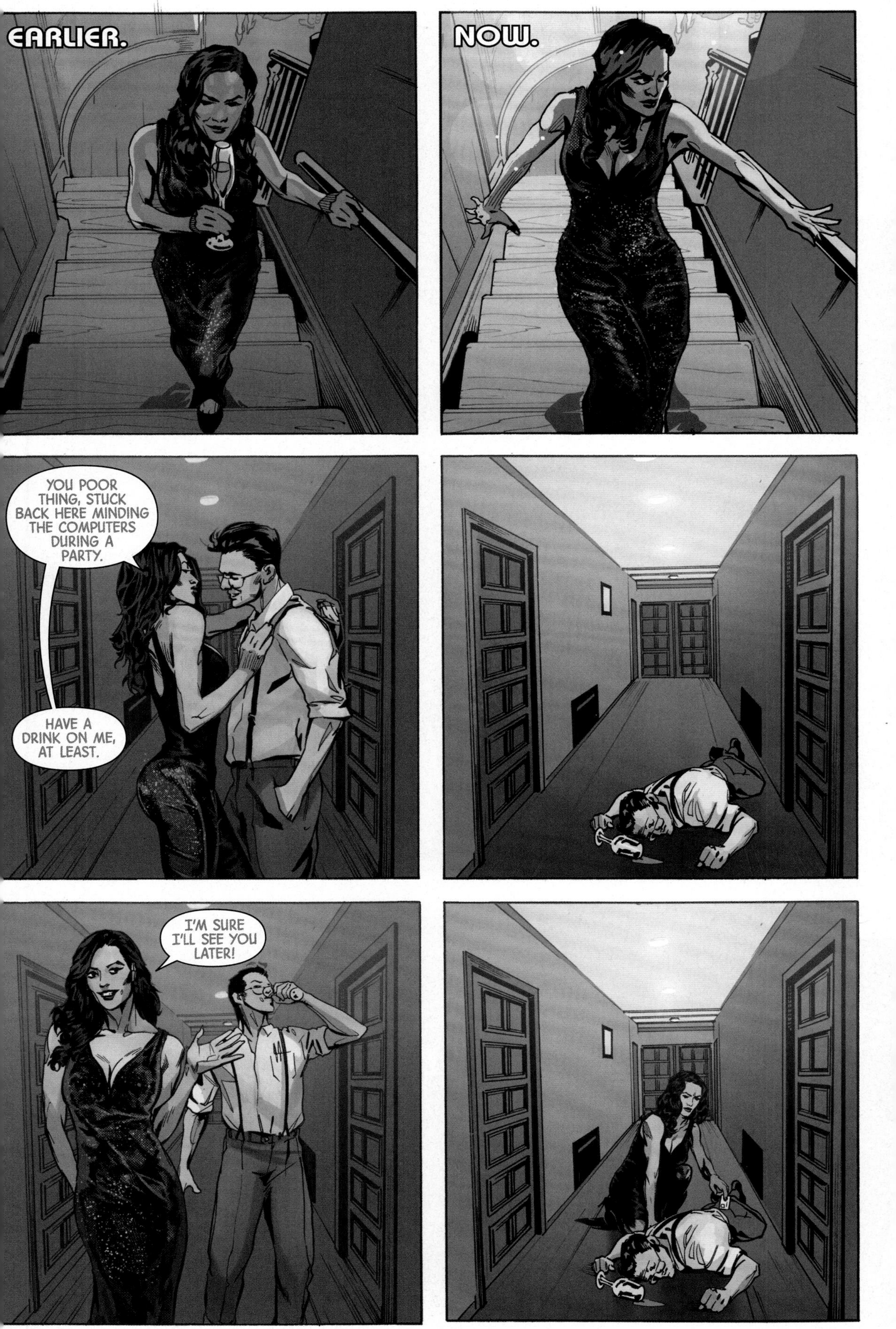
EARLIER.
NOW.
YOU POOR THING, STUCK BACK HERE MINDING THE COMPUTERS DURING A PARTY.
HAVE A DRINK ON ME, AT LEAST.
I'M SURE I'LL SEE YOU LATER!

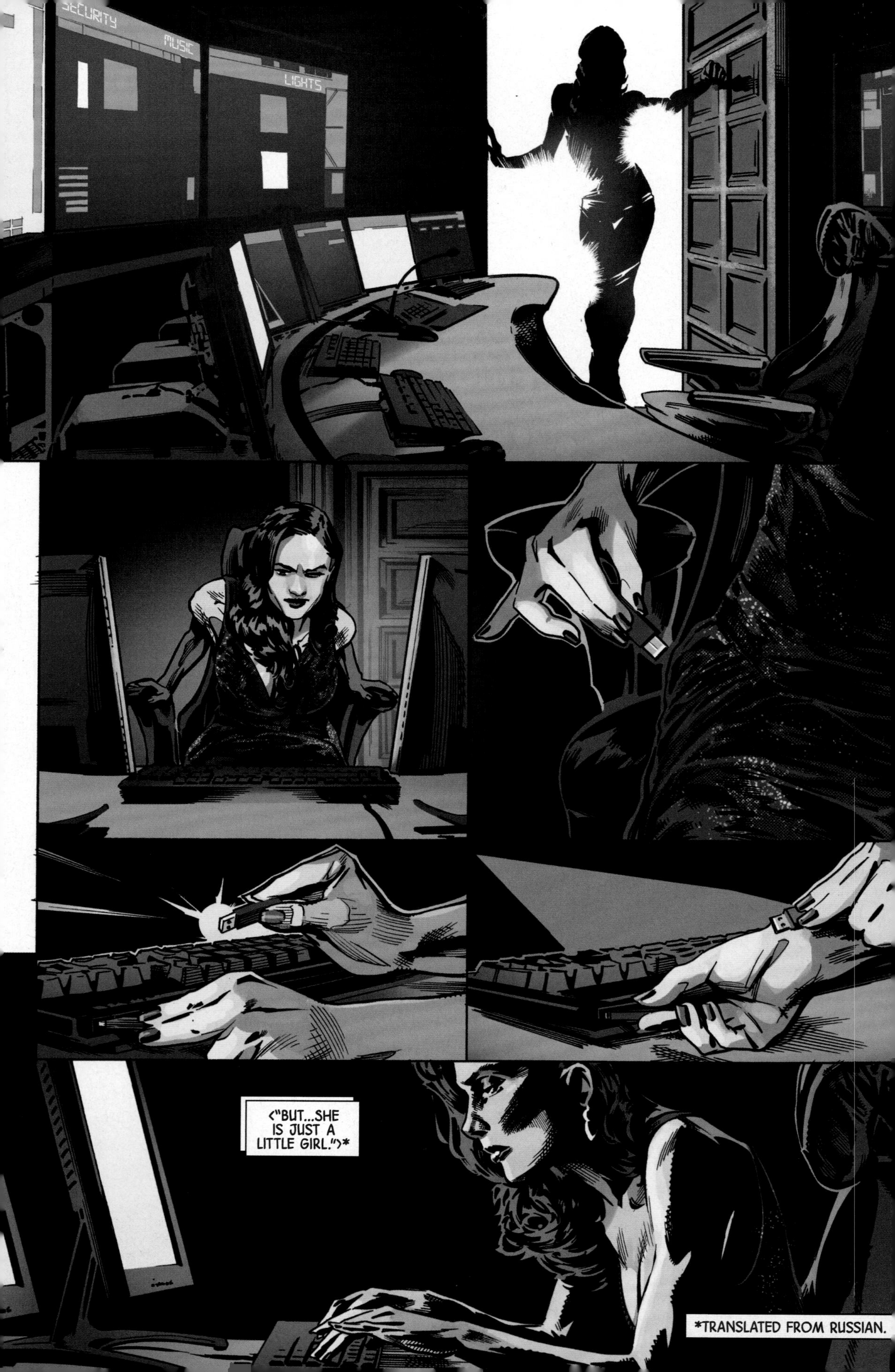
SECURITY
MUSIC
LIGHTS
<"BUT...SHE IS JUST A LITTLE GIRL.">*
*TRANSLATED FROM RUSSIAN.

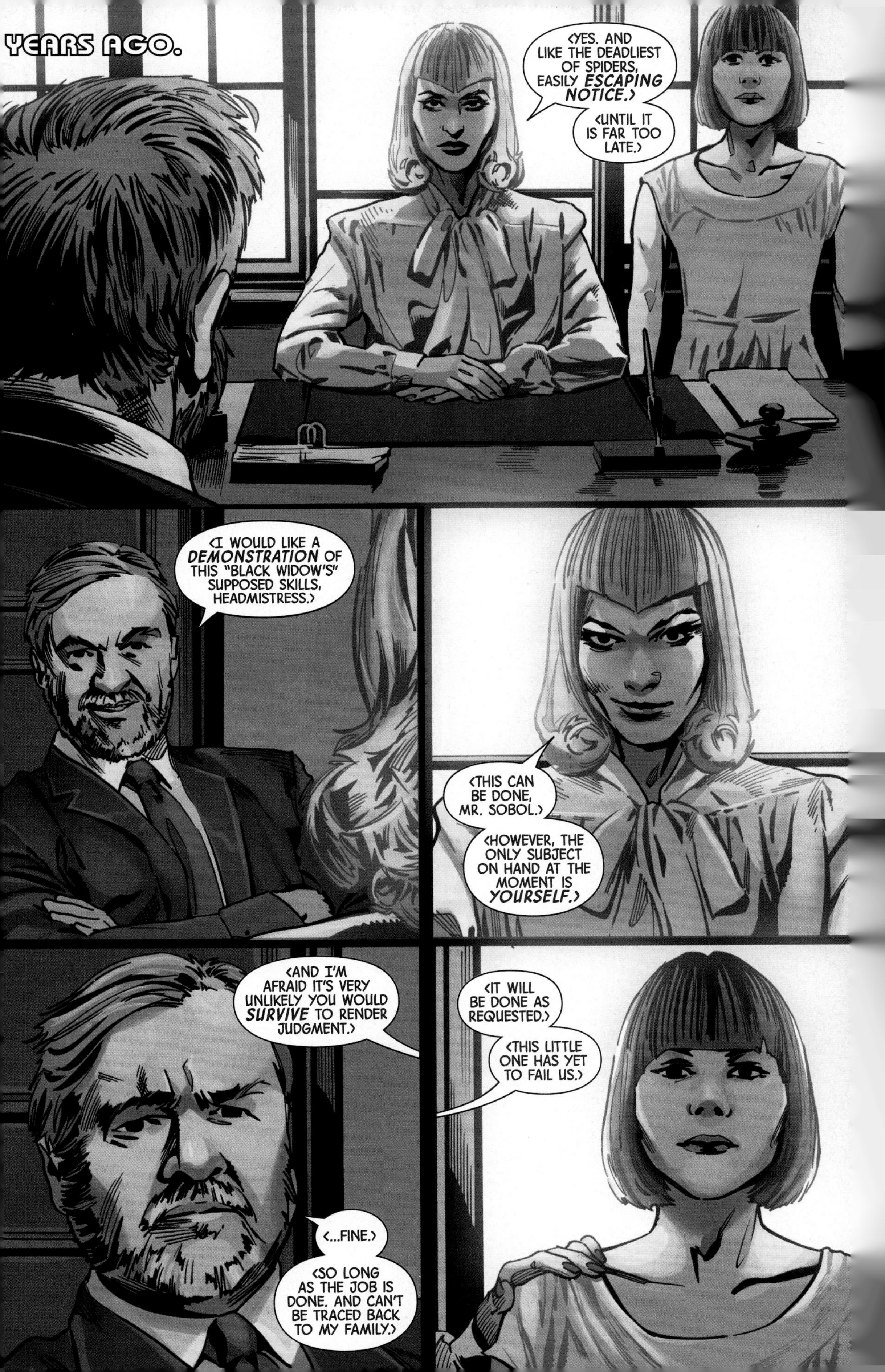
YEARS AGO.
<YES. AND LIKE THE DEADLIEST OF SPIDERS, EASILY ESCAPING NOTICE.>
<UNTIL IT IS FAR TOO LATE.>
<I WOULD LIKE A DEMONSTRATION OF THIS "BLACK WIDOW'S" SUPPOSED SKILLS, HEADMISTRESS.>
<THIS CAN BE DONE, MR. SOBOL.>
<HOWEVER, THE ONLY SUBJECT ON HAND AT THE MOMENT IS YOURSELF.>
<AND I'M AFRAID IT'S VERY UNLIKELY YOU WOULD SURVIVE TO RENDER JUDGMENT.>
<IT WILL BE DONE AS REQUESTED.>
<THIS LITTLE ONE HAS YET TO FAIL US.>
<...FINE.>
<SO LONG AS THE JOB IS DONE. AND CAN'T BE TRACED BACK TO MY FAMILY.>

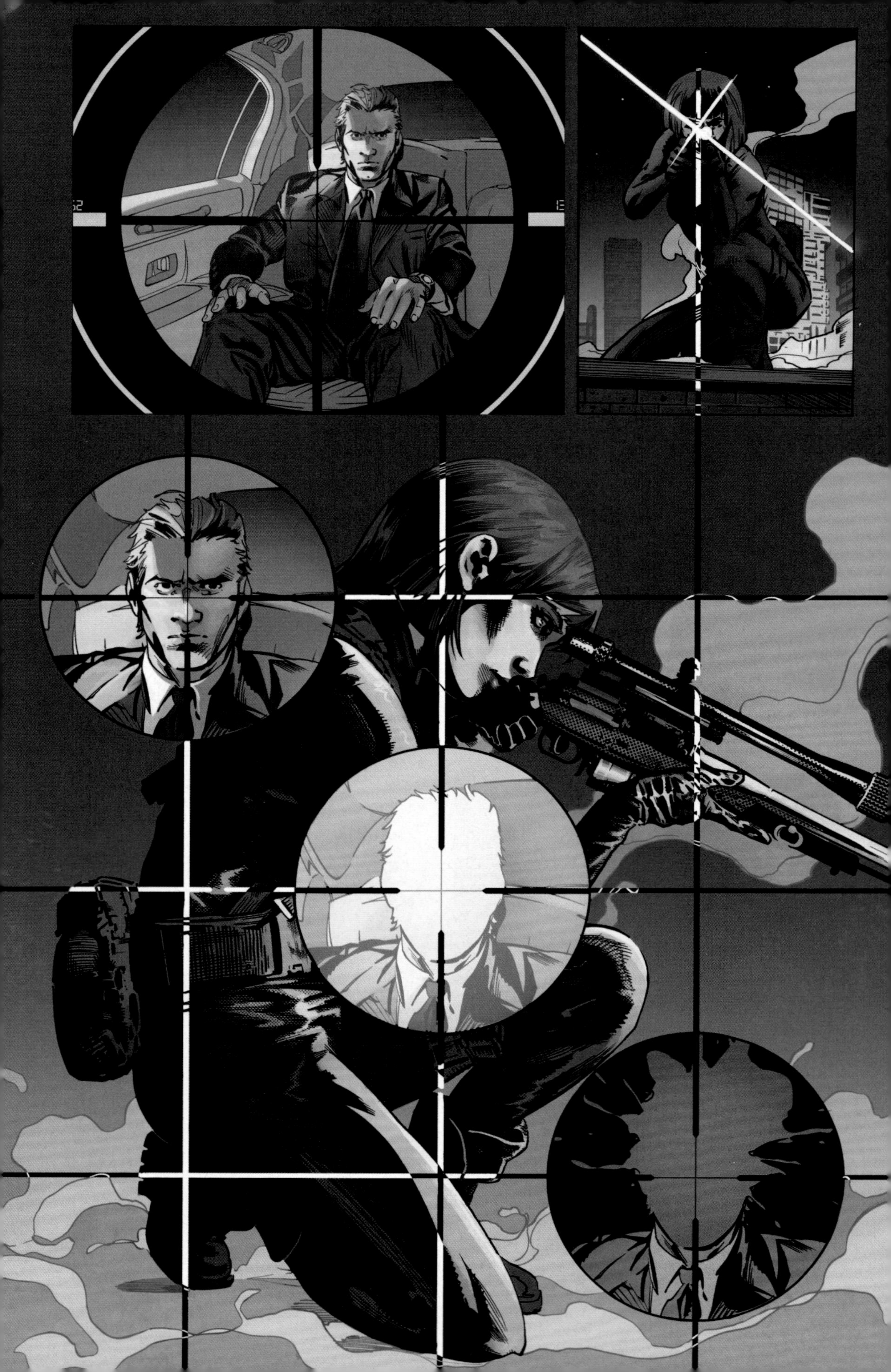

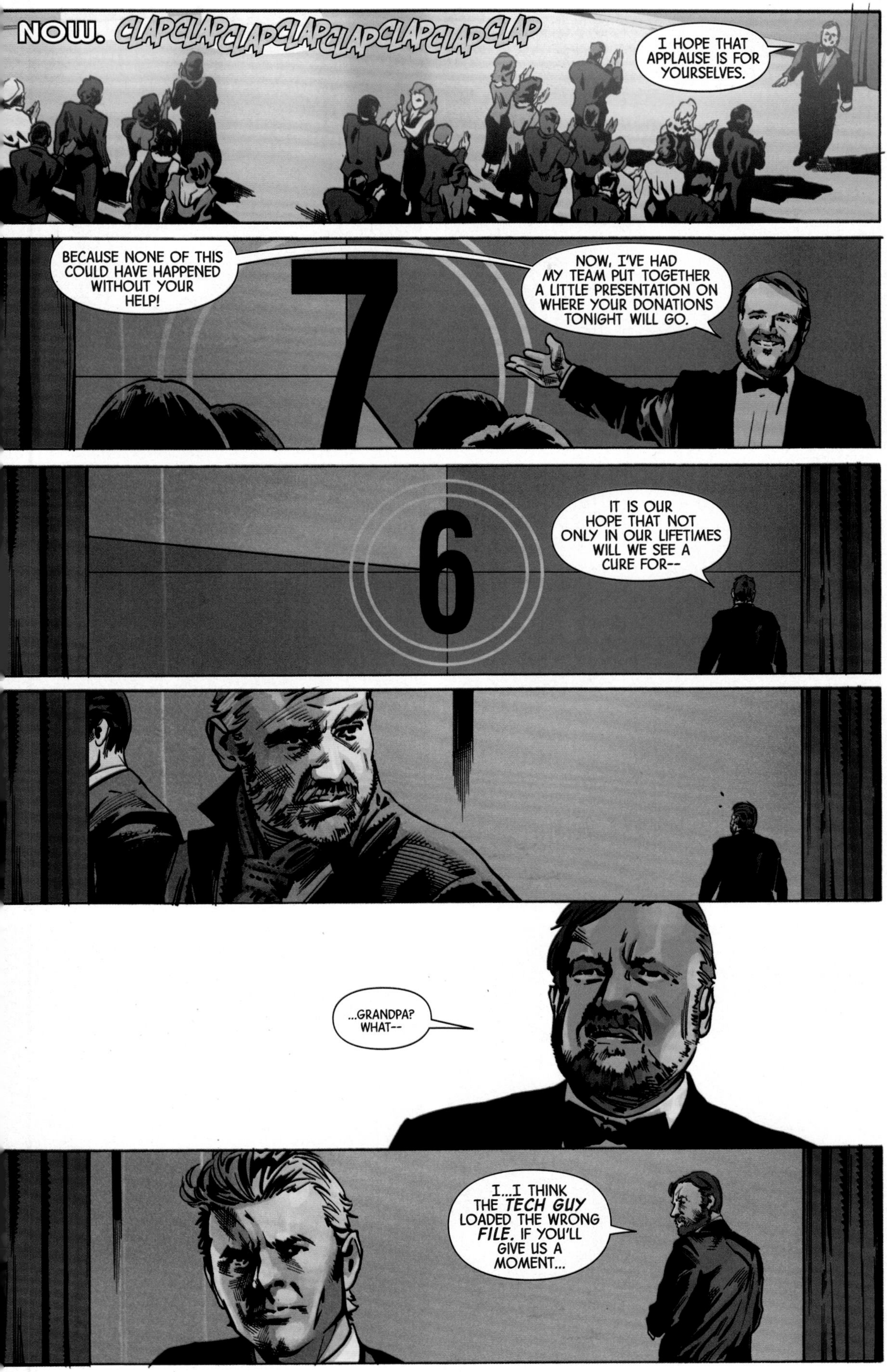
NOW.
CLAPCLAPCLAPCLAPCLAPCLAPCLAPCLAP
I HOPE THAT APPLAUSE IS FOR YOURSELVES.
BECAUSE NONE OF THIS COULD HAVE HAPPENED WITHOUT YOUR HELP!
NOW, I'VE HAD MY TEAM PUT TOGETHER A LITTLE PRESENTATION ON WHERE YOUR DONATIONS TONIGHT WILL GO.
7
6
IT IS OUR HOPE THAT NOT ONLY IN OUR LIFETIMES WILL WE SEE A CURE FOR--
...GRANDPA? WHAT--
I...I THINK THE *TECH GUY* LOADED THE WRONG *FILE.* IF YOU'LL GIVE US A MOMENT...

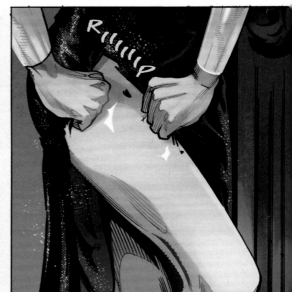

SLOW...

TROMP TROMP TROMP

THERE THEY ARE...

THUUD THUUD THUUD

HEY! WHO'S IN THERE?!

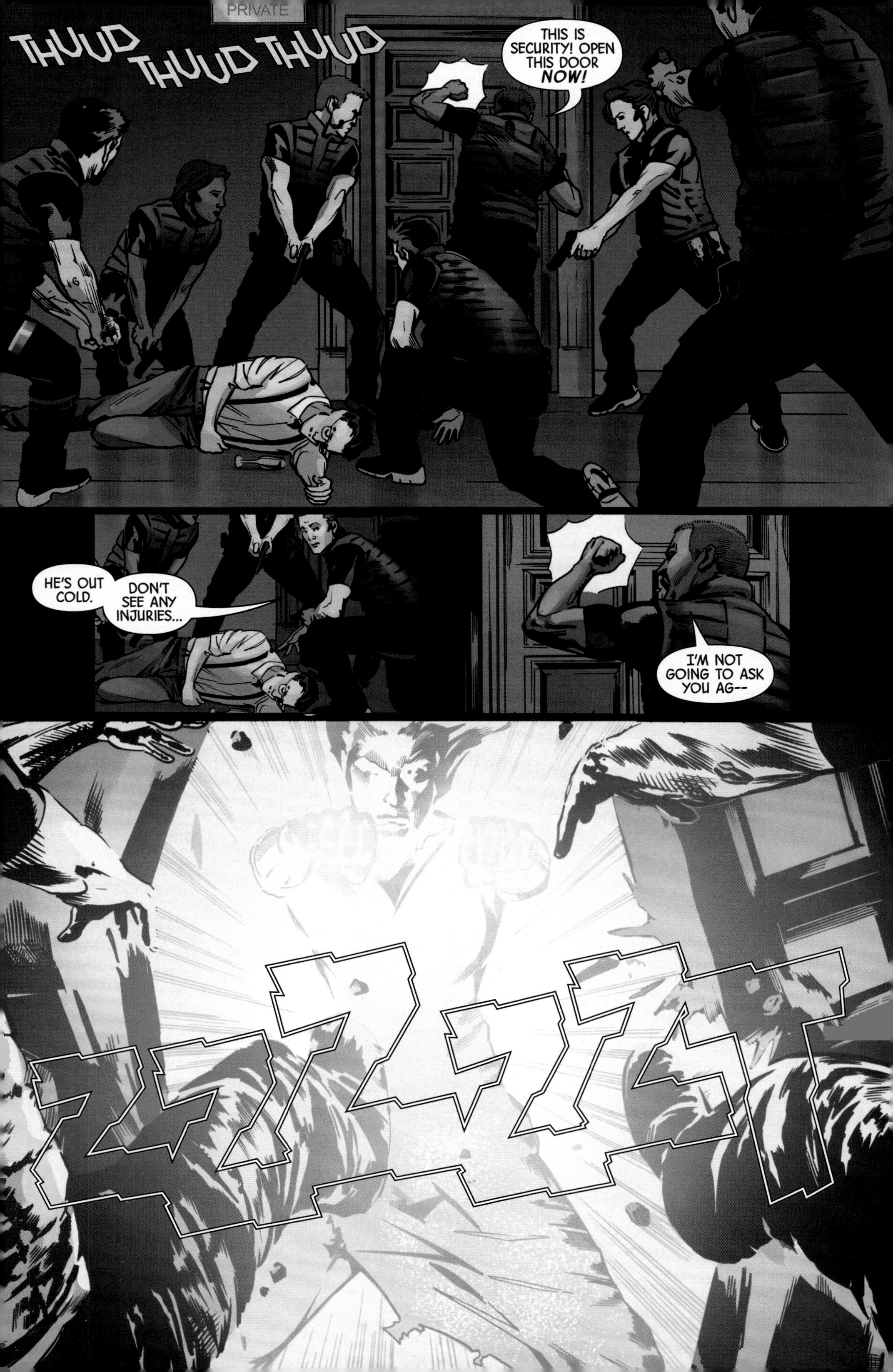
PRIVATE
THUUD THUUD THUUD
THIS IS SECURITY! OPEN THIS DOOR NOW!
HE'S OUT COLD.
DON'T SEE ANY INJURIES...
I'M NOT GOING TO ASK YOU AG--

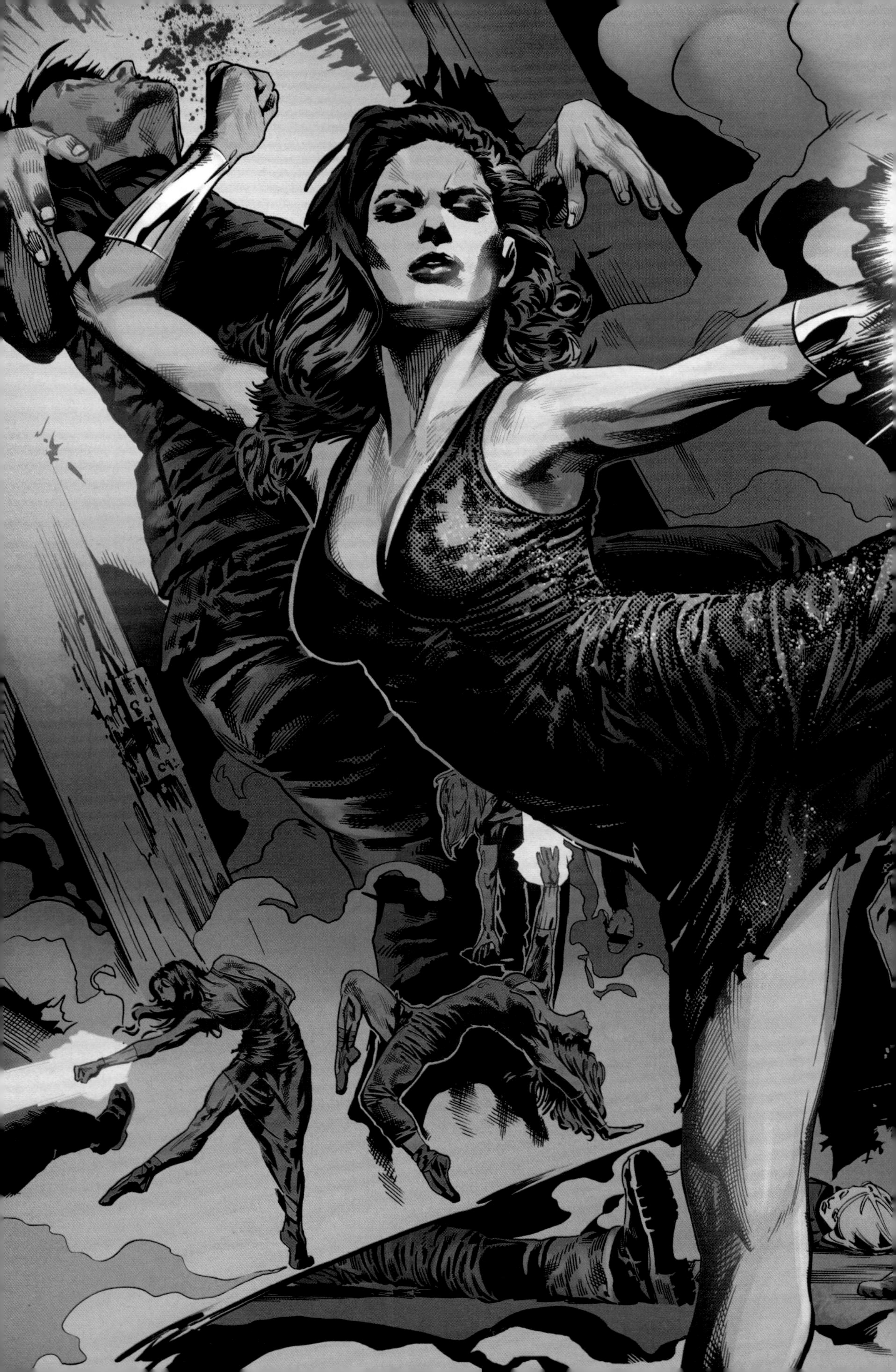

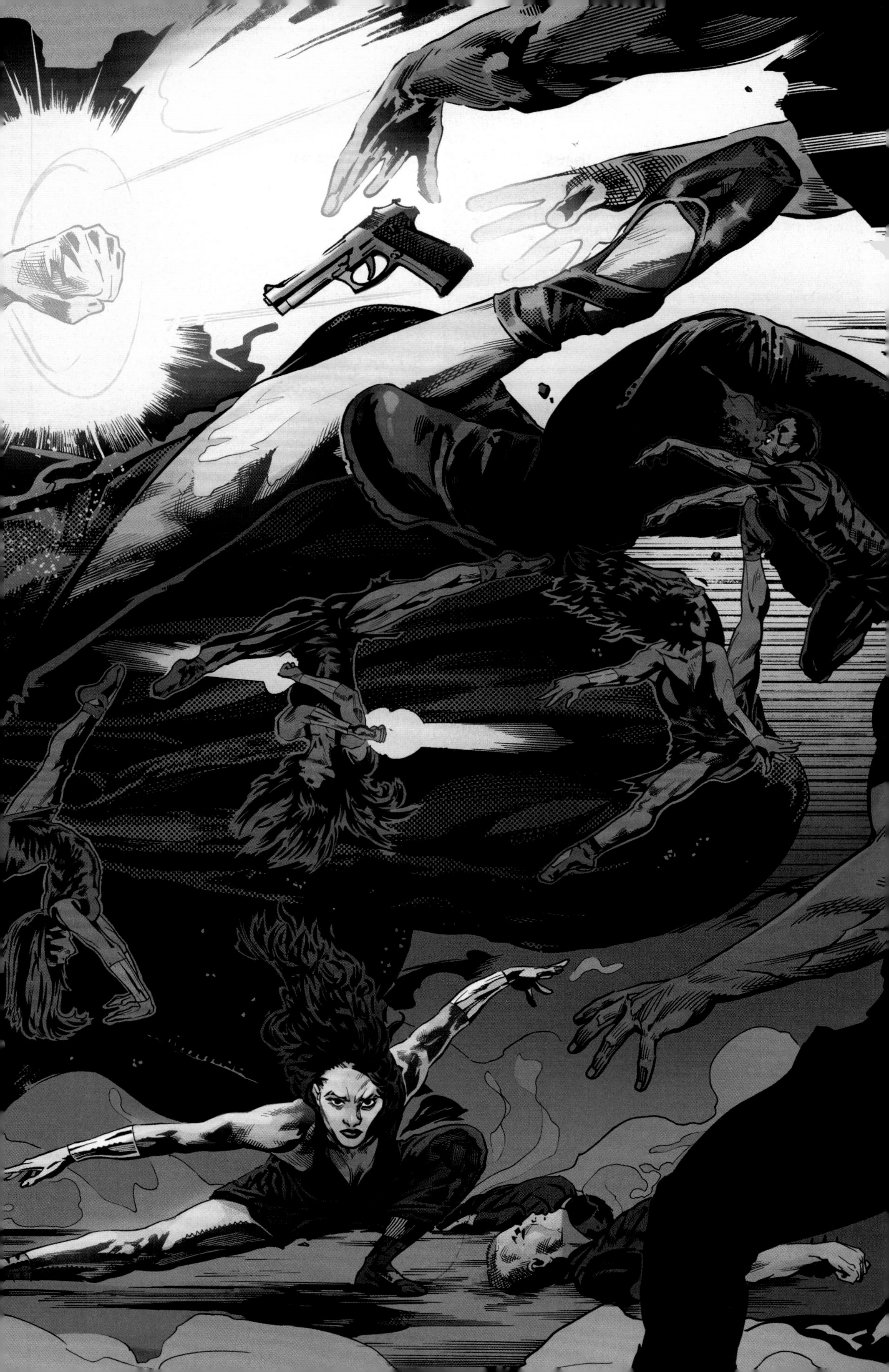

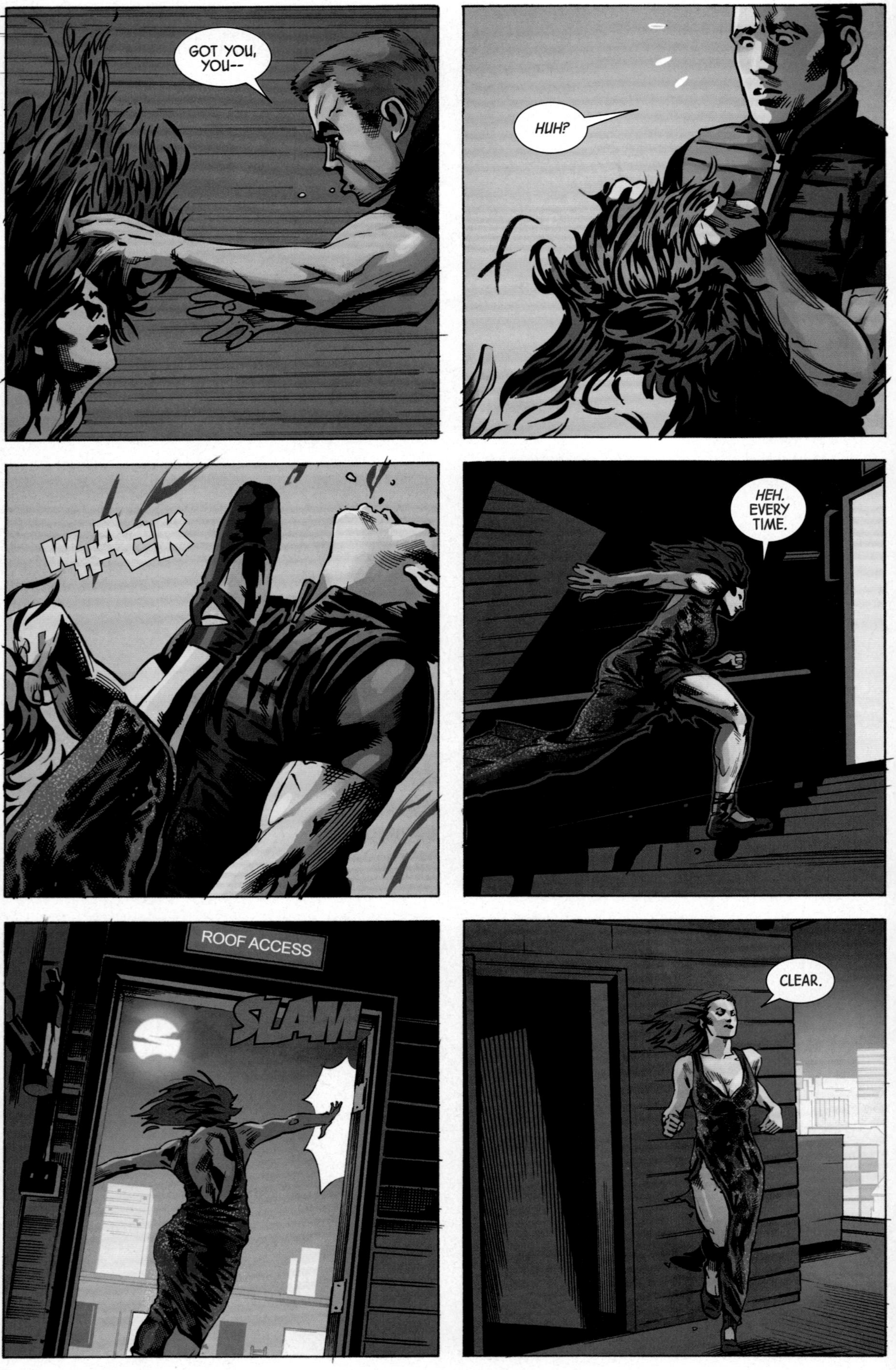
GOT YOU, YOU--
HUH?
WHACK
HEH. EVERY TIME.
ROOF ACCESS
SLAM
CLEAR.

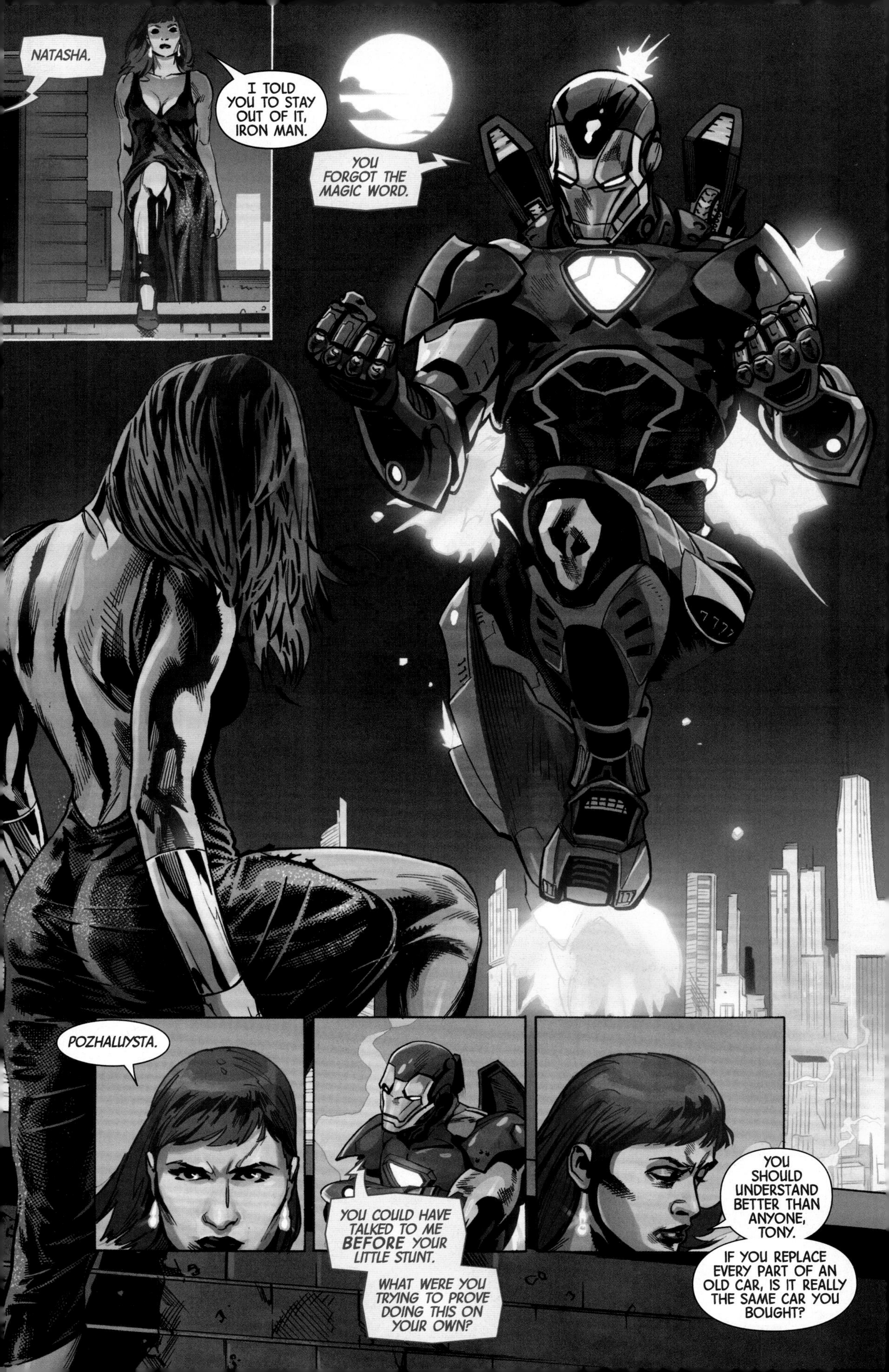
NATASHA.
I TOLD YOU TO STAY OUT OF IT, IRON MAN.
YOU FORGOT THE MAGIC WORD.
POZHALUYSTA.
YOU COULD HAVE TALKED TO ME **BEFORE** YOUR LITTLE STUNT.
WHAT WERE YOU TRYING TO PROVE DOING THIS ON YOUR OWN?
YOU SHOULD UNDERSTAND BETTER THAN ANYONE, TONY.
IF YOU REPLACE EVERY PART OF AN OLD CAR, IS IT REALLY THE SAME CAR YOU BOUGHT?

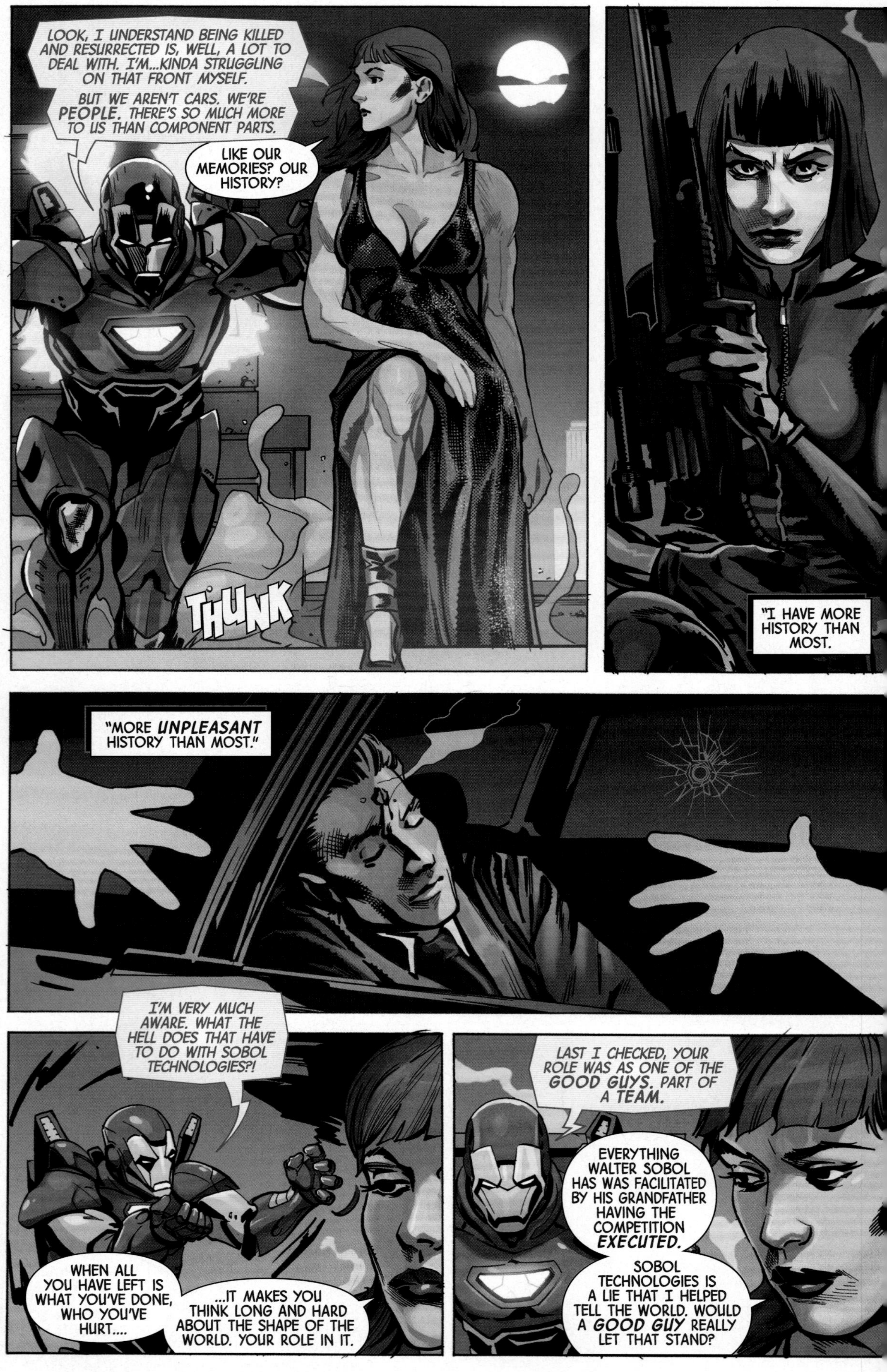
LOOK, I UNDERSTAND BEING KILLED AND RESURRECTED IS, WELL, A LOT TO DEAL WITH. I'M...KINDA STRUGGLING ON THAT FRONT MYSELF.
BUT WE AREN'T CARS. WE'RE PEOPLE. THERE'S SO MUCH MORE TO US THAN COMPONENT PARTS.
LIKE OUR MEMORIES? OUR HISTORY?
THUNK
"I HAVE MORE HISTORY THAN MOST.
"MORE UNPLEASANT HISTORY THAN MOST."
I'M VERY MUCH AWARE. WHAT THE HELL DOES THAT HAVE TO DO WITH SOBOL TECHNOLOGIES?!
WHEN ALL YOU HAVE LEFT IS WHAT YOU'VE DONE, WHO YOU'VE HURT....
...IT MAKES YOU THINK LONG AND HARD ABOUT THE SHAPE OF THE WORLD. YOUR ROLE IN IT.
LAST I CHECKED, YOUR ROLE WAS AS ONE OF THE GOOD GUYS. PART OF A TEAM.
EVERYTHING WALTER SOBOL HAS WAS FACILITATED BY HIS GRANDFATHER HAVING THE COMPETITION EXECUTED.
SOBOL TECHNOLOGIES IS A LIE THAT I HELPED TELL THE WORLD. WOULD A GOOD GUY REALLY LET THAT STAND?

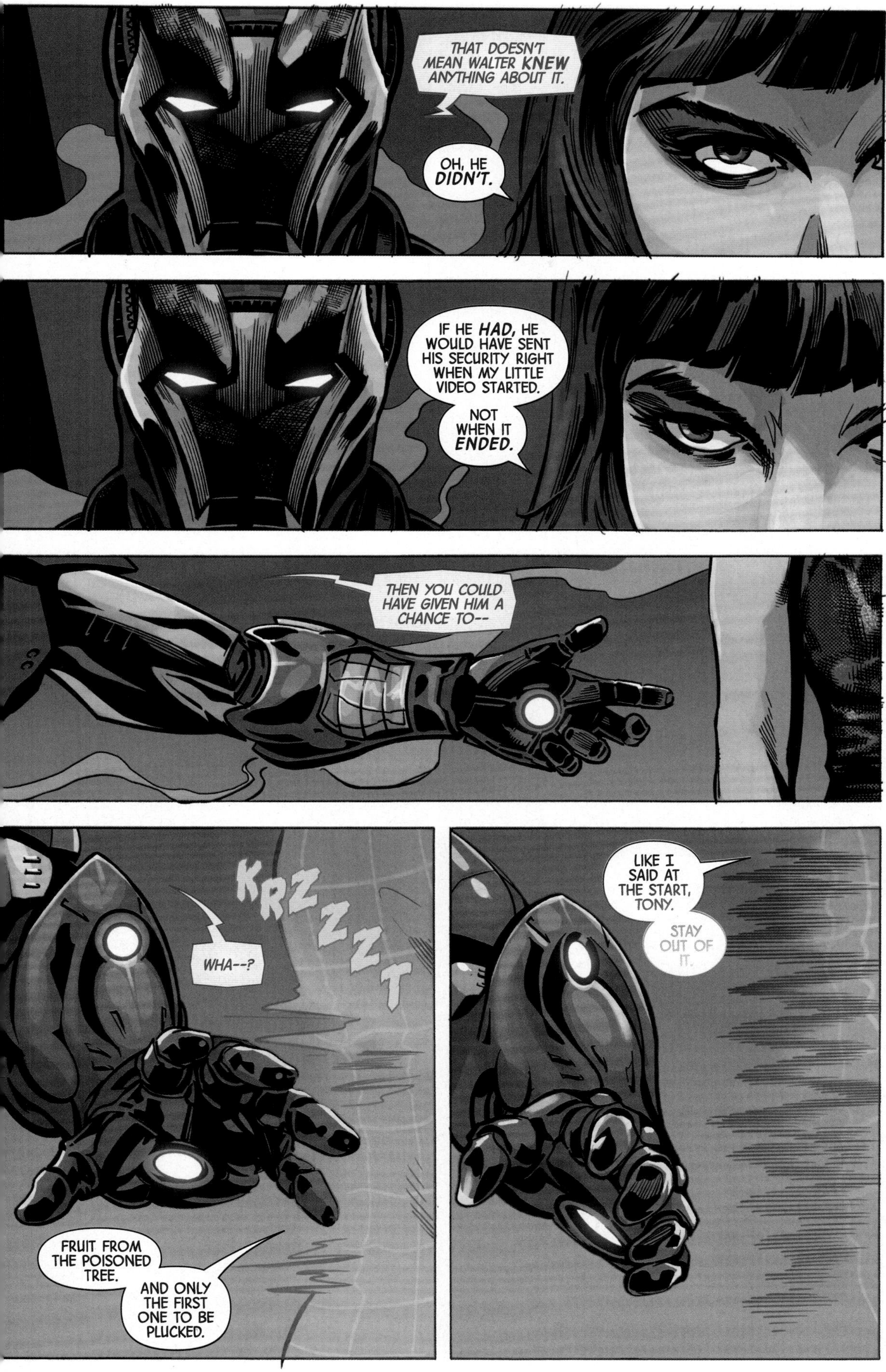
THAT DOESN'T MEAN WALTER KNEW ANYTHING ABOUT IT.
OH, HE DIDN'T.
IF HE HAD, HE WOULD HAVE SENT HIS SECURITY RIGHT WHEN MY LITTLE VIDEO STARTED.
NOT WHEN IT ENDED.
THEN YOU COULD HAVE GIVEN HIM A CHANCE TO--
KRZZZZT
WHA--?
FRUIT FROM THE POISONED TREE.
AND ONLY THE FIRST ONE TO BE PLUCKED.
LIKE I SAID AT THE START, TONY.
STAY OUT OF IT.

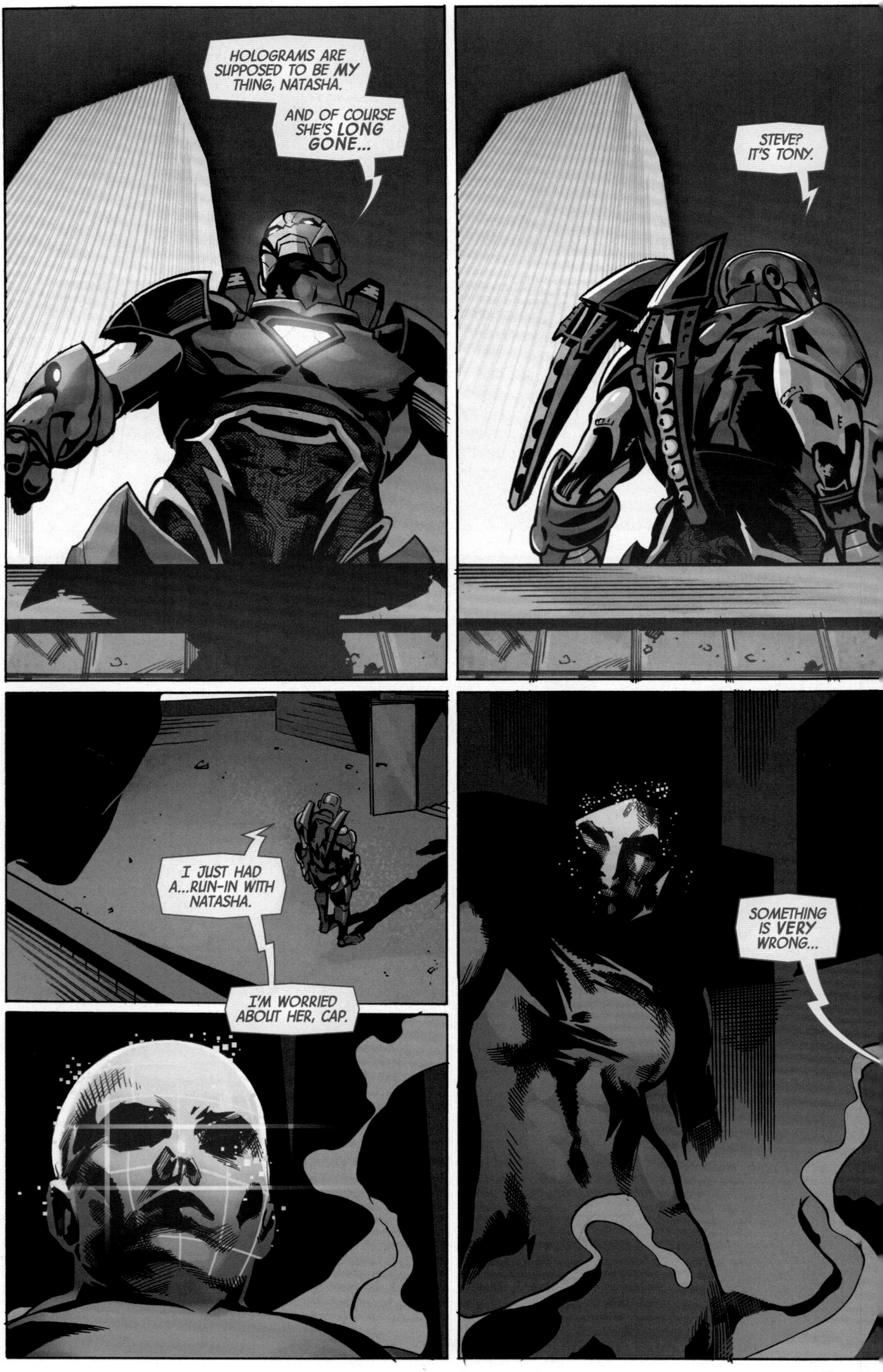
HOLOGRAMS ARE SUPPOSED TO BE MY THING, NATASHA.
AND OF COURSE SHE'S LONG GONE...
STEVE? IT'S TONY.
I JUST HAD A...RUN-IN WITH NATASHA.
I'M WORRIED ABOUT HER, CAP.
SOMETHING IS VERY WRONG...

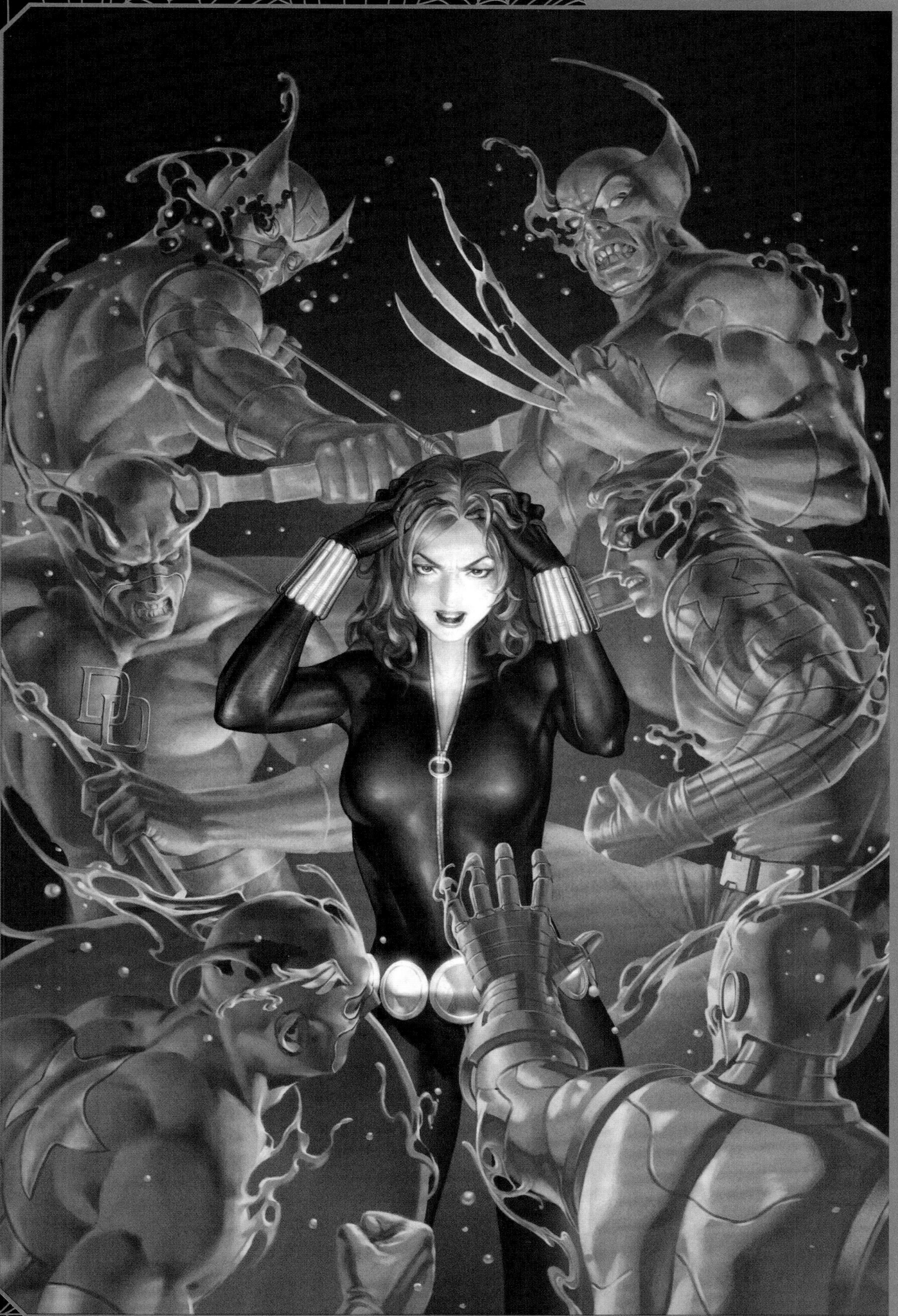

TWO

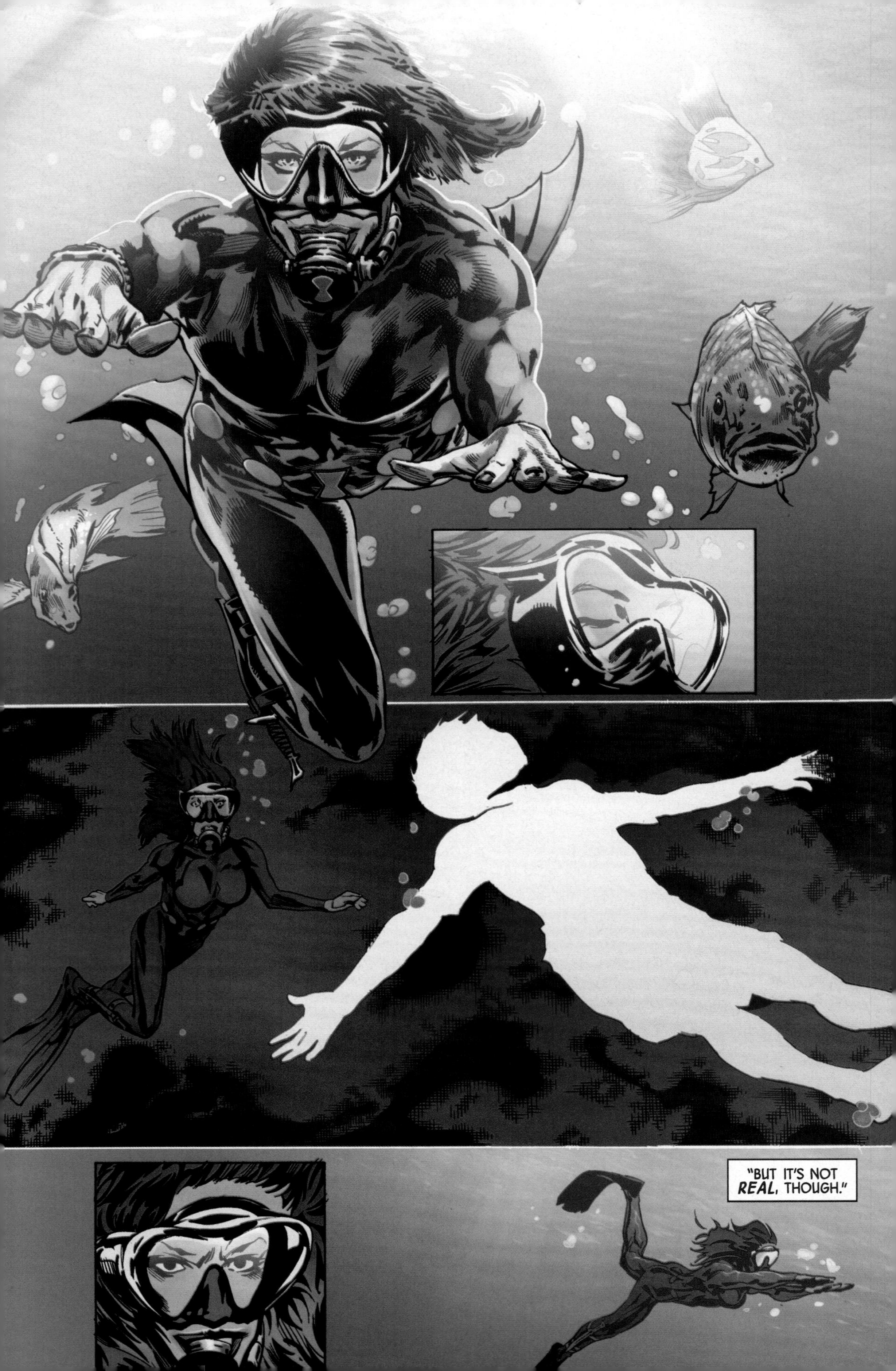
"BUT IT'S NOT REAL, THOUGH."

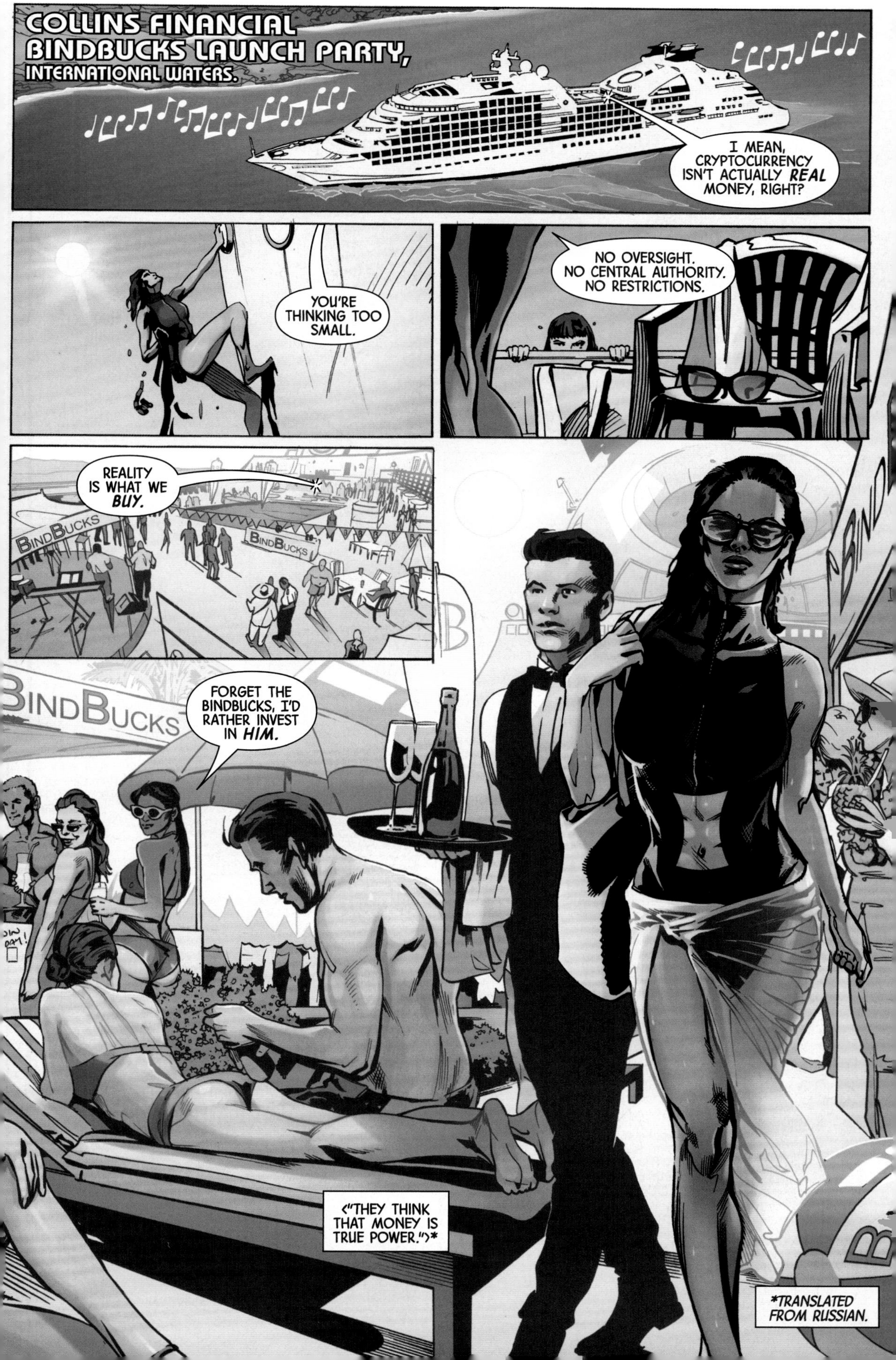
COLLINS FINANCIAL BINDBUCKS LAUNCH PARTY, INTERNATIONAL WATERS.
I MEAN, CRYPTOCURRENCY ISN'T ACTUALLY REAL MONEY, RIGHT?
YOU'RE THINKING TOO SMALL.
NO OVERSIGHT. NO CENTRAL AUTHORITY. NO RESTRICTIONS.
REALITY IS WHAT WE BUY.
BINDBUCKS
BINDBUCKS
BINDBUCKS
FORGET THE BINDBUCKS, I'D RATHER INVEST IN HIM.
<"THEY THINK THAT MONEY IS TRUE POWER.">*
*TRANSLATED FROM RUSSIAN.

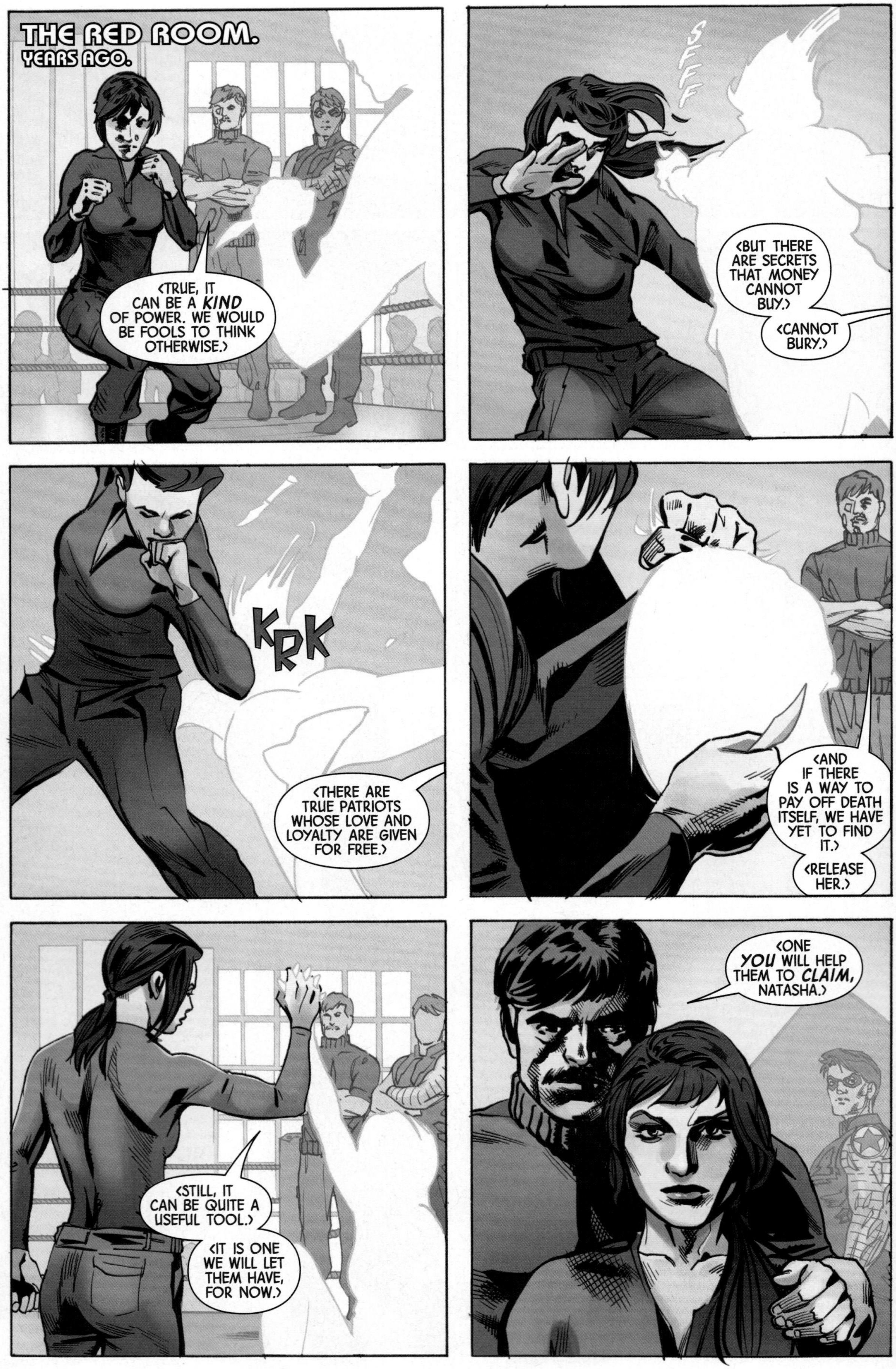
THE RED ROOM.
YEARS AGO.
<TRUE, IT CAN BE A KIND OF POWER. WE WOULD BE FOOLS TO THINK OTHERWISE.>
SFFF
<BUT THERE ARE SECRETS THAT MONEY CANNOT BUY.>
<CANNOT BURY.>
KRK
<THERE ARE TRUE PATRIOTS WHOSE LOVE AND LOYALTY ARE GIVEN FOR FREE.>
<AND IF THERE IS A WAY TO PAY OFF DEATH ITSELF, WE HAVE YET TO FIND IT.>
<RELEASE HER.>
<STILL, IT CAN BE QUITE A USEFUL TOOL.>
<IT IS ONE WE WILL LET THEM HAVE, FOR NOW.>
<ONE YOU WILL HELP THEM TO CLAIM, NATASHA.>

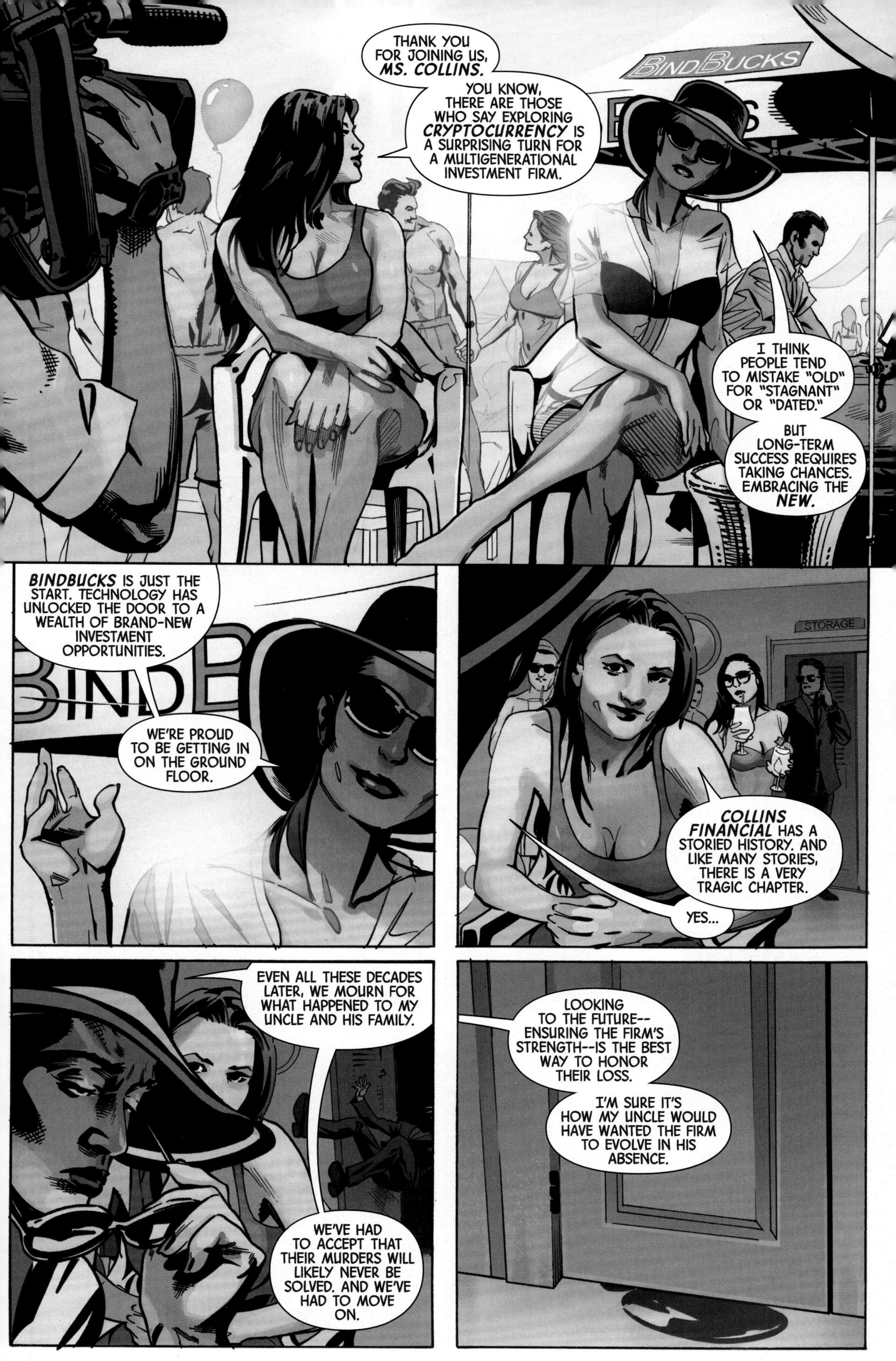
BINDBUCKS
THANK YOU FOR JOINING US, MS. COLLINS.
YOU KNOW, THERE ARE THOSE WHO SAY EXPLORING CRYPTOCURRENCY IS A SURPRISING TURN FOR A MULTIGENERATIONAL INVESTMENT FIRM.
I THINK PEOPLE TEND TO MISTAKE "OLD" FOR "STAGNANT" OR "DATED."
BUT LONG-TERM SUCCESS REQUIRES TAKING CHANCES. EMBRACING THE NEW.
BINDBUCKS IS JUST THE START. TECHNOLOGY HAS UNLOCKED THE DOOR TO A WEALTH OF BRAND-NEW INVESTMENT OPPORTUNITIES.
WE'RE PROUD TO BE GETTING IN ON THE GROUND FLOOR.
STORAGE
COLLINS FINANCIAL HAS A STORIED HISTORY. AND LIKE MANY STORIES, THERE IS A VERY TRAGIC CHAPTER.
YES...
EVEN ALL THESE DECADES LATER, WE MOURN FOR WHAT HAPPENED TO MY UNCLE AND HIS FAMILY.
WE'VE HAD TO ACCEPT THAT THEIR MURDERS WILL LIKELY NEVER BE SOLVED. AND WE'VE HAD TO MOVE ON.
LOOKING TO THE FUTURE--ENSURING THE FIRM'S STRENGTH--IS THE BEST WAY TO HONOR THEIR LOSS.
I'M SURE IT'S HOW MY UNCLE WOULD HAVE WANTED THE FIRM TO EVOLVE IN HIS ABSENCE.

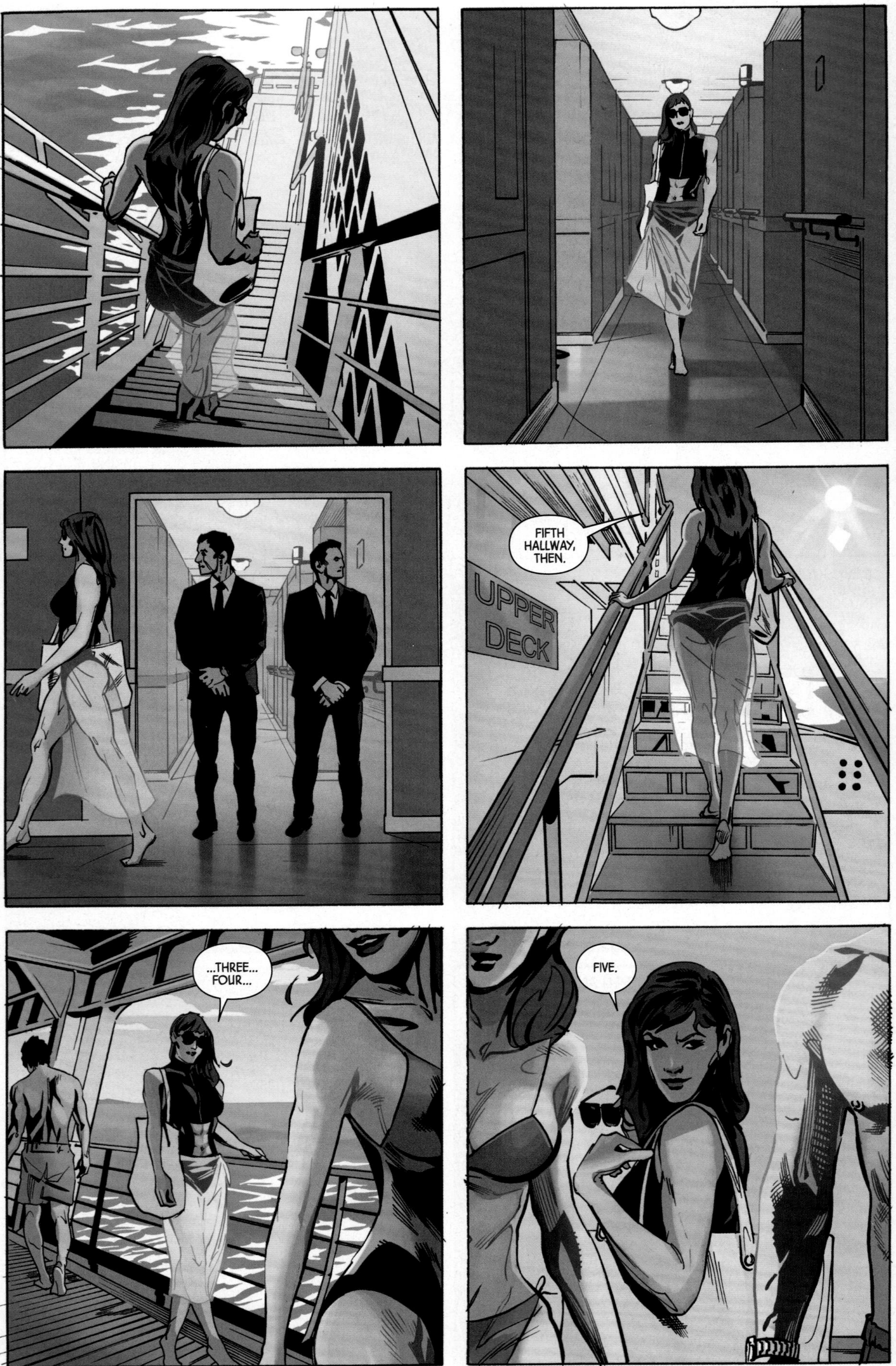
FIFTH HALLWAY, THEN.
UPPER DECK
...THREE... FOUR...
FIVE.

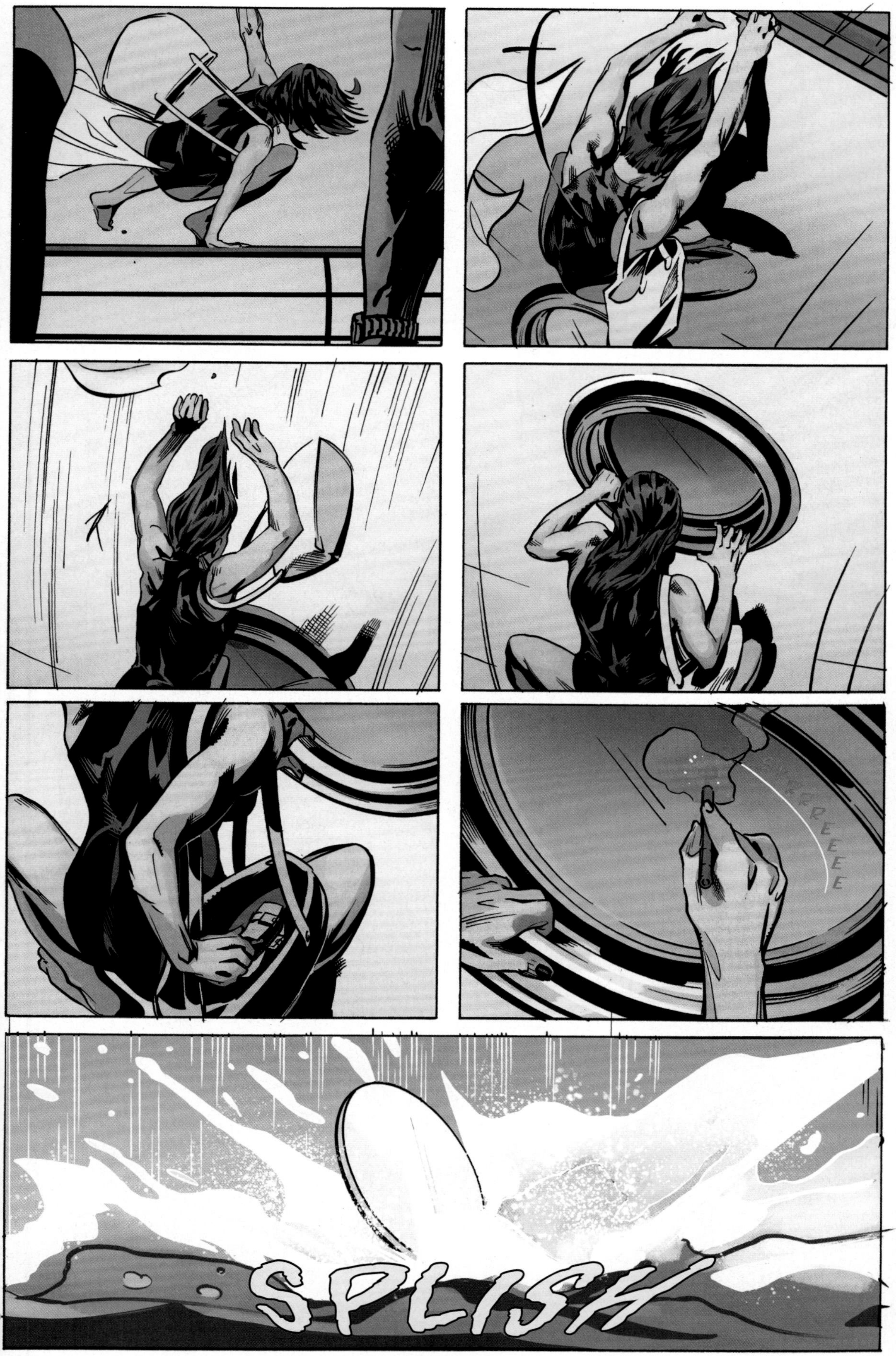
SKRREEEE
SPLISH

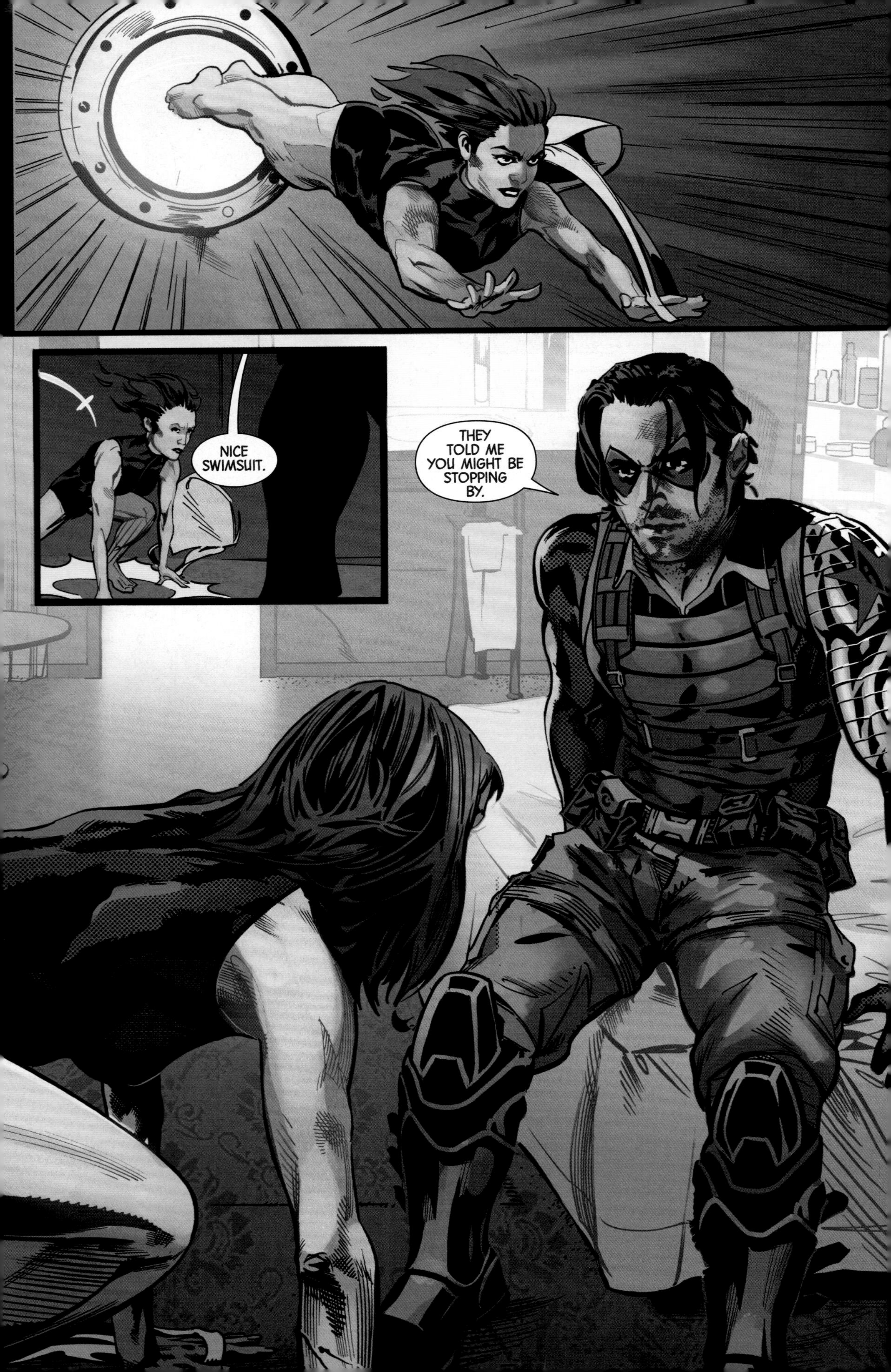
NICE SWIMSUIT.
THEY TOLD ME YOU MIGHT BE STOPPING BY.

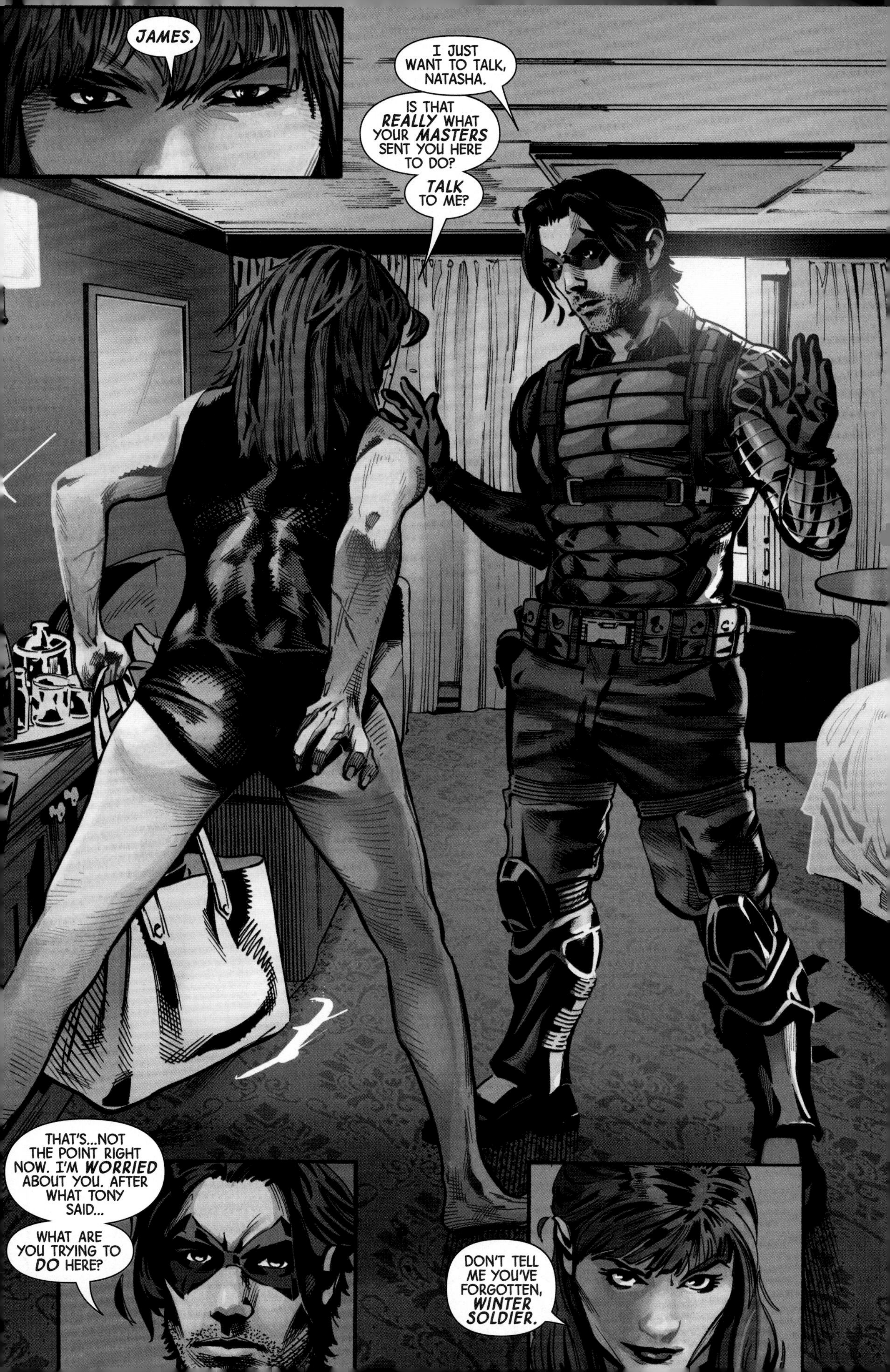
JAMES.
I JUST WANT TO TALK, NATASHA.
IS THAT REALLY WHAT YOUR MASTERS SENT YOU HERE TO DO?
TALK TO ME?
THAT'S...NOT THE POINT RIGHT NOW. I'M WORRIED ABOUT YOU. AFTER WHAT TONY SAID...
WHAT ARE YOU TRYING TO DO HERE?
DON'T TELL ME YOU'VE FORGOTTEN, WINTER SOLDIER.

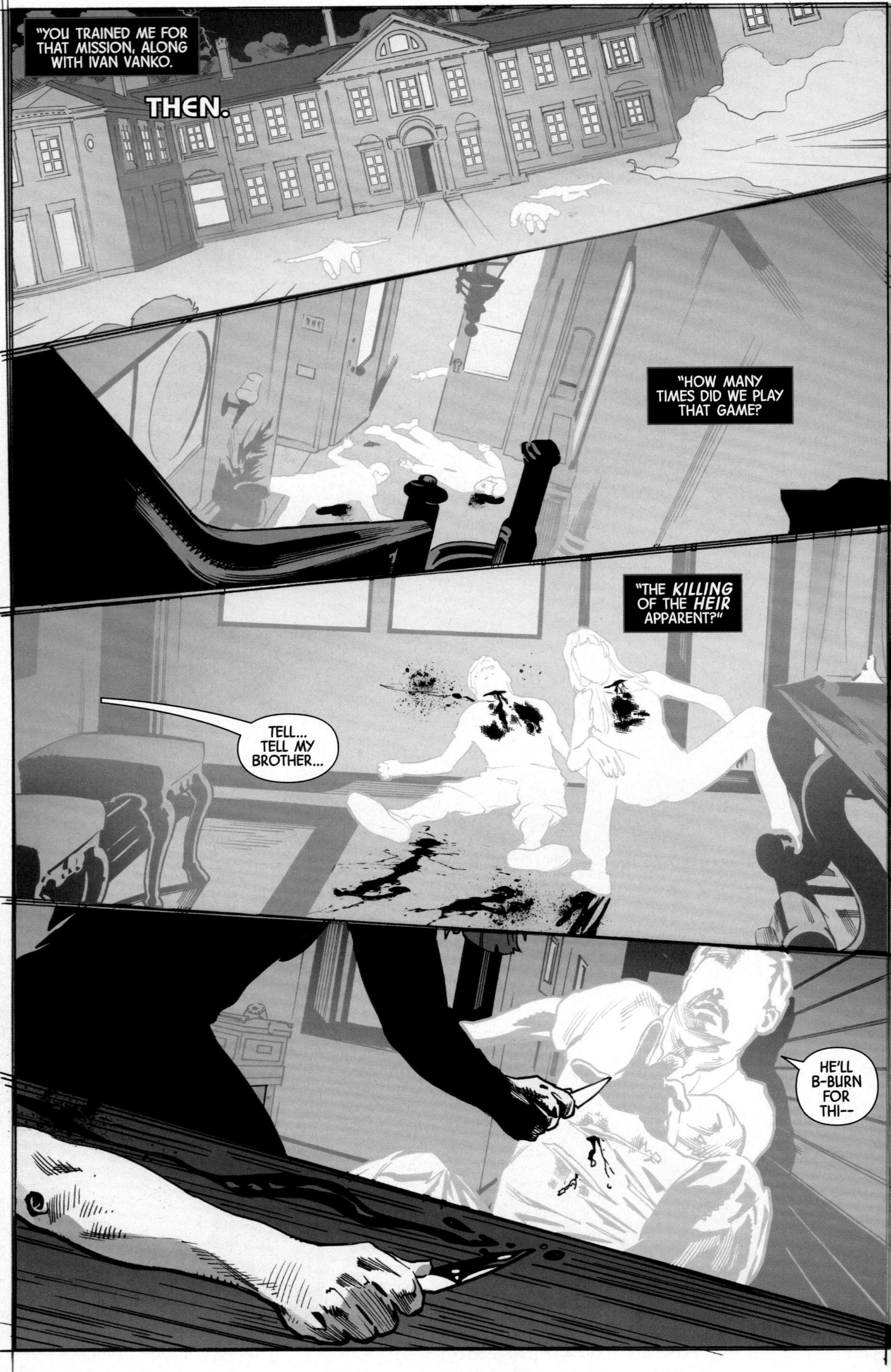
"YOU TRAINED ME FOR THAT MISSION, ALONG WITH IVAN VANKO.
THEN.
"HOW MANY TIMES DID WE PLAY THAT GAME?
"THE KILLING OF THE HEIR APPARENT?"
TELL... TELL MY BROTHER...
HE'LL B-BURN FOR THI--

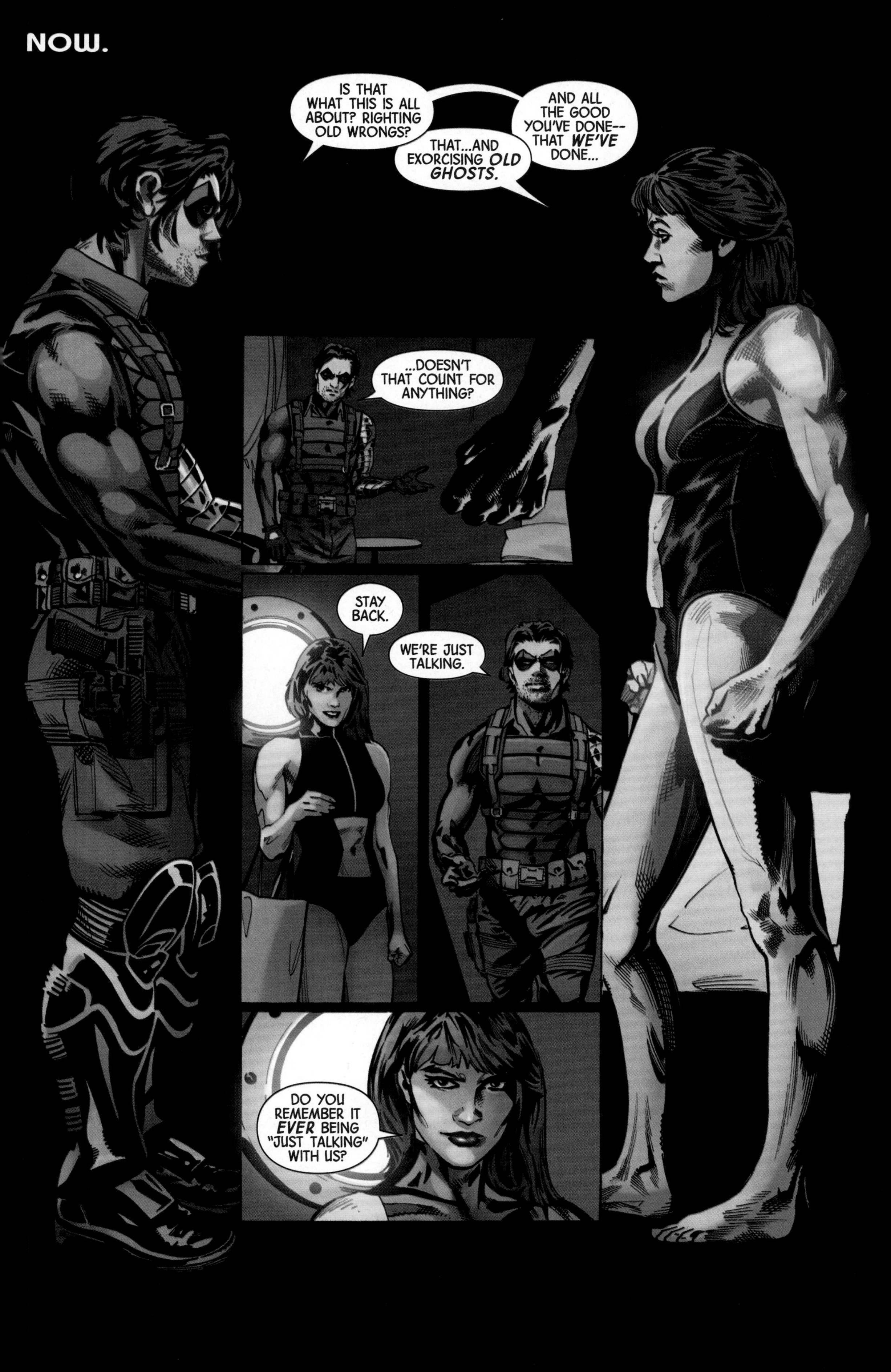
NOW.
IS THAT WHAT THIS IS ALL ABOUT? RIGHTING OLD WRONGS?
THAT...AND EXORCISING OLD GHOSTS.
AND ALL THE GOOD YOU'VE DONE-- THAT WE'VE DONE...
...DOESN'T THAT COUNT FOR ANYTHING?
STAY BACK.
WE'RE JUST TALKING.
DO YOU REMEMBER IT EVER BEING "JUST TALKING" WITH US?

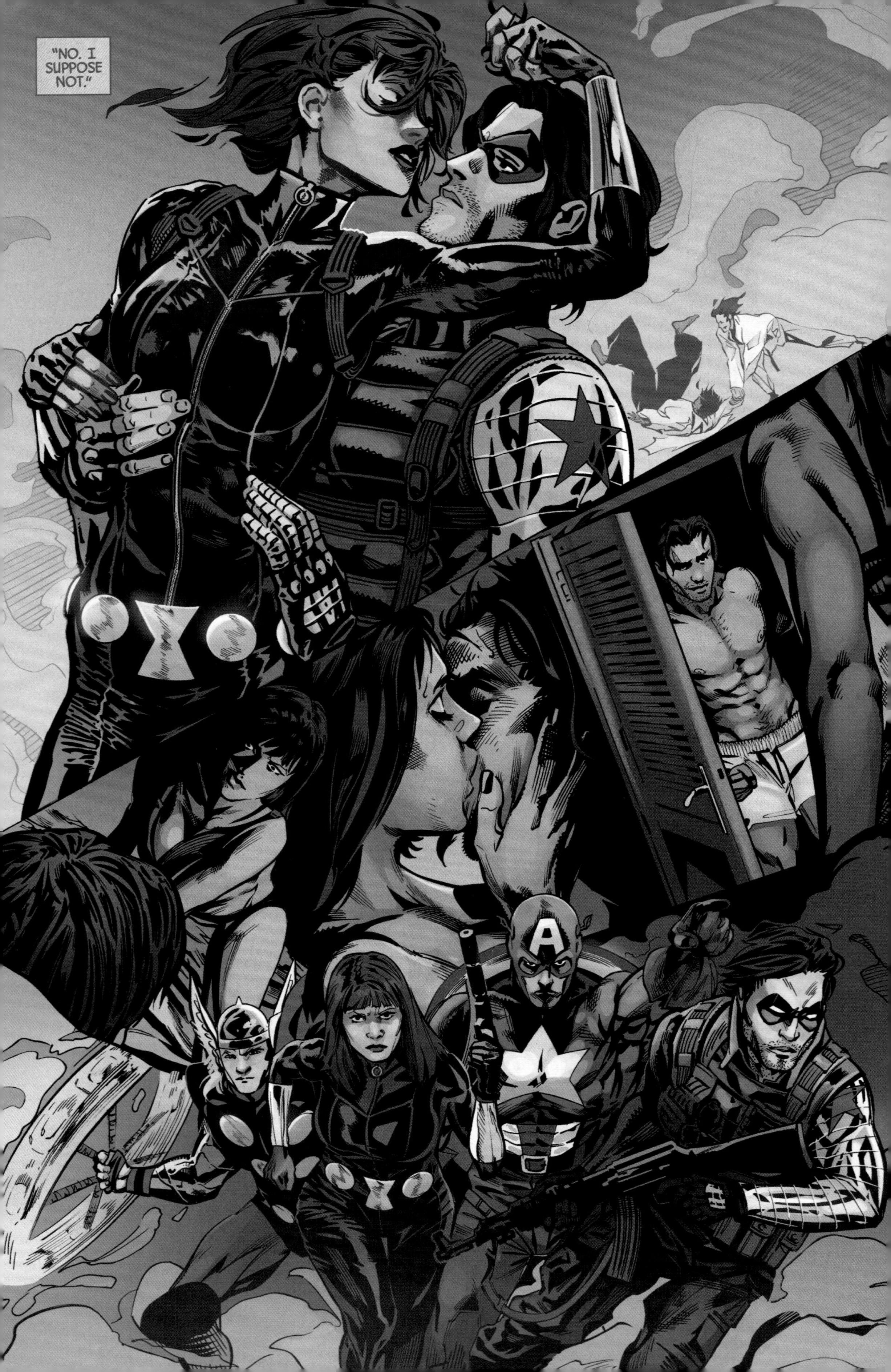
"NO. I SUPPOSE NOT."

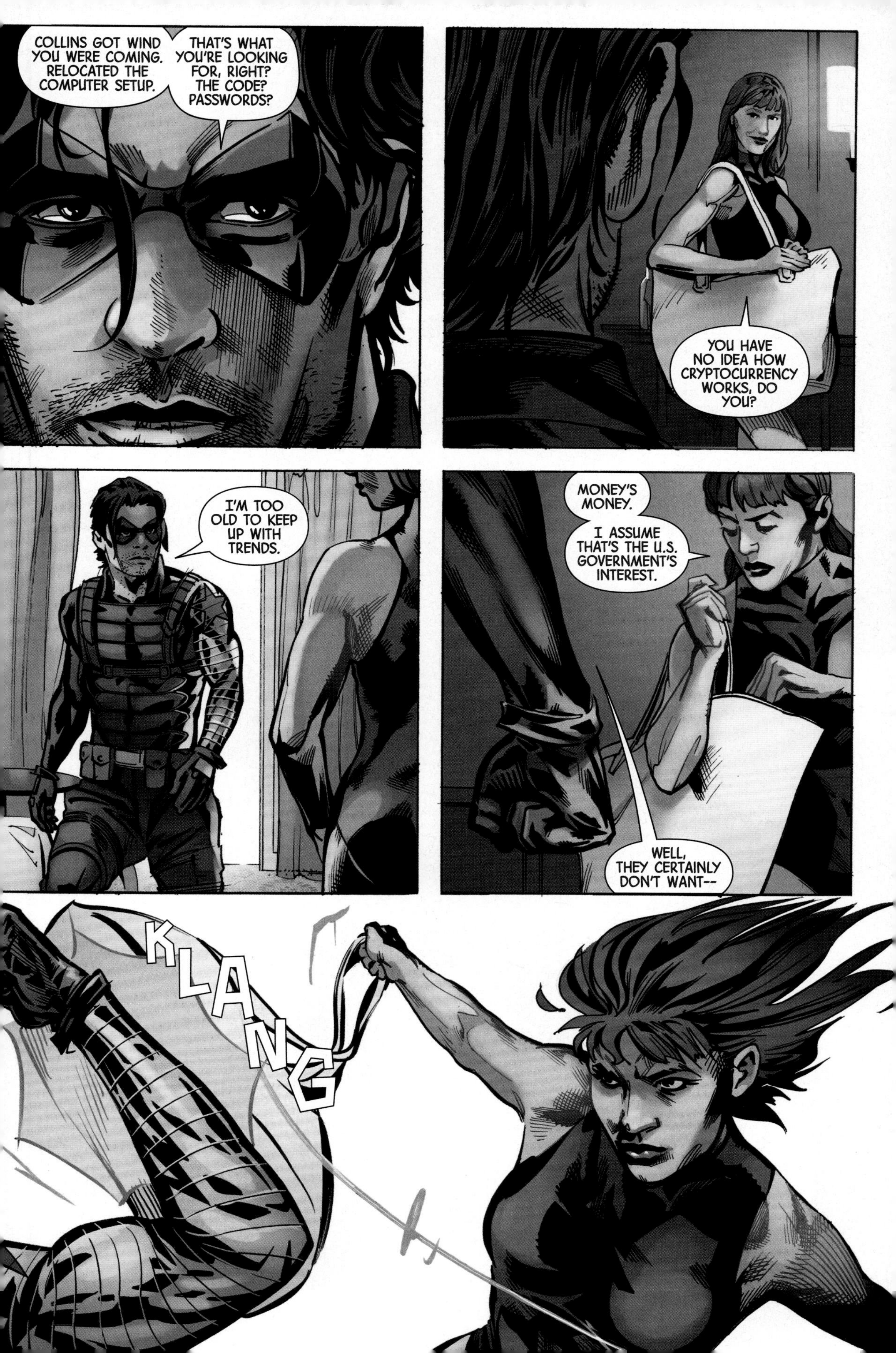
COLLINS GOT WIND YOU WERE COMING. RELOCATED THE COMPUTER SETUP.
THAT'S WHAT YOU'RE LOOKING FOR, RIGHT? THE CODE? PASSWORDS?
YOU HAVE NO IDEA HOW CRYPTOCURRENCY WORKS, DO YOU?
I'M TOO OLD TO KEEP UP WITH TRENDS.
MONEY'S MONEY.
I ASSUME THAT'S THE U.S. GOVERNMENT'S INTEREST.
WELL, THEY CERTAINLY DON'T WANT--
KLANG

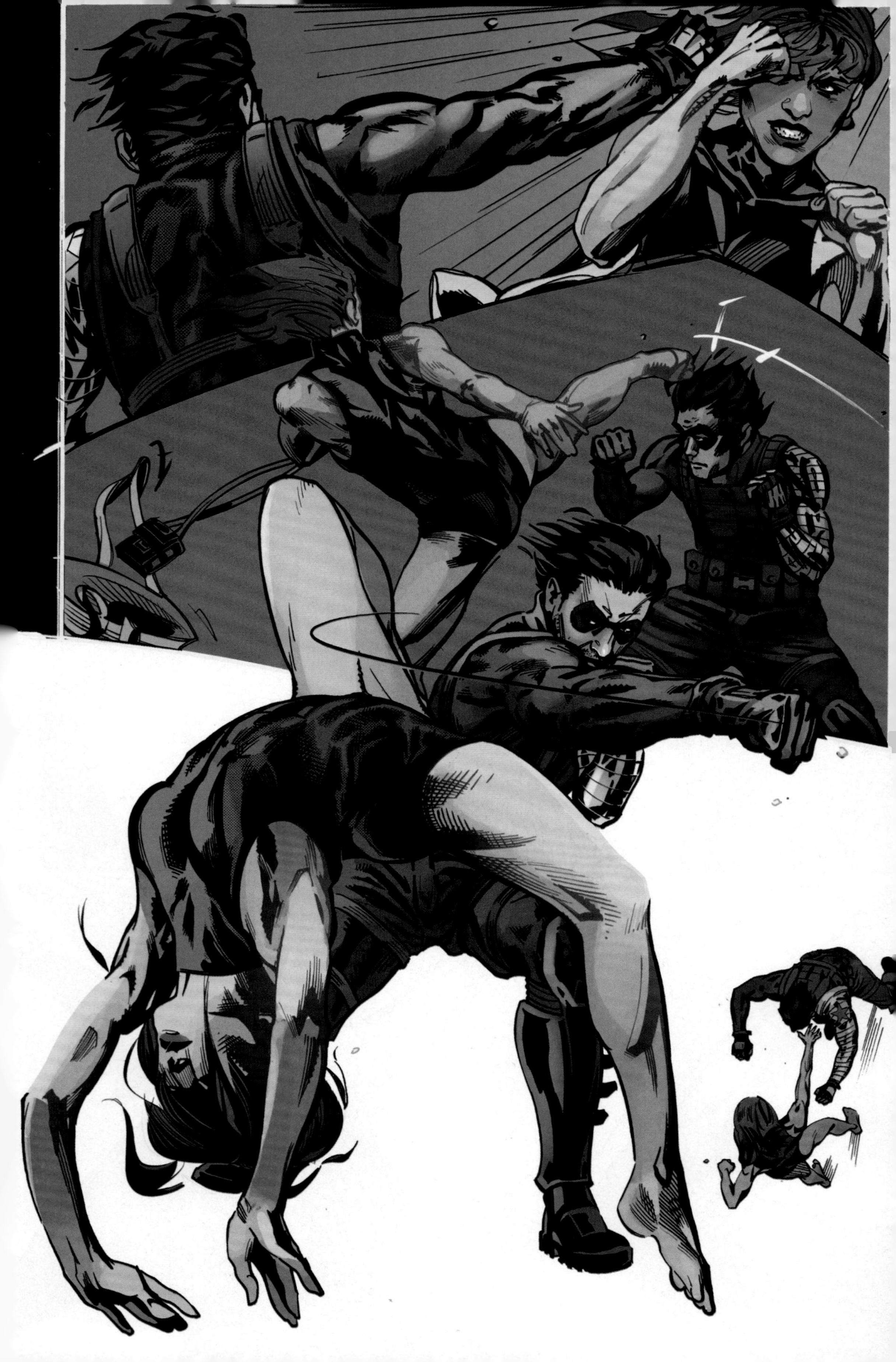

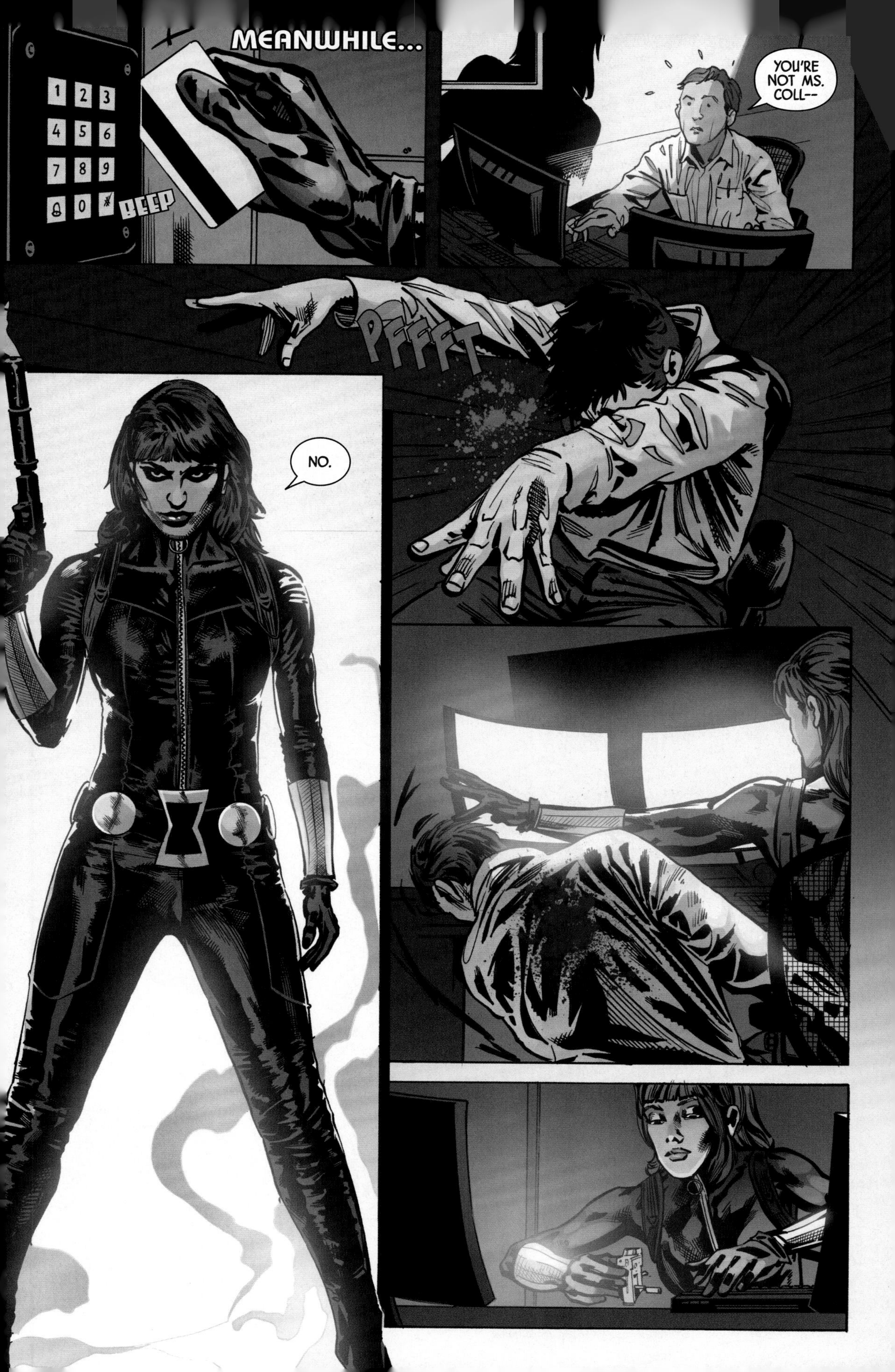
MEANWHILE...
BEEP
YOU'RE NOT MS. COLL--
PFFFT
NO.

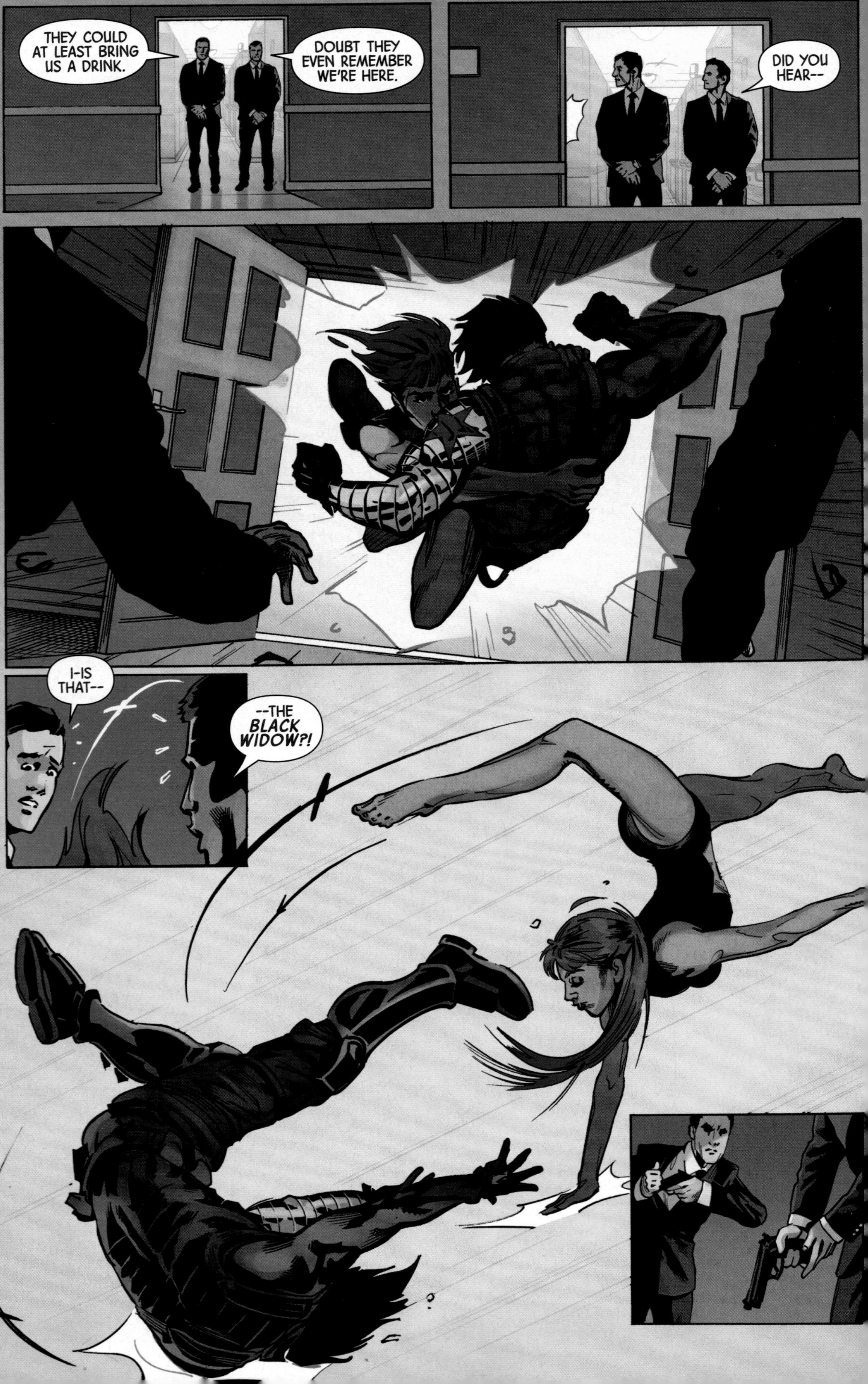
THEY COULD AT LEAST BRING US A DRINK.
DOUBT THEY EVEN REMEMBER WE'RE HERE.
DID YOU HEAR--
I-IS THAT--
--THE BLACK WIDOW?!

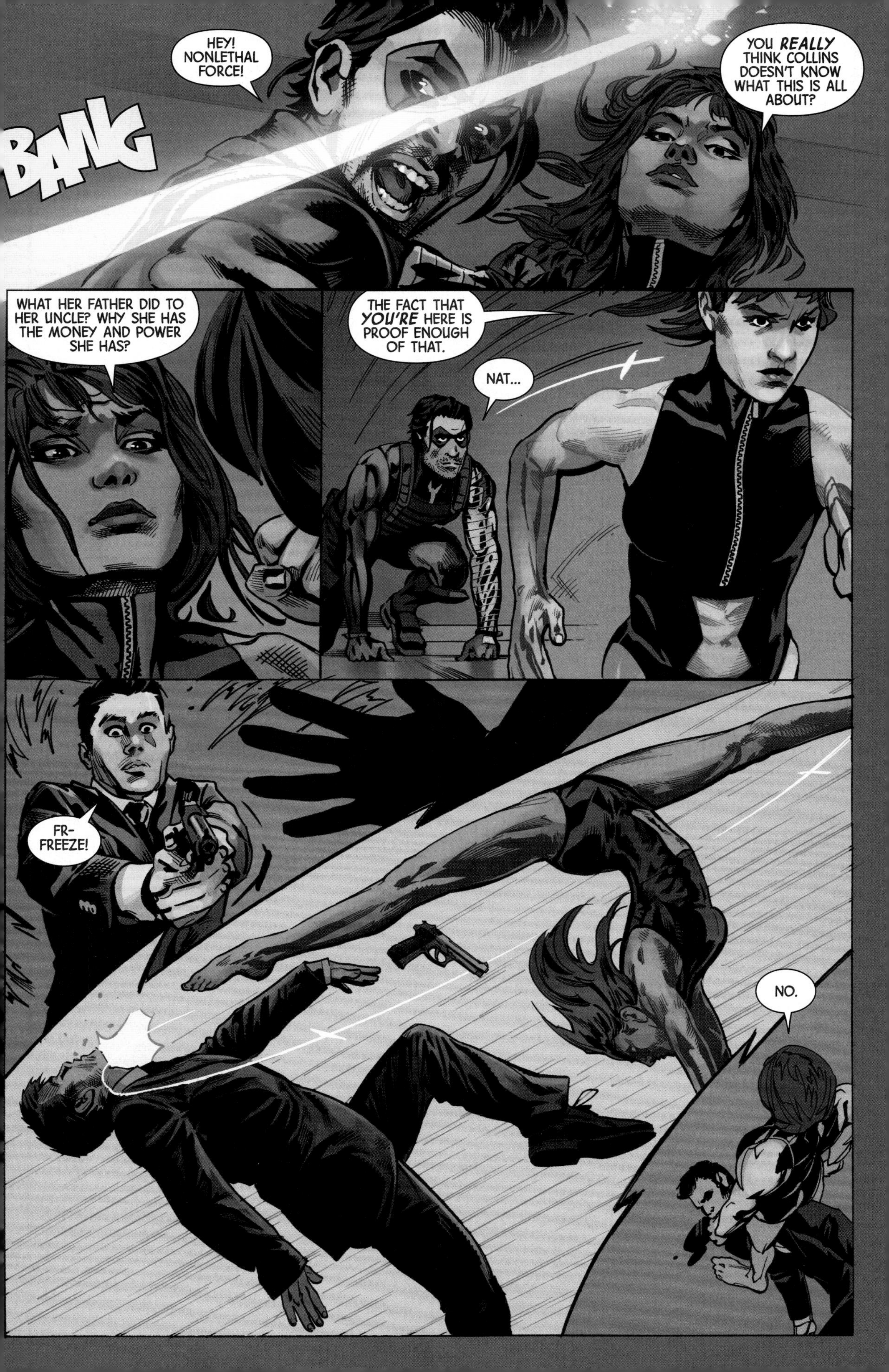
BANG
HEY! NONLETHAL FORCE!
YOU REALLY THINK COLLINS DOESN'T KNOW WHAT THIS IS ALL ABOUT?
WHAT HER FATHER DID TO HER UNCLE? WHY SHE HAS THE MONEY AND POWER SHE HAS?
THE FACT THAT YOU'RE HERE IS PROOF ENOUGH OF THAT.
NAT...
FR- FREEZE!
NO.

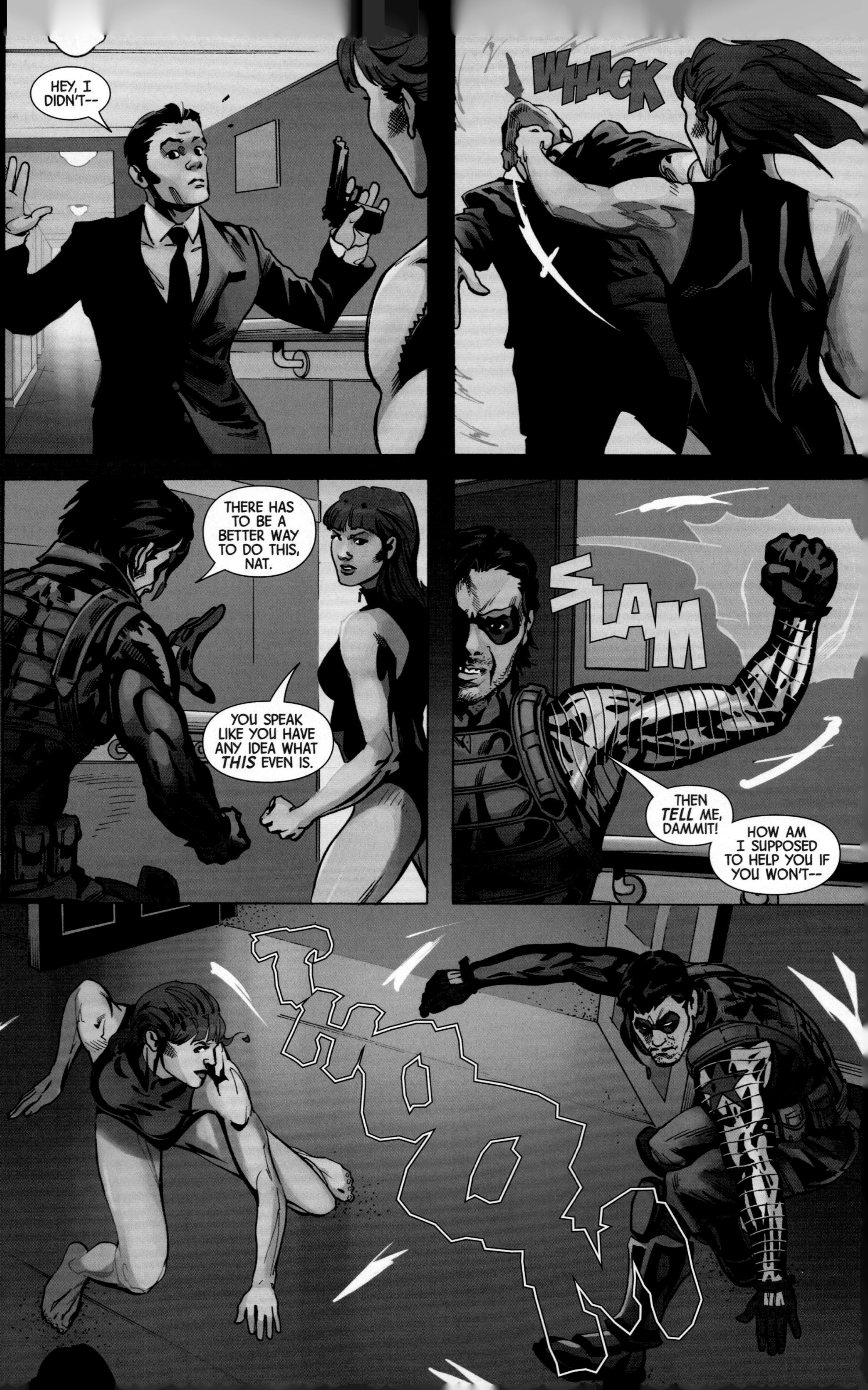
HEY, I DIDN'T--
WHACK
THERE HAS TO BE A BETTER WAY TO DO THIS, NAT.
YOU SPEAK LIKE YOU HAVE ANY IDEA WHAT *THIS* EVEN IS.
SLAM
THEN *TELL* ME, DAMMIT!
HOW AM I SUPPOSED TO HELP YOU IF YOU WON'T--
THOOM

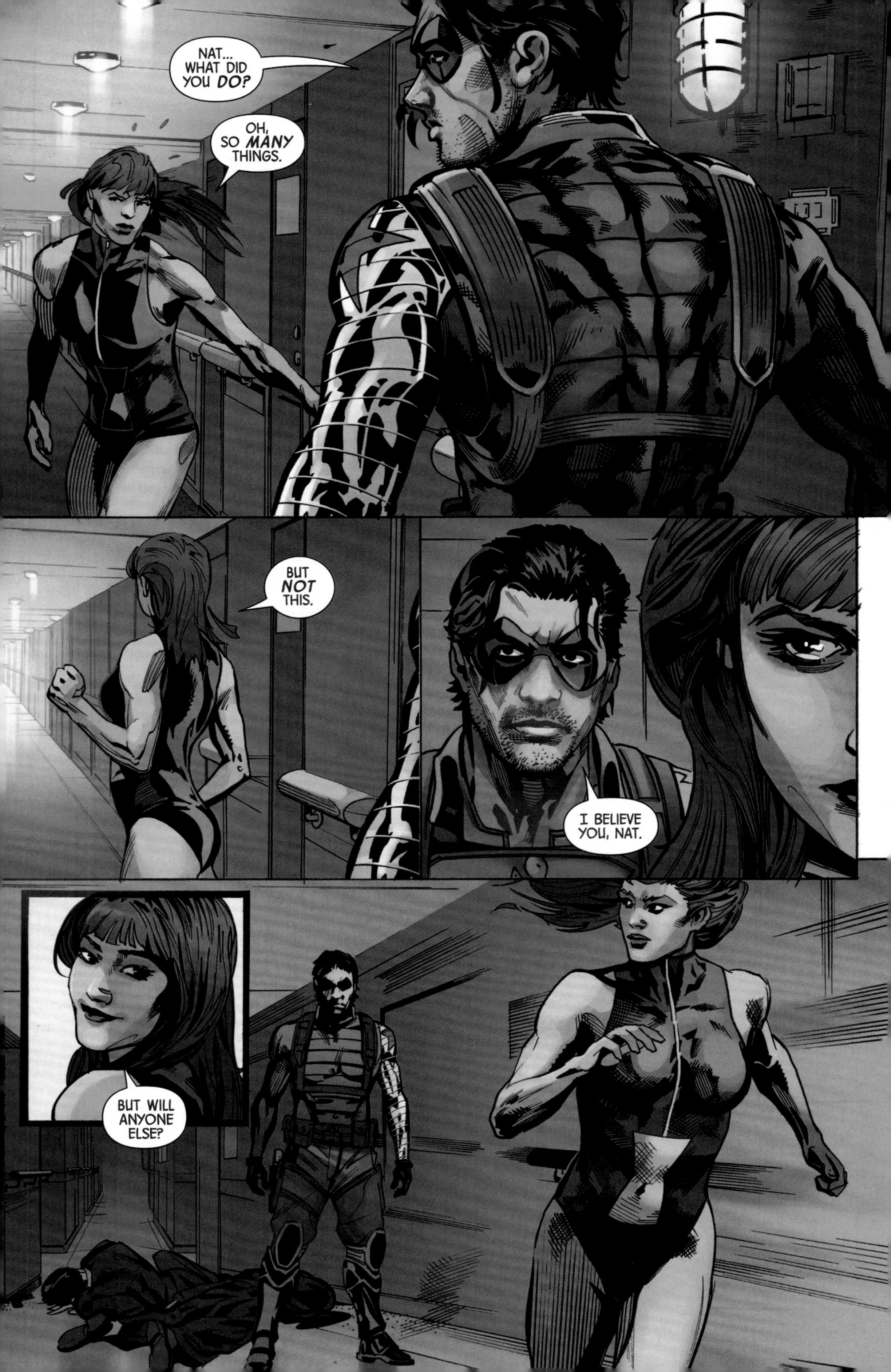
NAT... WHAT DID YOU DO?
OH, SO MANY THINGS.
BUT NOT THIS.
I BELIEVE YOU, NAT.
BUT WILL ANYONE ELSE?

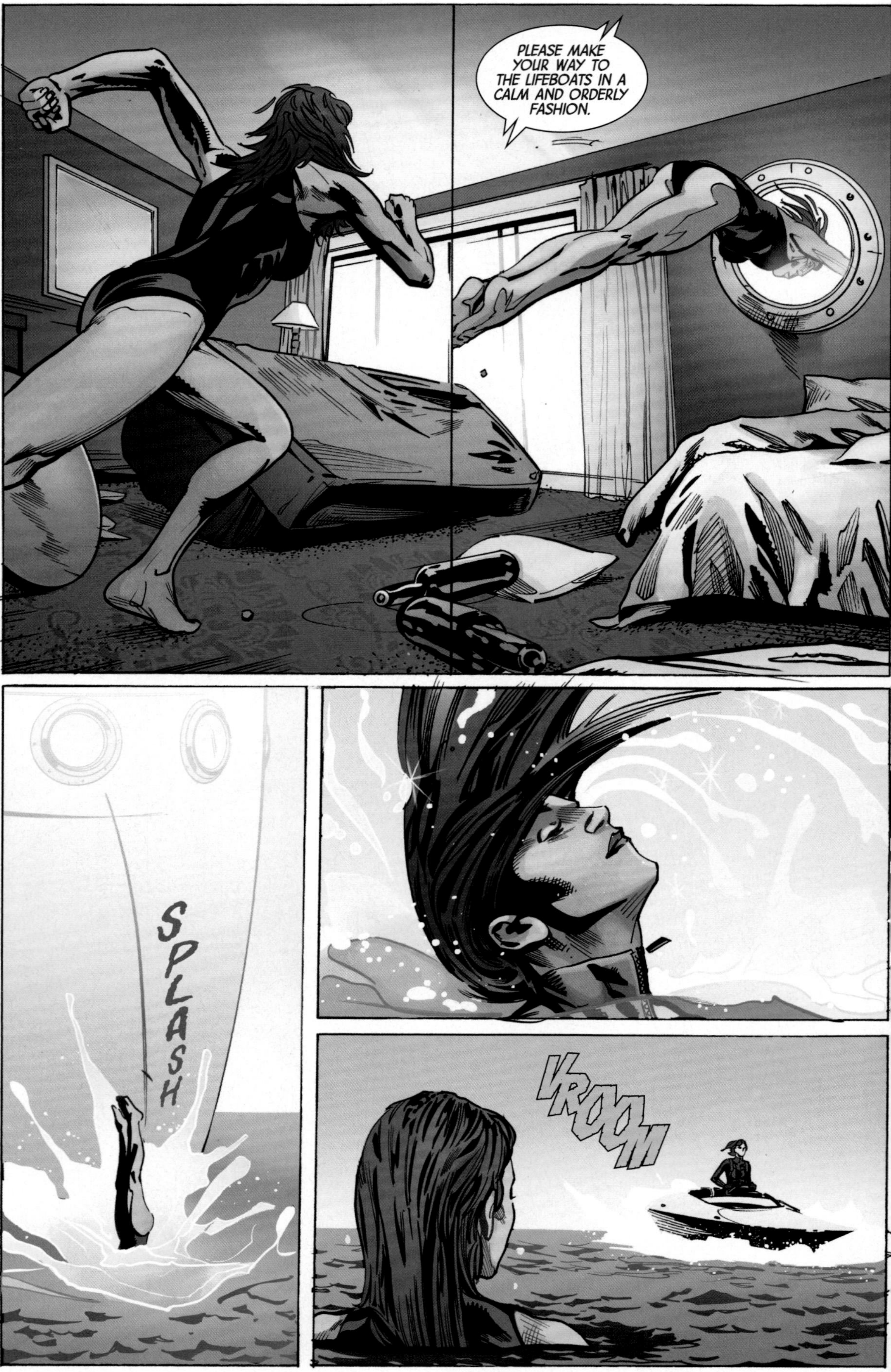
PLEASE MAKE YOUR WAY TO THE LIFEBOATS IN A CALM AND ORDERLY FASHION.
SPLASH
VROOOM

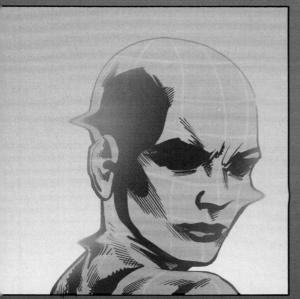

BE SEEING YOU, NATASHA...

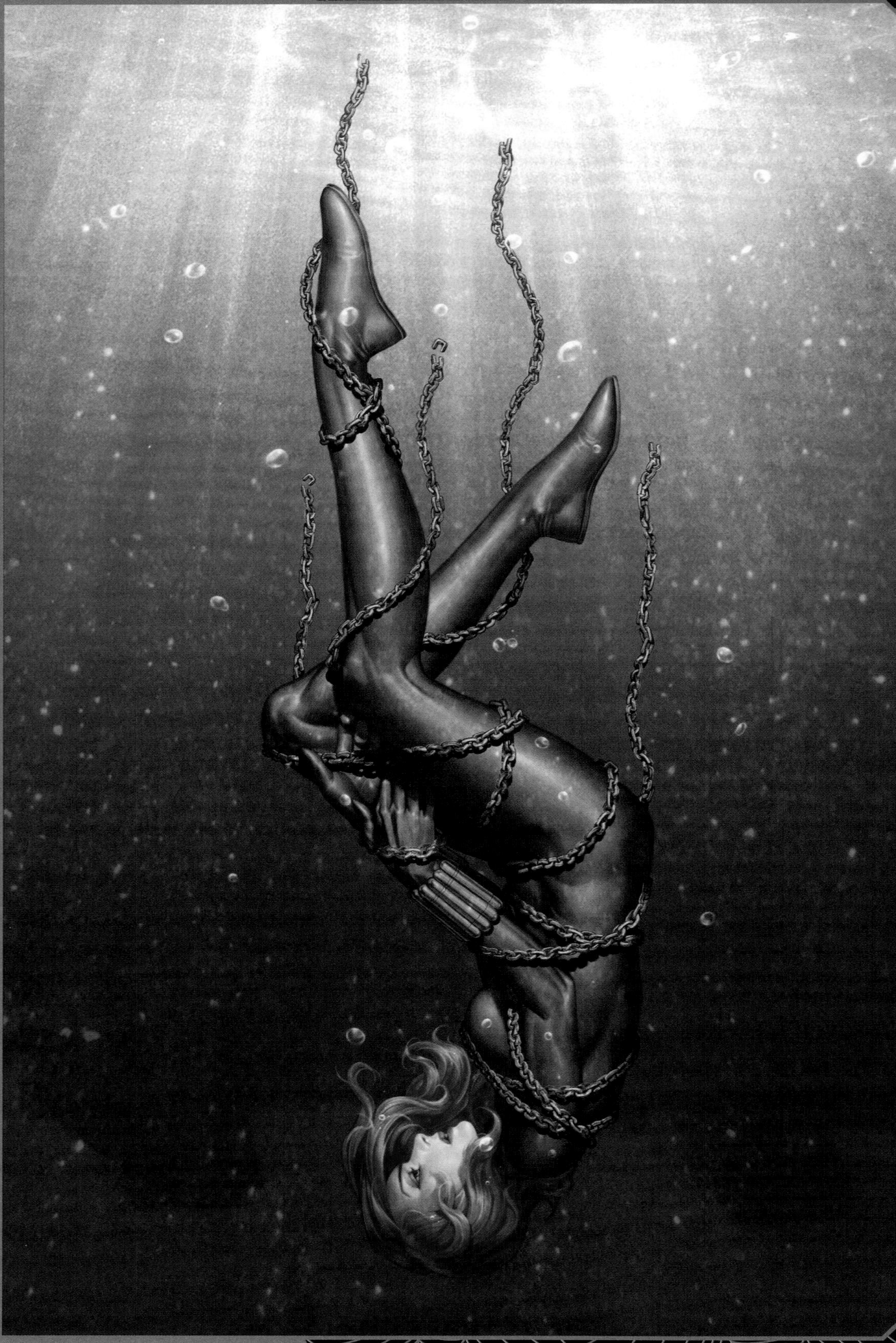

THREE

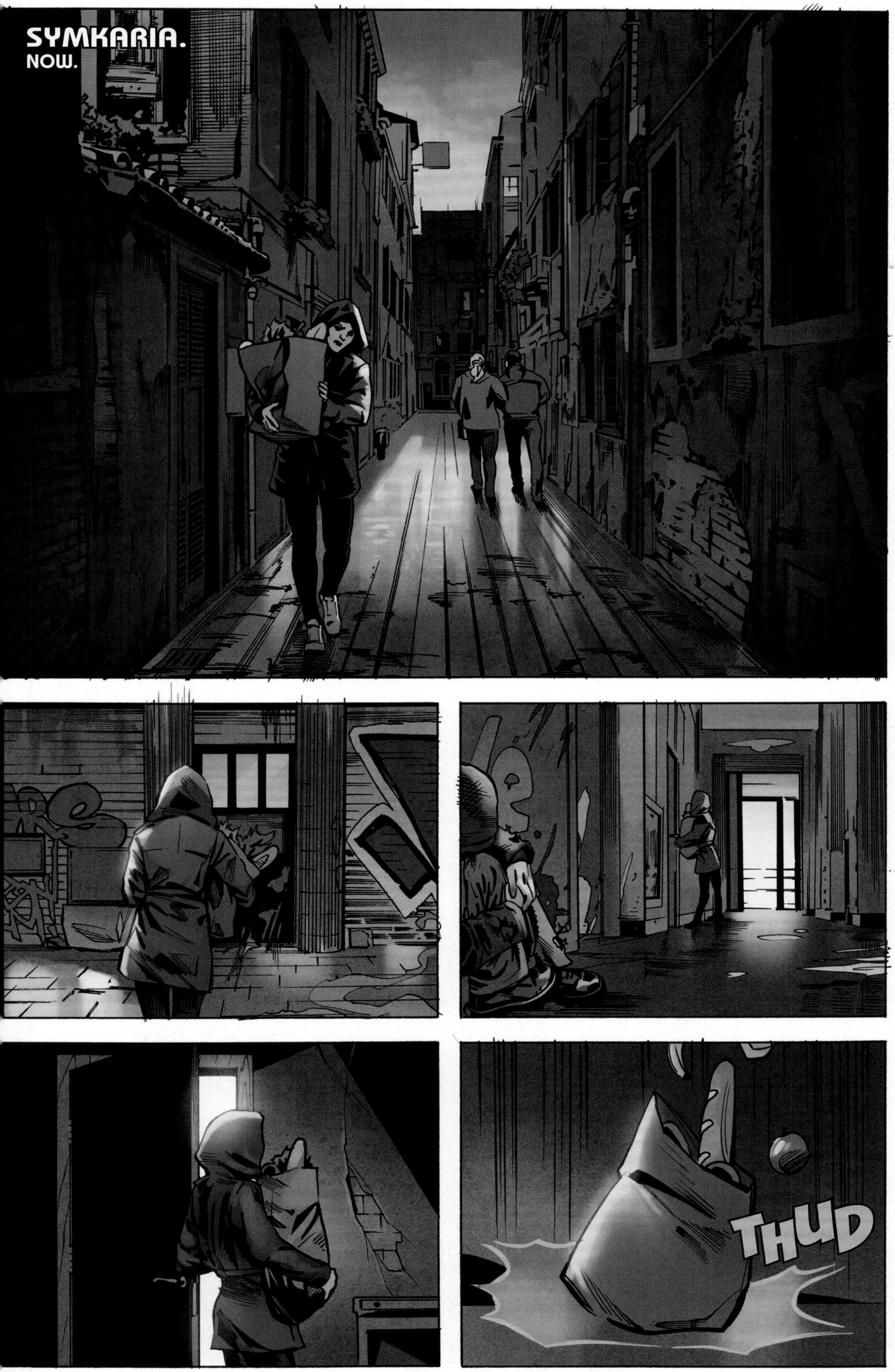
SYMKARIA.
NOW.
THUD

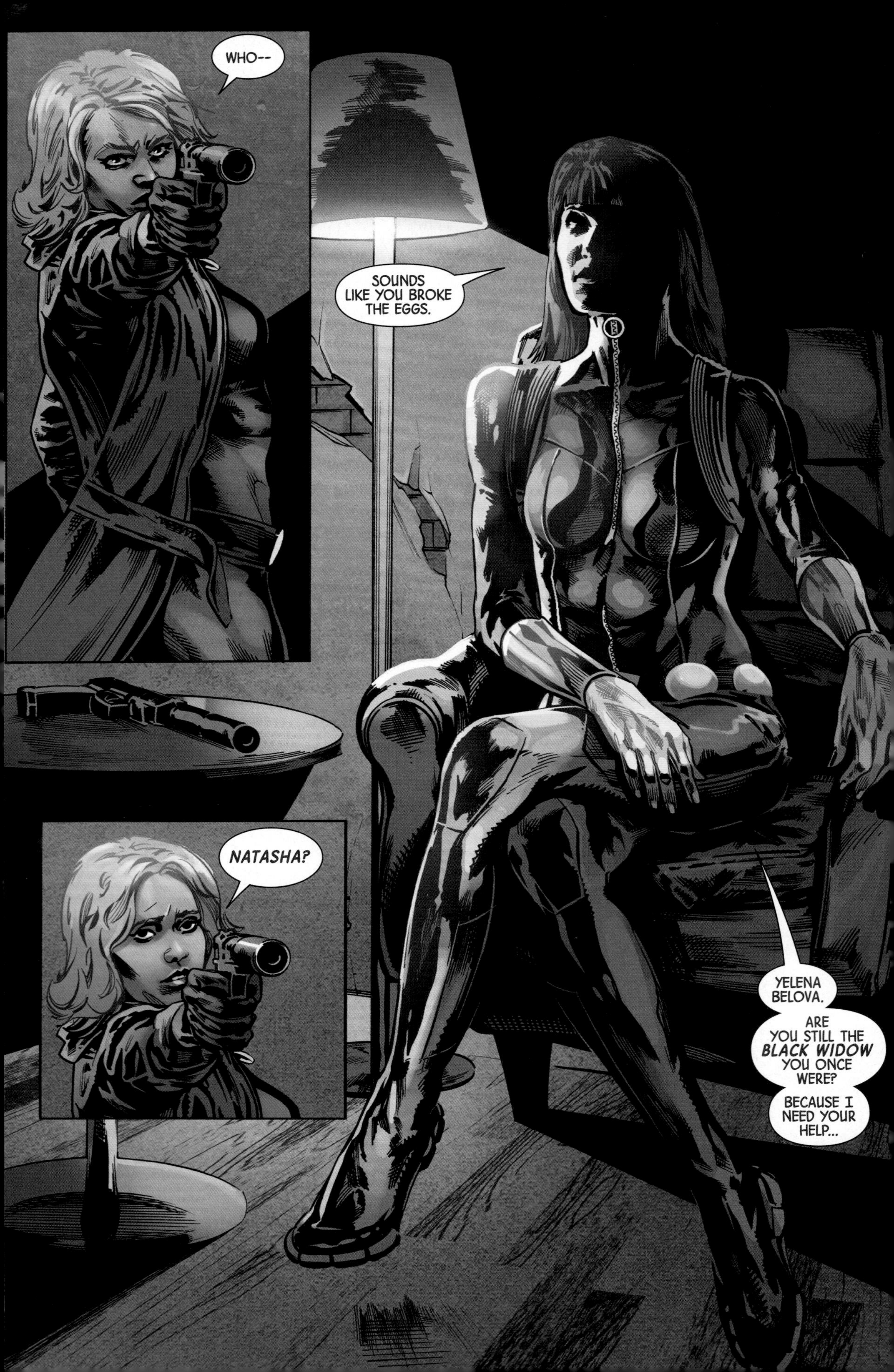
WHO--
SOUNDS LIKE YOU BROKE THE EGGS.
NATASHA?
YELENA BELOVA.
ARE YOU STILL THE BLACK WIDOW YOU ONCE WERE?
BECAUSE I NEED YOUR HELP...

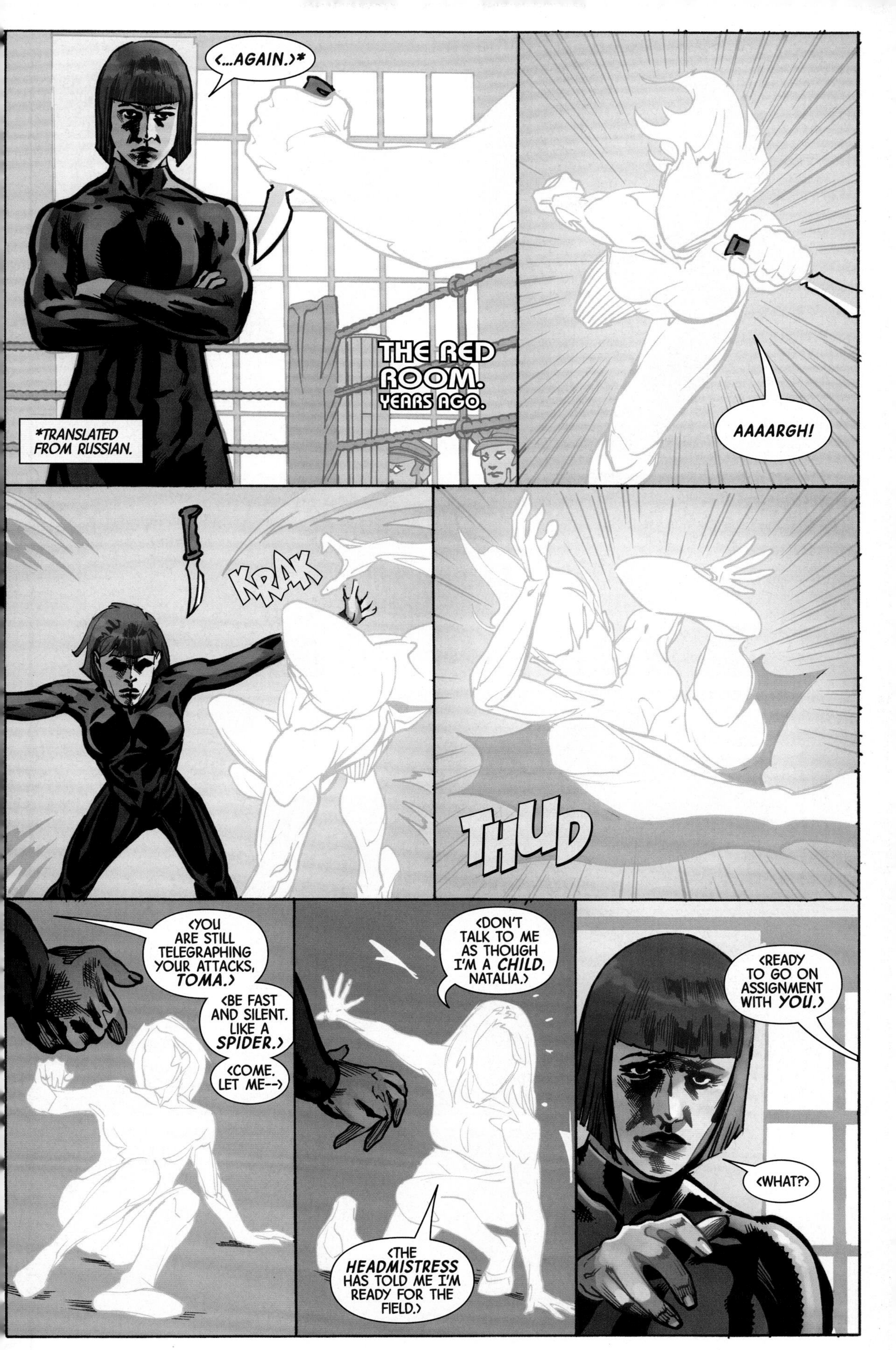
<...AGAIN.>*
*TRANSLATED FROM RUSSIAN.
THE RED ROOM. YEARS AGO.
AAAARGH!
KRAK
THUD
<YOU ARE STILL TELEGRAPHING YOUR ATTACKS, TOMA.>
<BE FAST AND SILENT. LIKE A SPIDER.>
<COME. LET ME-->
<DON'T TALK TO ME AS THOUGH I'M A CHILD, NATALIA.>
<THE HEADMISTRESS HAS TOLD ME I'M READY FOR THE FIELD.>
<READY TO GO ON ASSIGNMENT WITH YOU.>
<WHAT?>

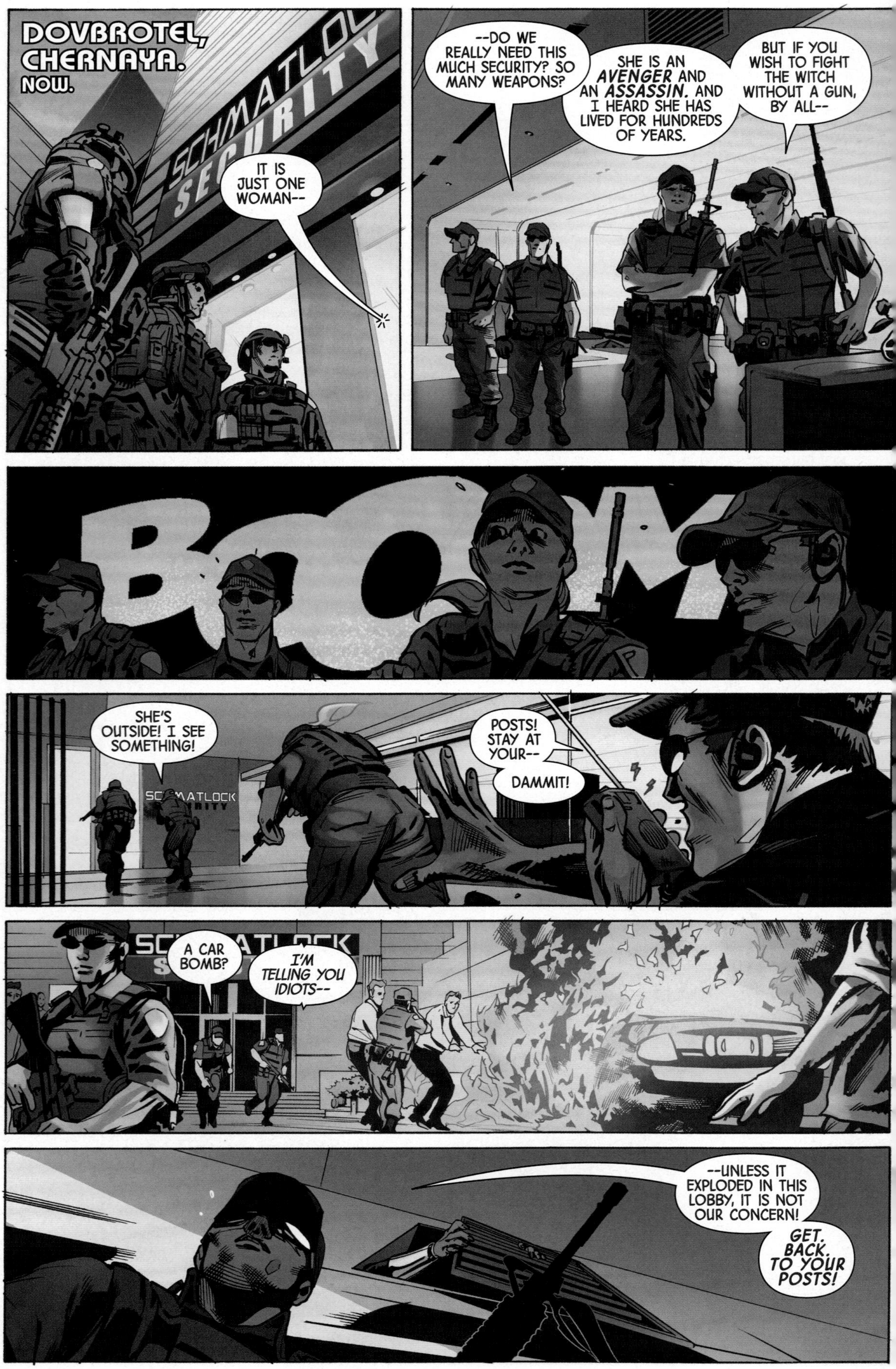
DOVBROTEL, CHERNAYA. NOW.
SCHMATLOCK SECURITY
IT IS JUST ONE WOMAN--
--DO WE REALLY NEED THIS MUCH SECURITY? SO MANY WEAPONS?
SHE IS AN AVENGER AND AN ASSASSIN. AND I HEARD SHE HAS LIVED FOR HUNDREDS OF YEARS.
BUT IF YOU WISH TO FIGHT THE WITCH WITHOUT A GUN, BY ALL--
BOOM
SHE'S OUTSIDE! I SEE SOMETHING!
SCHMATLOCK SECURITY
POSTS! STAY AT YOUR--
DAMMIT!
A CAR BOMB?
I'M TELLING YOU IDIOTS--
--UNLESS IT EXPLODED IN THIS LOBBY, IT IS NOT OUR CONCERN!
GET. BACK. TO YOUR POSTS!

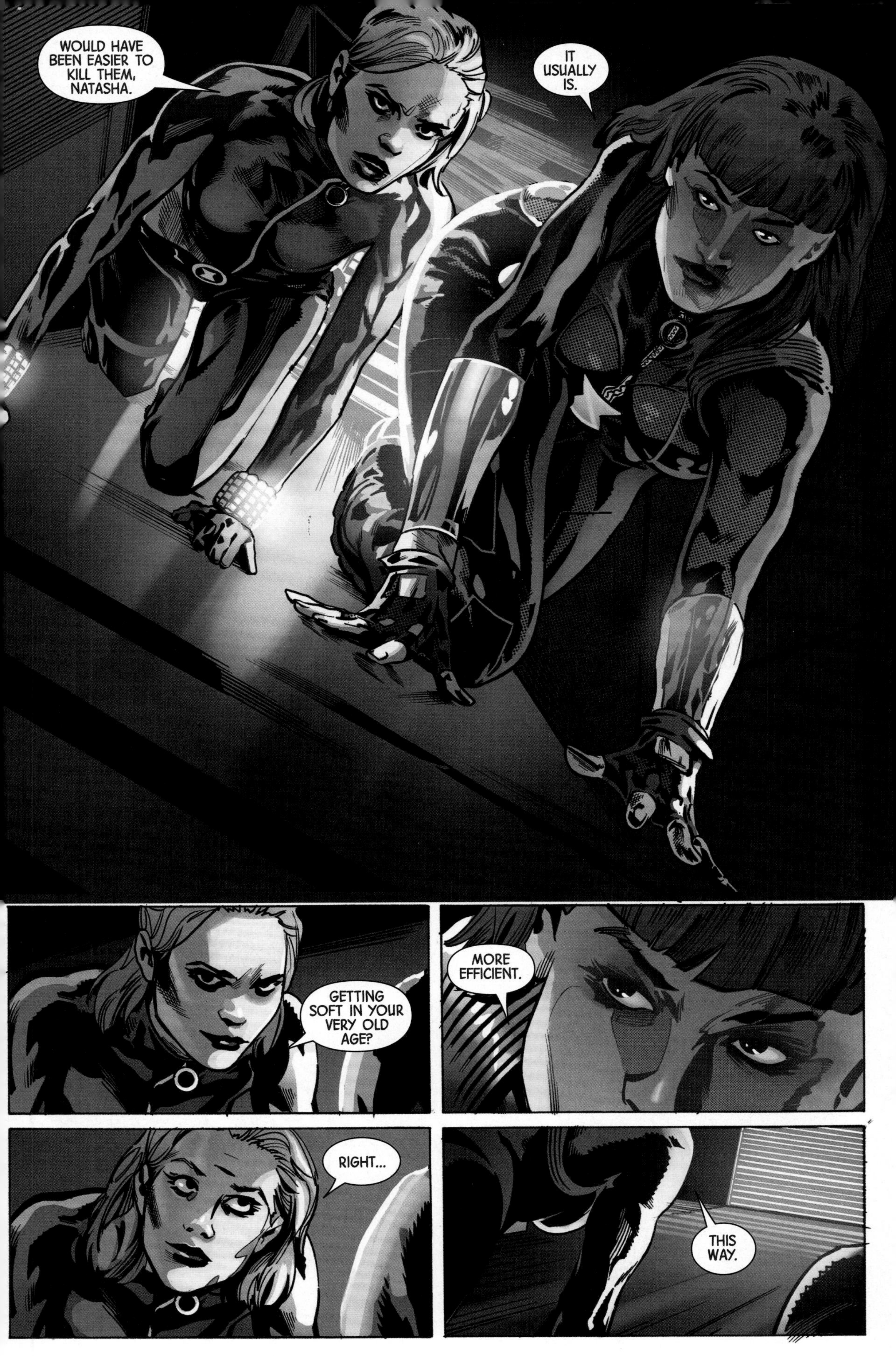
WOULD HAVE BEEN EASIER TO KILL THEM, NATASHA.
IT USUALLY IS.
GETTING SOFT IN YOUR VERY OLD AGE?
MORE EFFICIENT.
RIGHT...
THIS WAY.

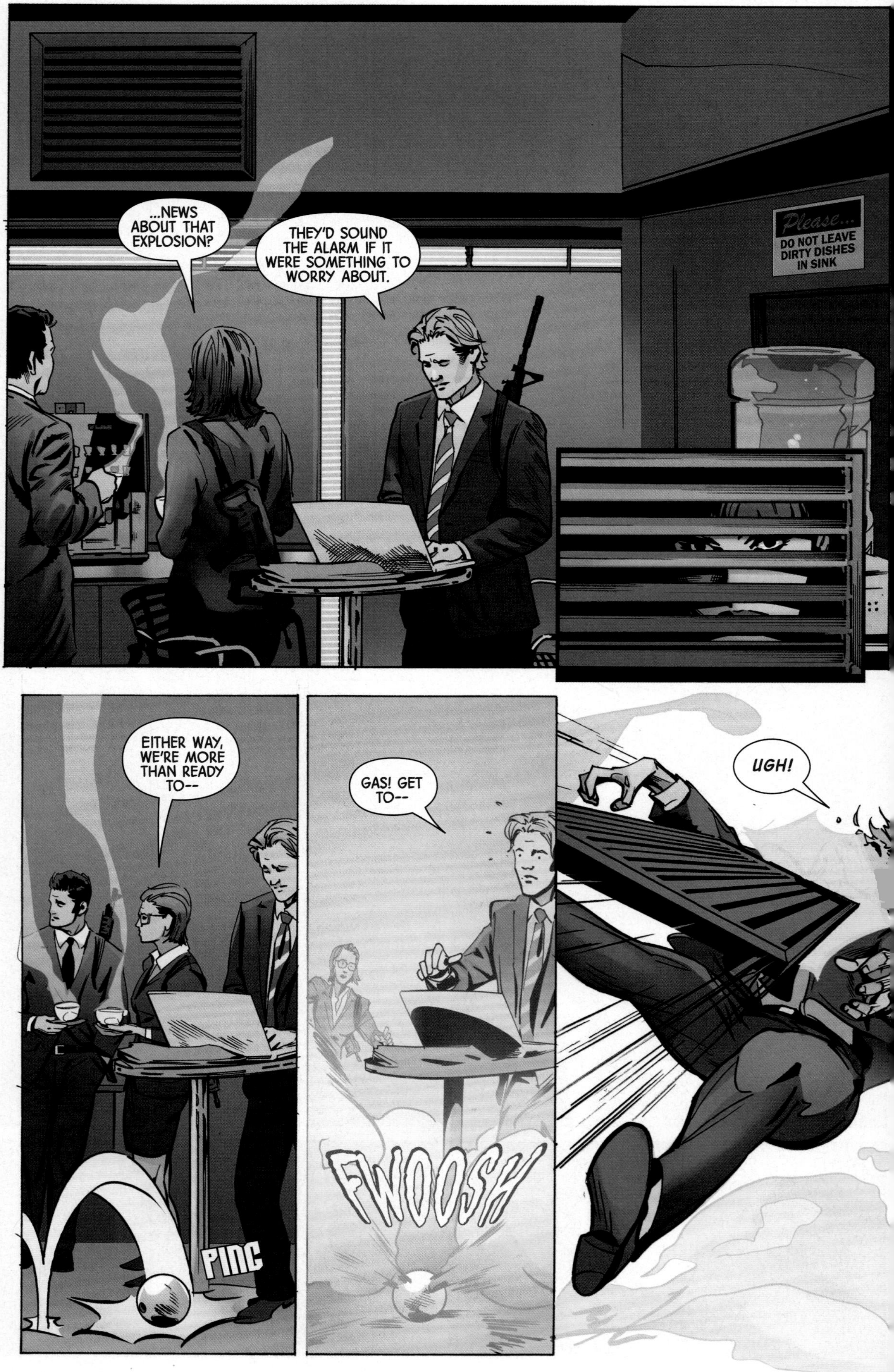
...NEWS ABOUT THAT EXPLOSION?
THEY'D SOUND THE ALARM IF IT WERE SOMETHING TO WORRY ABOUT.
Please... DO NOT LEAVE DIRTY DISHES IN SINK
EITHER WAY, WE'RE MORE THAN READY TO--
PING
GAS! GET TO--
FWOOSH
UGH!

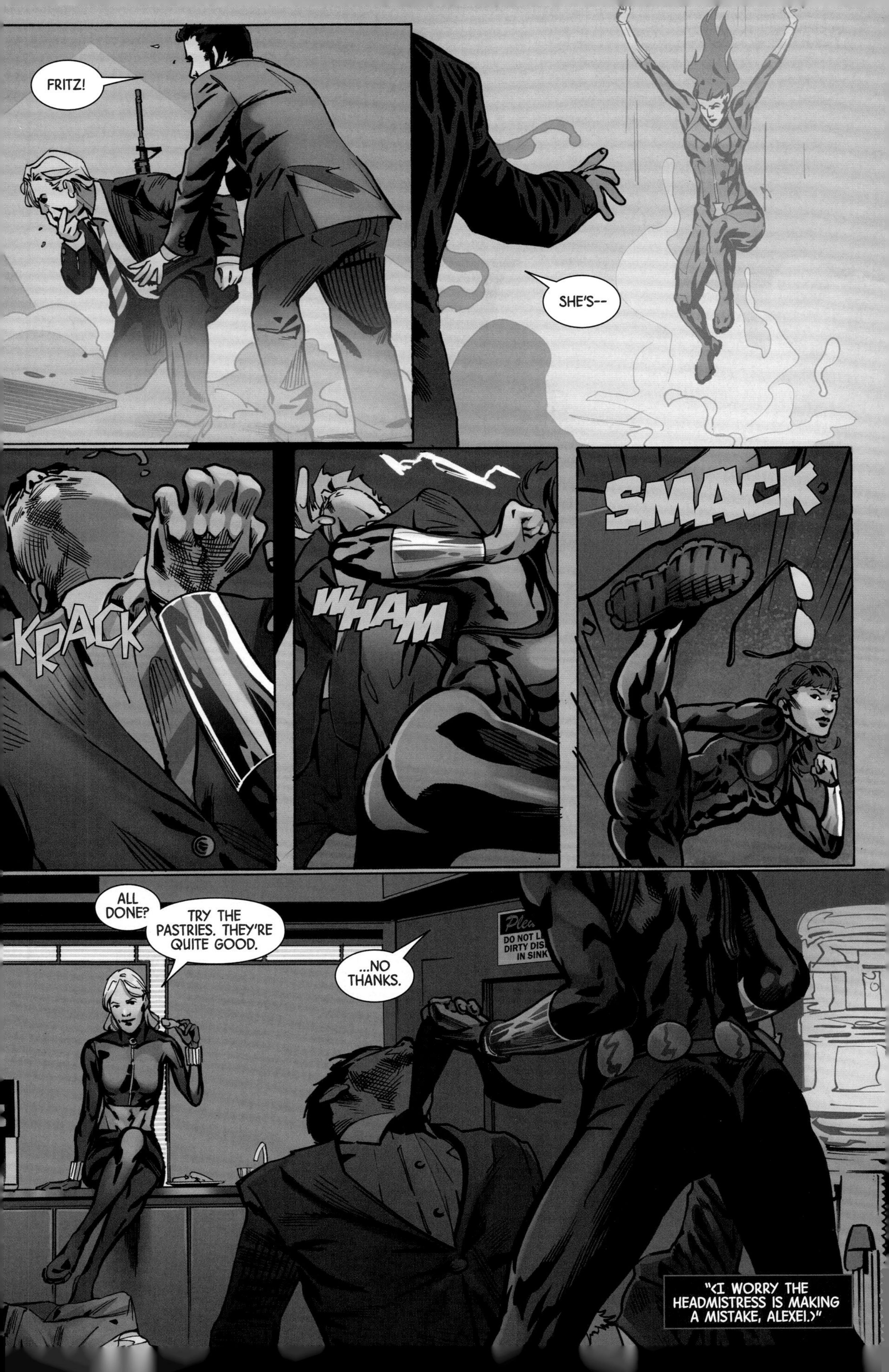
FRITZ!
SHE'S--
KRACK
WHAM
SMACK
ALL DONE?
TRY THE PASTRIES. THEY'RE QUITE GOOD.
...NO THANKS.
DO NOT LEAVE DIRTY DISHES IN SINK
"<I WORRY THE HEADMISTRESS IS MAKING A MISTAKE, ALEXEI.>"

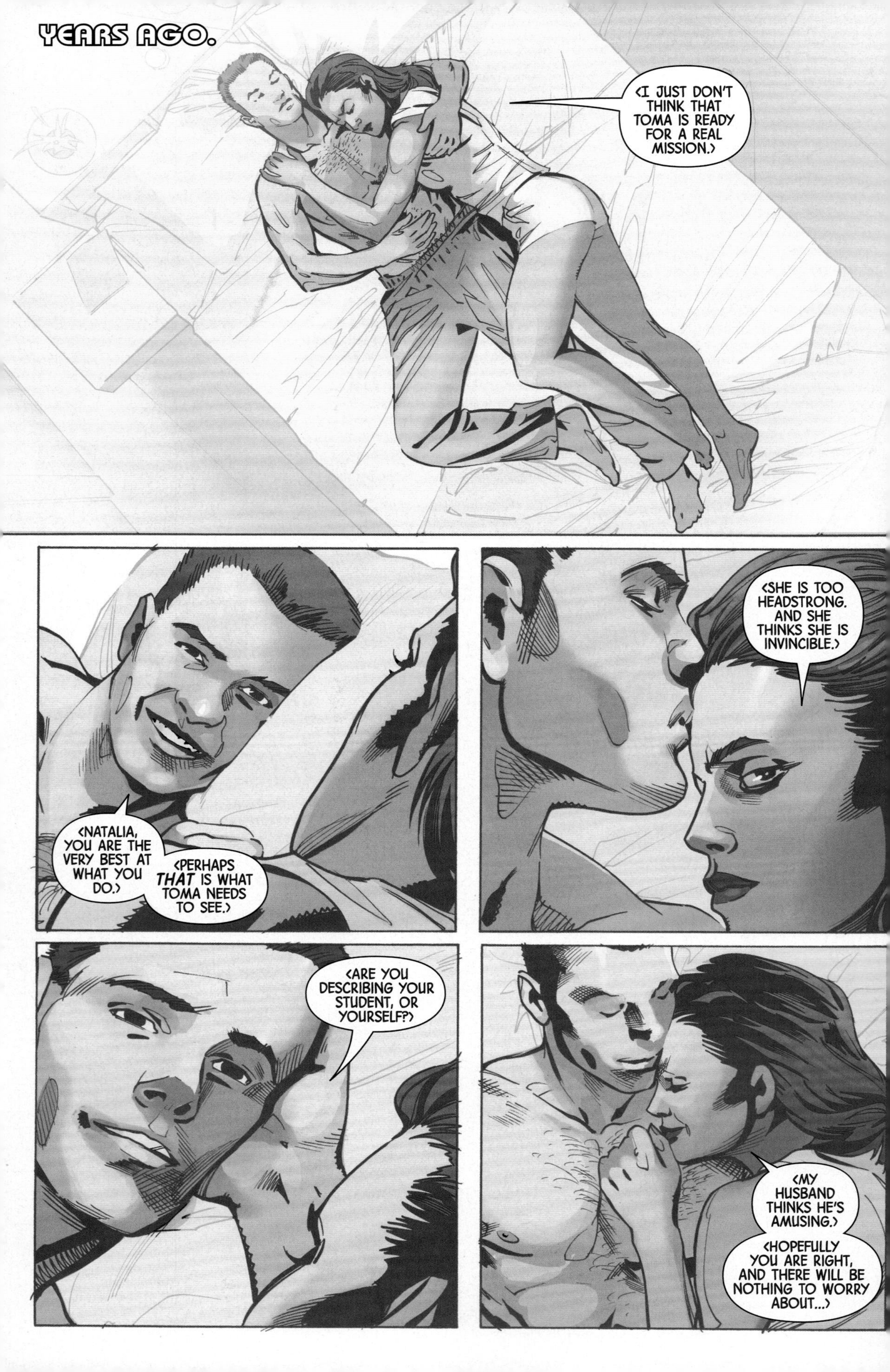
YEARS AGO.
<I JUST DON'T THINK THAT TOMA IS READY FOR A REAL MISSION.>
<NATALIA, YOU ARE THE VERY BEST AT WHAT YOU DO.>
<PERHAPS *THAT* IS WHAT TOMA NEEDS TO SEE.>
<SHE IS TOO HEADSTRONG. AND SHE THINKS SHE IS INVINCIBLE.>
<ARE YOU DESCRIBING YOUR STUDENT, OR YOURSELF?>
<MY HUSBAND THINKS HE'S AMUSING.>
<HOPEFULLY YOU ARE RIGHT, AND THERE WILL BE NOTHING TO WORRY ABOUT...>

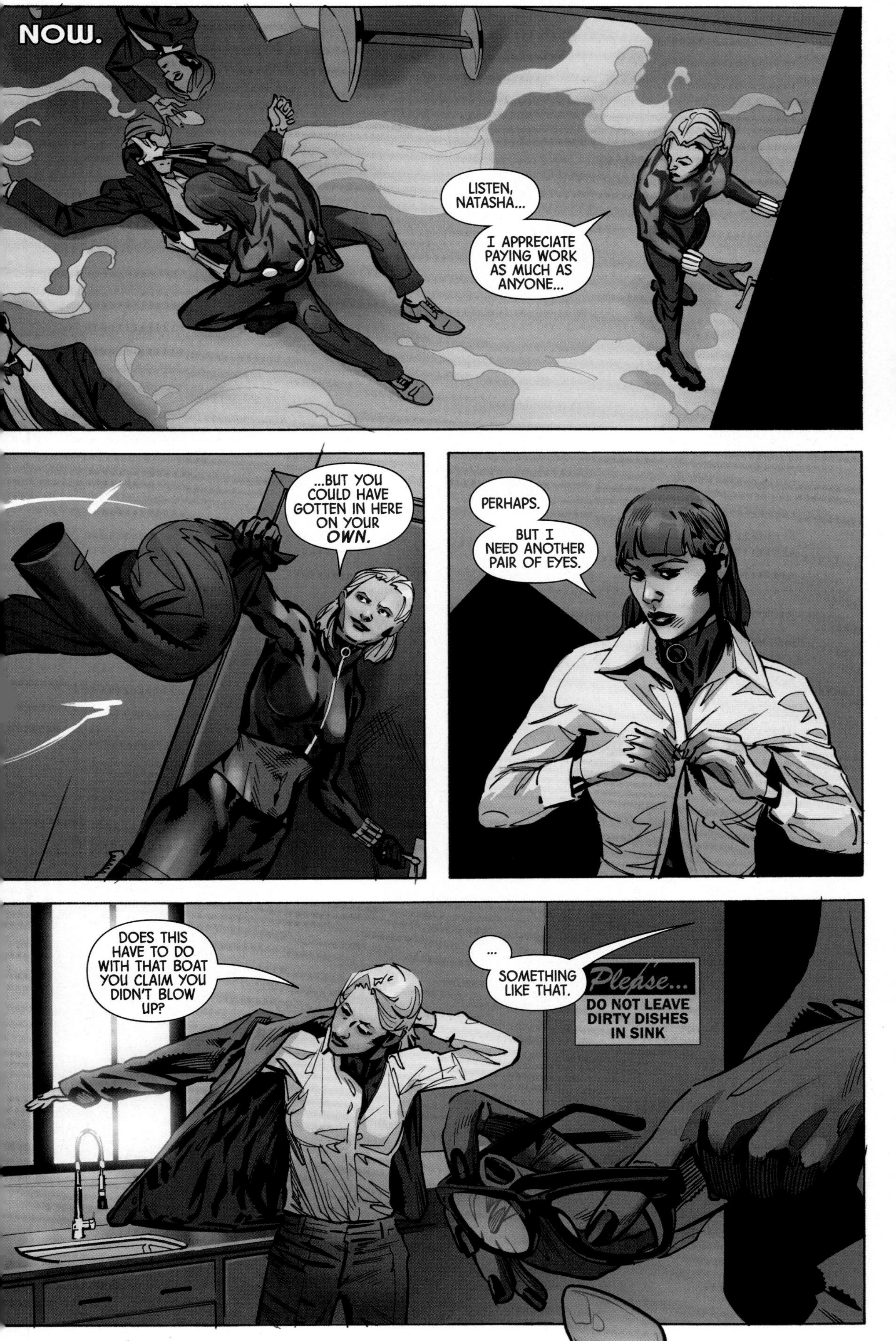
NOW.
LISTEN, NATASHA...
I APPRECIATE PAYING WORK AS MUCH AS ANYONE...
...BUT YOU COULD HAVE GOTTEN IN HERE ON YOUR *OWN.*
PERHAPS.
BUT I NEED ANOTHER PAIR OF EYES.
DOES THIS HAVE TO DO WITH THAT BOAT YOU CLAIM YOU DIDN'T BLOW UP?
...
SOMETHING LIKE THAT.
Please...
DO NOT LEAVE DIRTY DISHES IN SINK

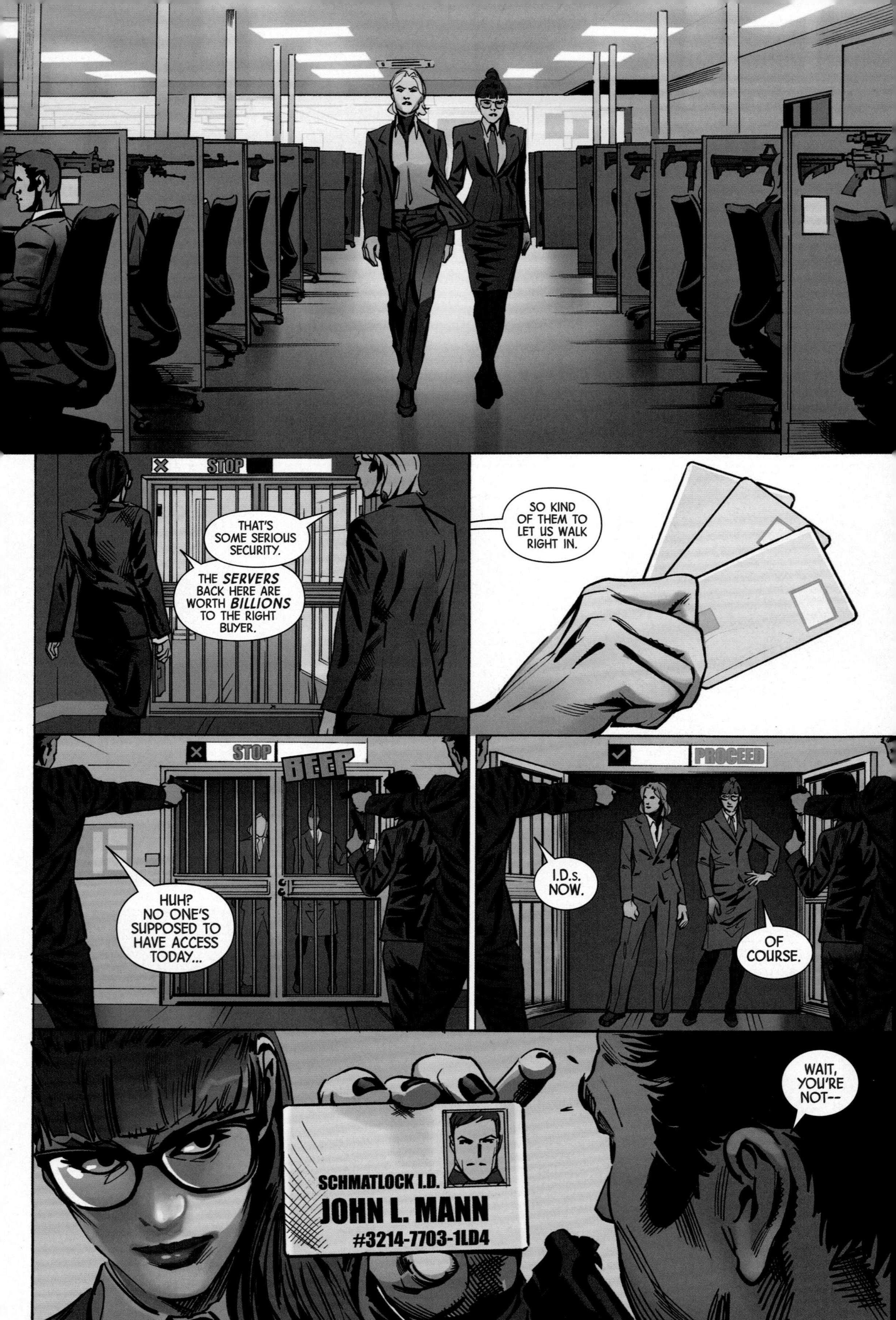

STOP
THAT'S SOME SERIOUS SECURITY.
THE SERVERS BACK HERE ARE WORTH BILLIONS TO THE RIGHT BUYER.
SO KIND OF THEM TO LET US WALK RIGHT IN.
STOP
BEEP
HUH? NO ONE'S SUPPOSED TO HAVE ACCESS TODAY...
PROCEED
I.D.s. NOW.
OF COURSE.
SCHMATLOCK I.D.
JOHN L. MANN
#3214-7703-1LD4
WAIT, YOU'RE NOT--

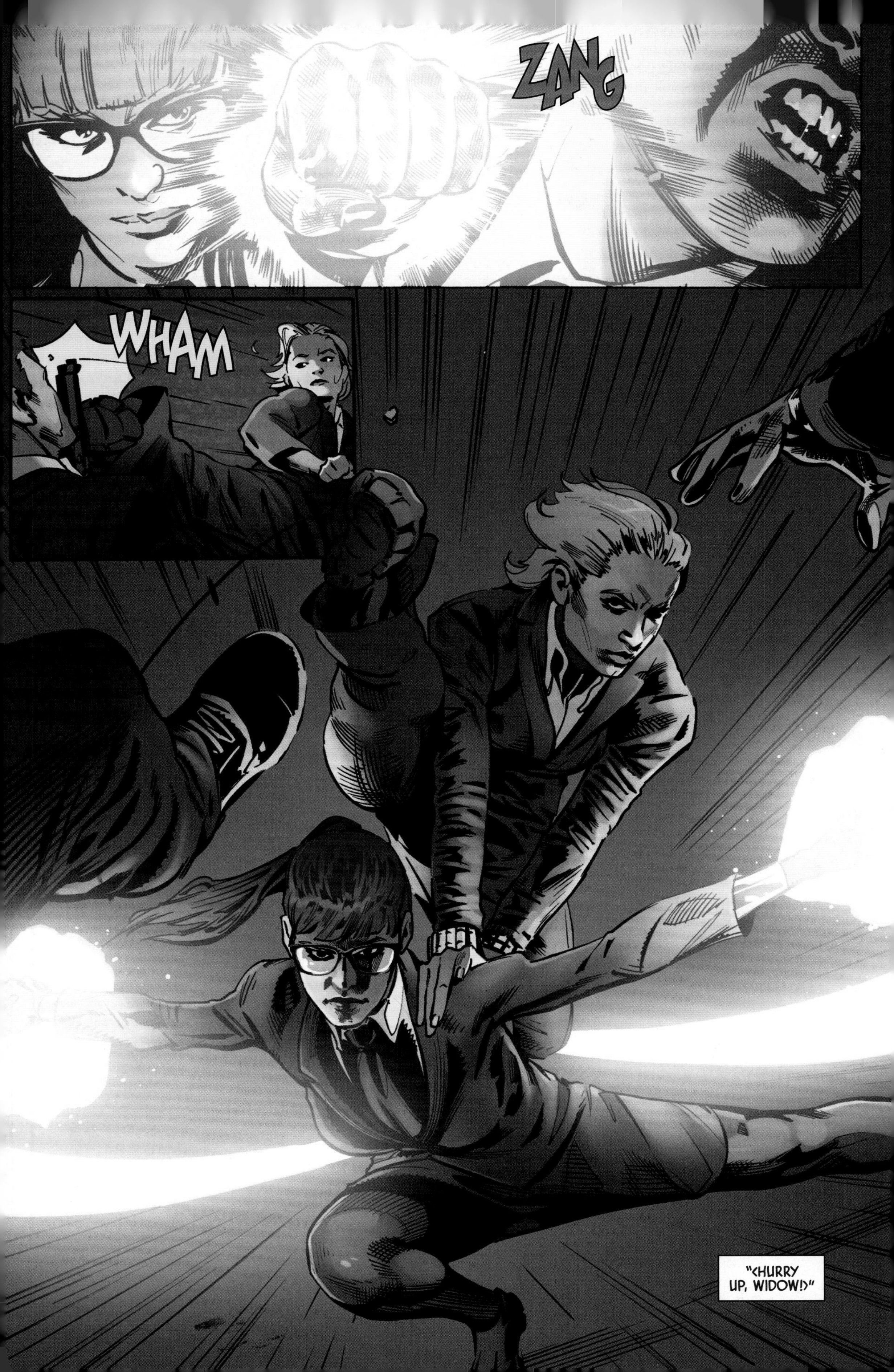
ZANG
WHAM
"<HURRY UP, WIDOW!>"

‹YOU ARE TAKING TOO LONG!›

‹SHH!›

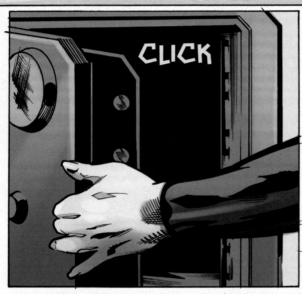

CLICK

CREEEAK

‹DID YOU HEAR THAT? SOMEONE'S COMING...›

‹IT DOESN'T MATTER. WE'VE GOT WHAT WE CAME FOR...›

‹...THE MASTER KEYS FOR SEIDEL SAFES.›

‹TOMA, WHAT ARE YOU DOING?›

‹THE HEADMISTRESS WOULDN'T HAVE SENT US BOTH FOR A SIMPLE THEFT.›

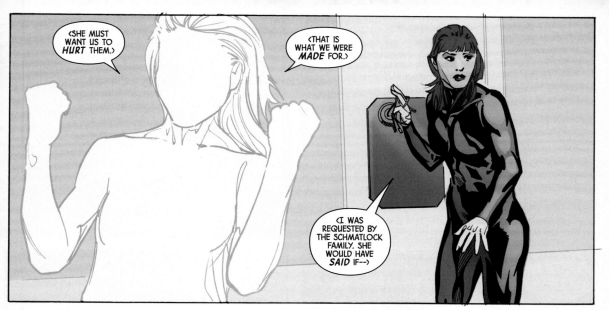

‹SHE MUST WANT US TO *HURT* THEM.›

‹THAT IS WHAT WE WERE *MADE* FOR.›

‹I WAS REQUESTED BY THE SCHMATLOCK FAMILY. SHE WOULD HAVE *SAID* IF—›

‹TOMA!›

‹DAMMIT.›

WHAM

UGH...

‹IT'S AN INTRUDER!›

‹KILL HER!›

RATATATATATATAT

‹WE NEED BACKUP!›

YOU MUST MISS THE DAYS WHEN "SECURITY" MERELY MEANT A LOCK TO PICK.

A KEY. A CODE. IT'S ALL THE SAME.

A WAY TO UNLOCK A DOOR.

A LONG TIME AGO, I STOLE A SET OF KEYS FOR THE SCHMATLOCKS.

TURNABOUT IS FAIR PLAY.

I CAN APPRECIATE THE SYMMETRY.

SO, WHAT ARE YOU GOING TO *DO* WITH THE CODE? RELEASE IT INTO THE WORLD?

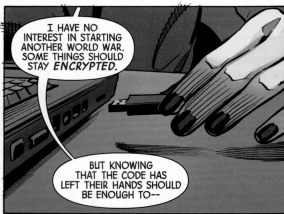

I HAVE NO INTEREST IN STARTING ANOTHER WORLD WAR. SOME THINGS SHOULD STAY *ENCRYPTED*.

BUT KNOWING THAT THE CODE HAS LEFT THEIR HANDS SHOULD BE ENOUGH TO--

WRAAAAAH WRAAAAAH WRAAAAAH

DID YOU HIT THE WRONG BUTTON?

YOU THINK SO LITTLE OF ME?

NO. THAT WASN'T US.

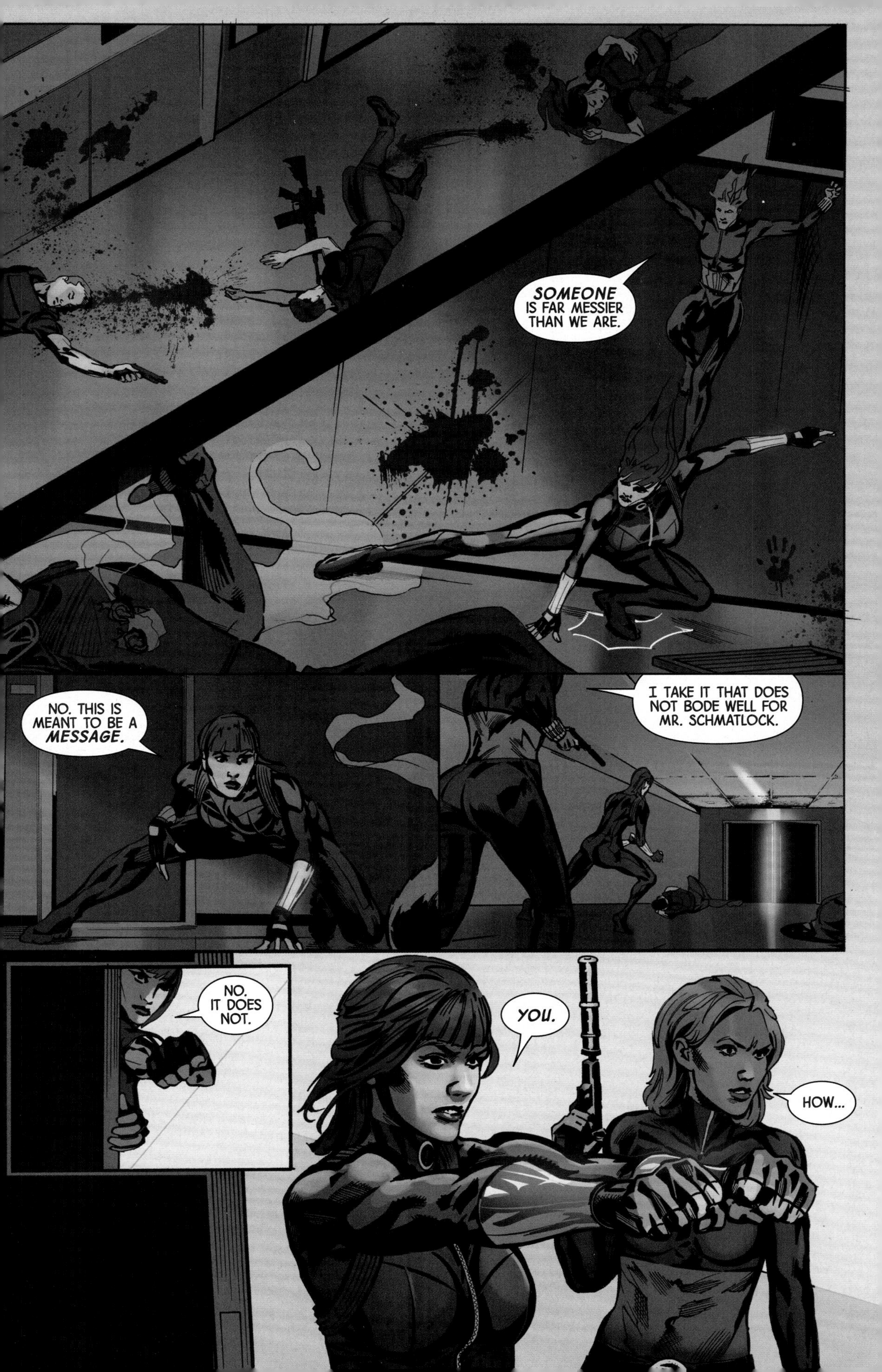
SOMEONE IS FAR MESSIER THAN WE ARE.
NO. THIS IS MEANT TO BE A MESSAGE.
I TAKE IT THAT DOES NOT BODE WELL FOR MR. SCHMATLOCK.
NO. IT DOES NOT.
YOU.
HOW...

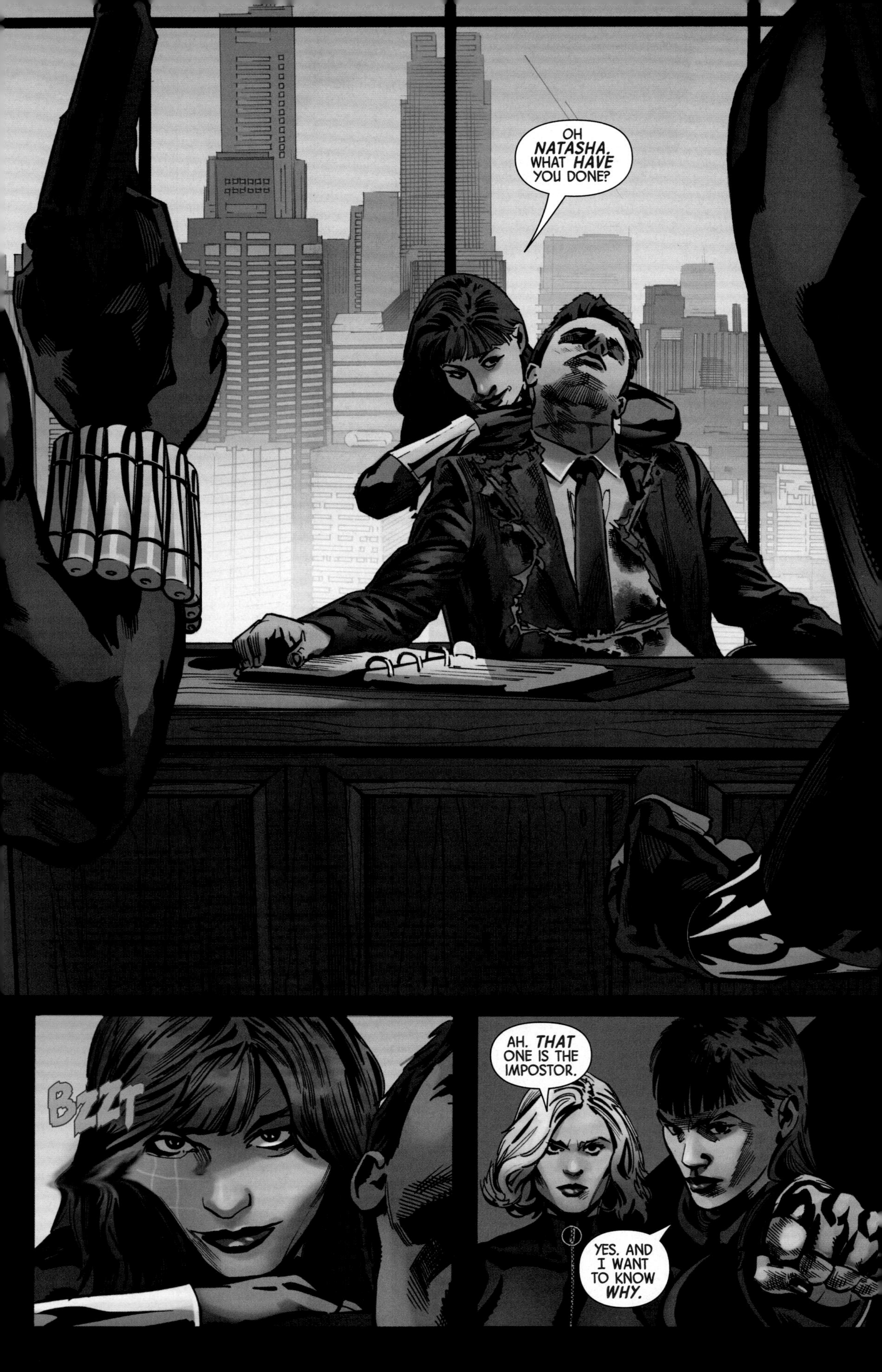
OH *NATASHA*, WHAT *HAVE* YOU DONE?
BZZT
AH. *THAT* ONE IS THE IMPOSTOR.
YES. AND I WANT TO KNOW *WHY*.

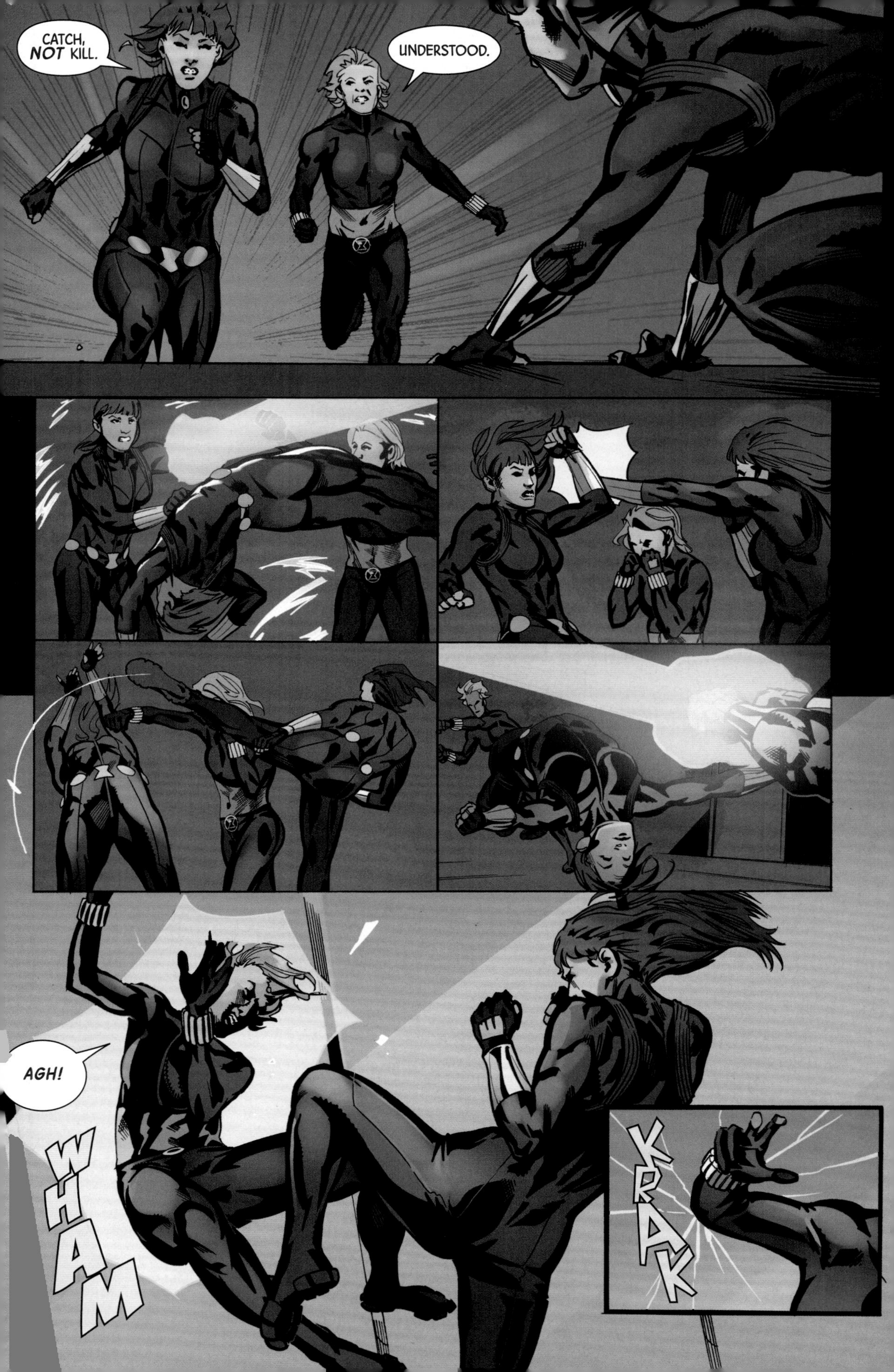
CATCH, NOT KILL.
UNDERSTOOD.
AGH!
WHAM
KRAK

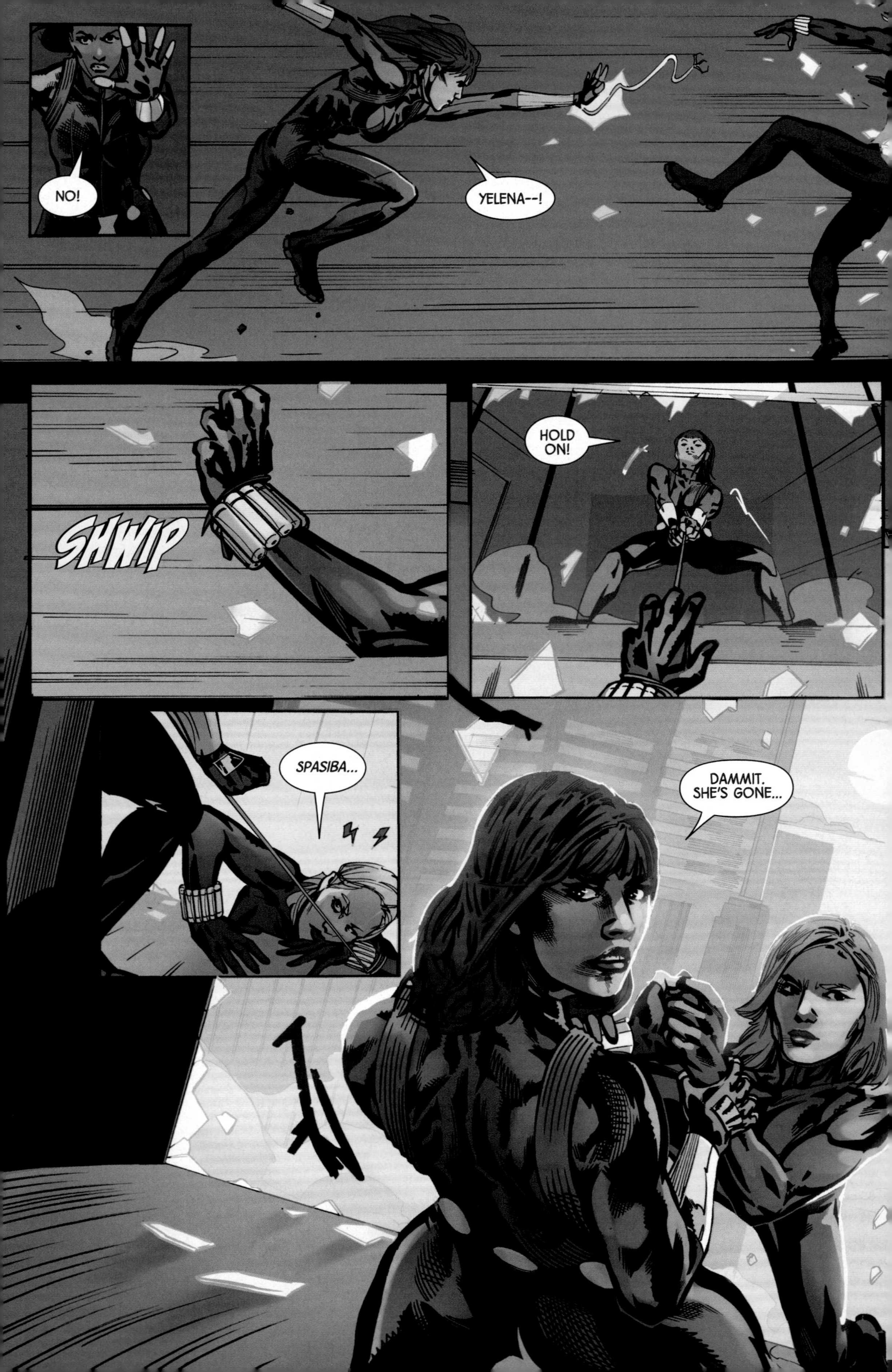
NO!
YELENA--!
SHWIP
HOLD ON!
SPASIBA...
DAMMIT. SHE'S GONE...

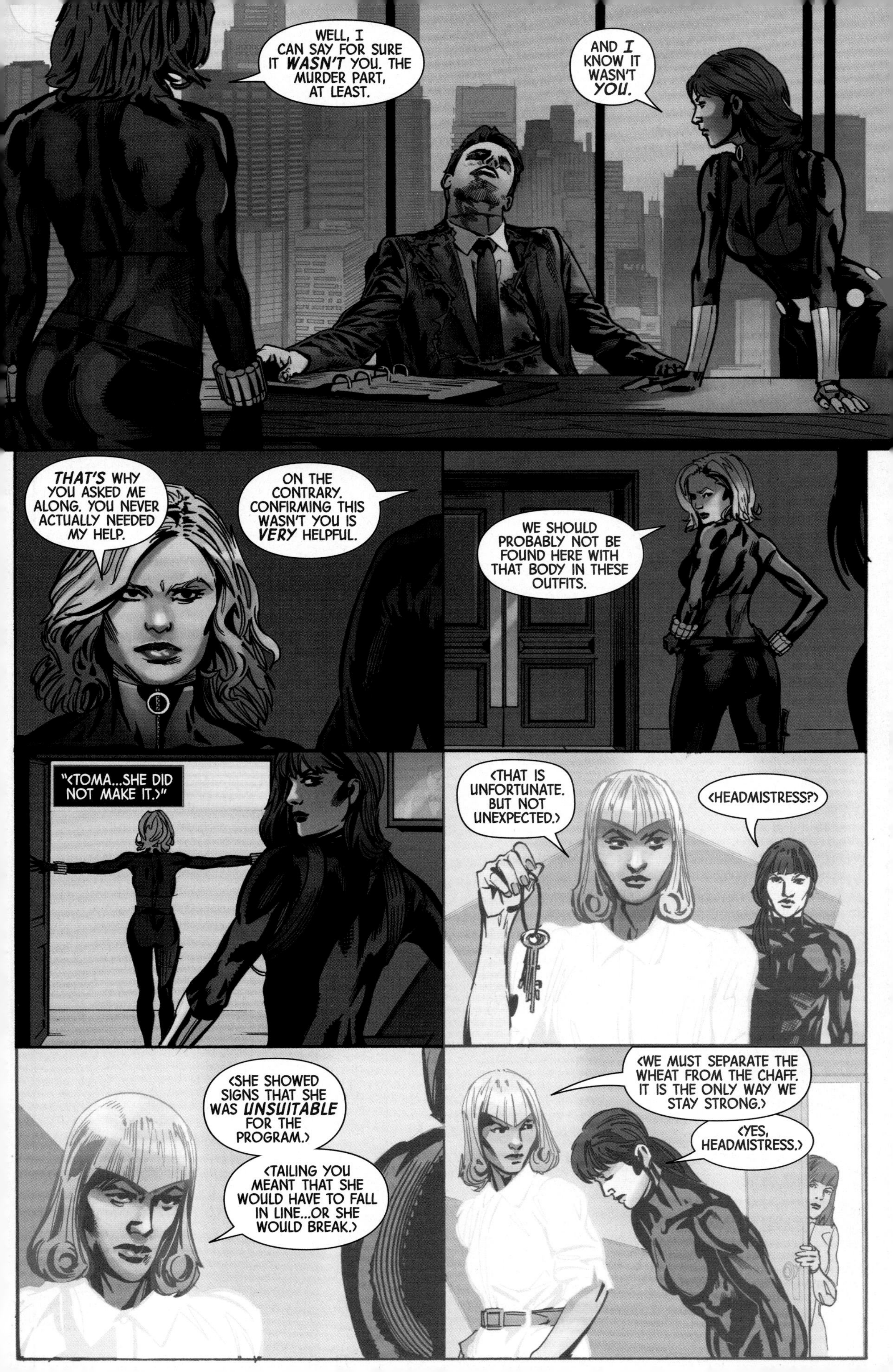
WELL, I CAN SAY FOR SURE IT WASN'T YOU. THE MURDER PART, AT LEAST.
AND I KNOW IT WASN'T YOU.
THAT'S WHY YOU ASKED ME ALONG. YOU NEVER ACTUALLY NEEDED MY HELP.
ON THE CONTRARY. CONFIRMING THIS WASN'T YOU IS VERY HELPFUL.
WE SHOULD PROBABLY NOT BE FOUND HERE WITH THAT BODY IN THESE OUTFITS.
"‹TOMA...SHE DID NOT MAKE IT.›"
‹THAT IS UNFORTUNATE. BUT NOT UNEXPECTED.›
‹HEADMISTRESS?›
‹SHE SHOWED SIGNS THAT SHE WAS UNSUITABLE FOR THE PROGRAM.›
‹TAILING YOU MEANT THAT SHE WOULD HAVE TO FALL IN LINE...OR SHE WOULD BREAK.›
‹WE MUST SEPARATE THE WHEAT FROM THE CHAFF. IT IS THE ONLY WAY WE STAY STRONG.›
‹YES, HEADMISTRESS.›

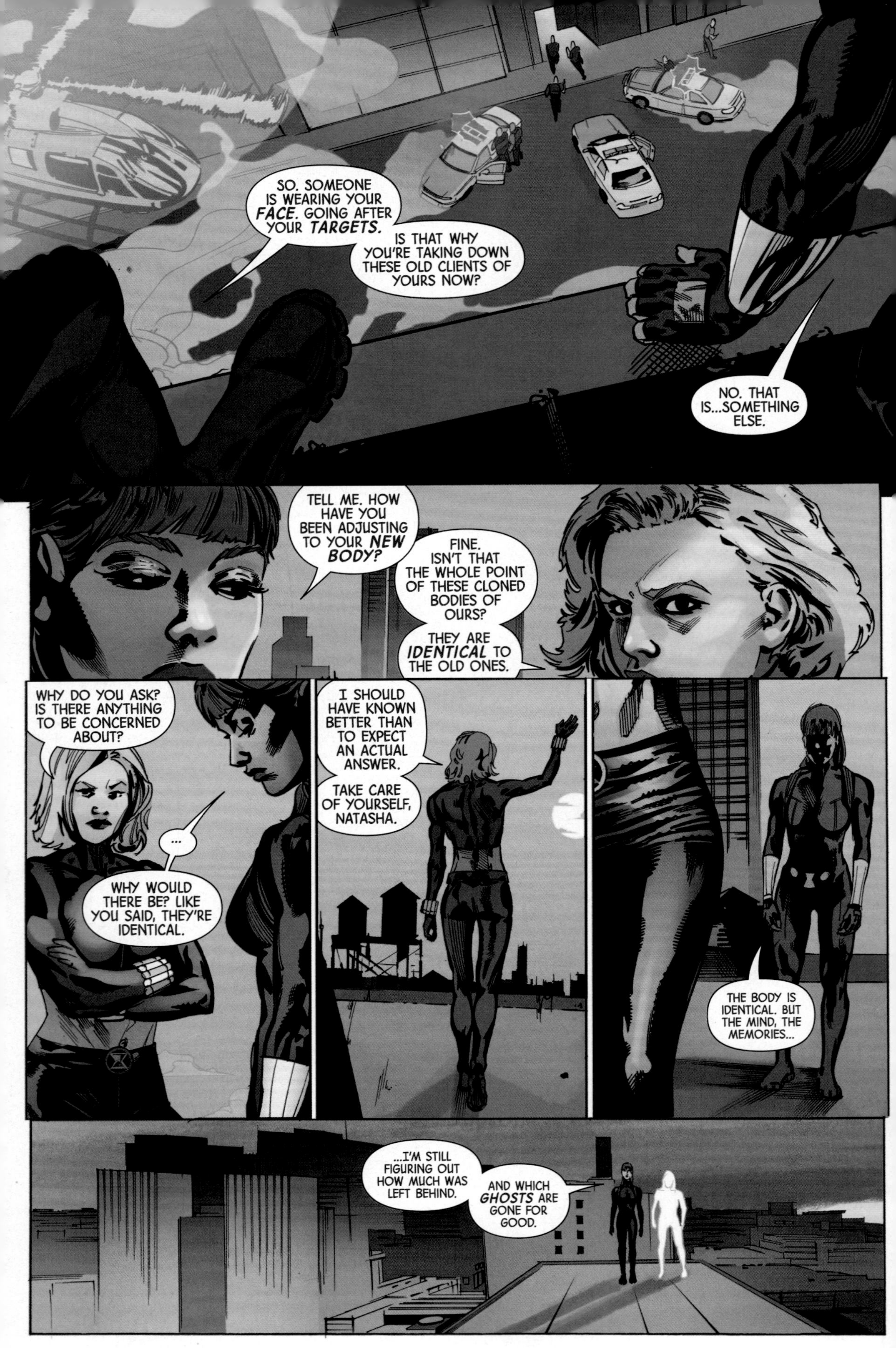
SO. SOMEONE IS WEARING YOUR FACE. GOING AFTER YOUR TARGETS.
IS THAT WHY YOU'RE TAKING DOWN THESE OLD CLIENTS OF YOURS NOW?
NO. THAT IS...SOMETHING ELSE.
TELL ME. HOW HAVE YOU BEEN ADJUSTING TO YOUR NEW BODY?
FINE. ISN'T THAT THE WHOLE POINT OF THESE CLONED BODIES OF OURS?
THEY ARE IDENTICAL TO THE OLD ONES.
WHY DO YOU ASK? IS THERE ANYTHING TO BE CONCERNED ABOUT?
...
WHY WOULD THERE BE? LIKE YOU SAID, THEY'RE IDENTICAL.
I SHOULD HAVE KNOWN BETTER THAN TO EXPECT AN ACTUAL ANSWER.
TAKE CARE OF YOURSELF, NATASHA.
THE BODY IS IDENTICAL. BUT THE MIND, THE MEMORIES...
...I'M STILL FIGURING OUT HOW MUCH WAS LEFT BEHIND.
AND WHICH GHOSTS ARE GONE FOR GOOD.

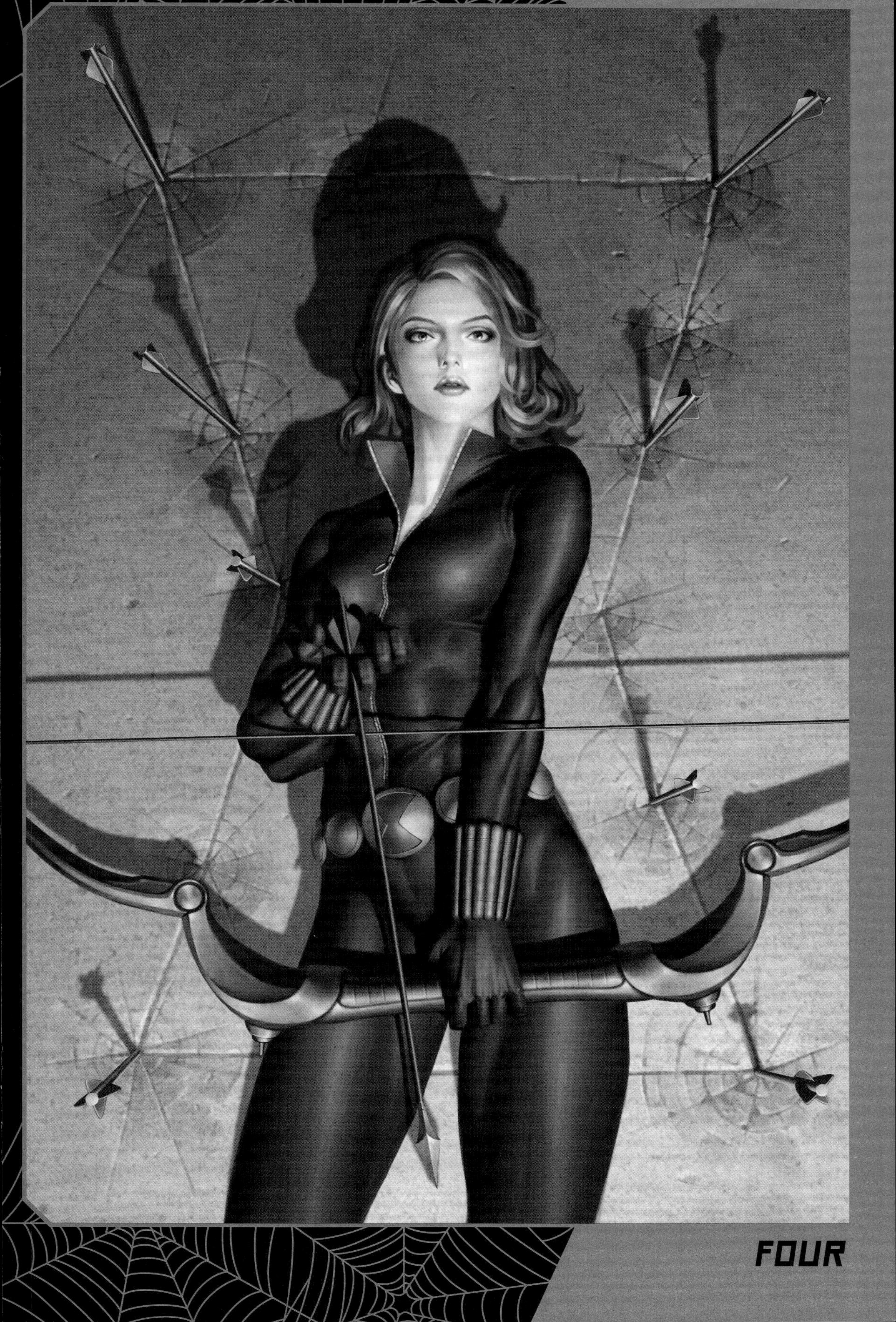

FOUR

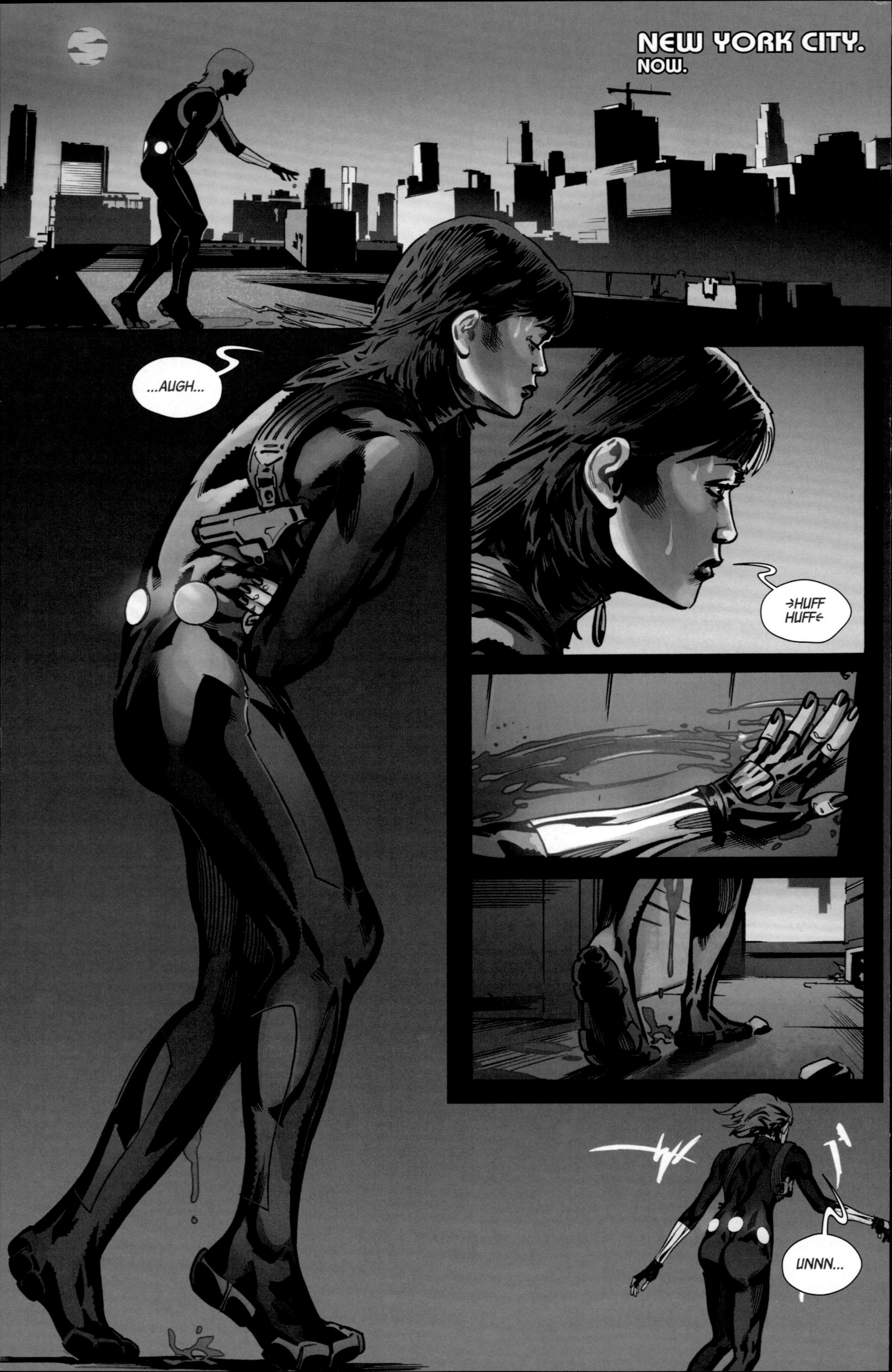
NEW YORK CITY.
NOW.
...AUGH...
HUFF HUFF
UNNN...

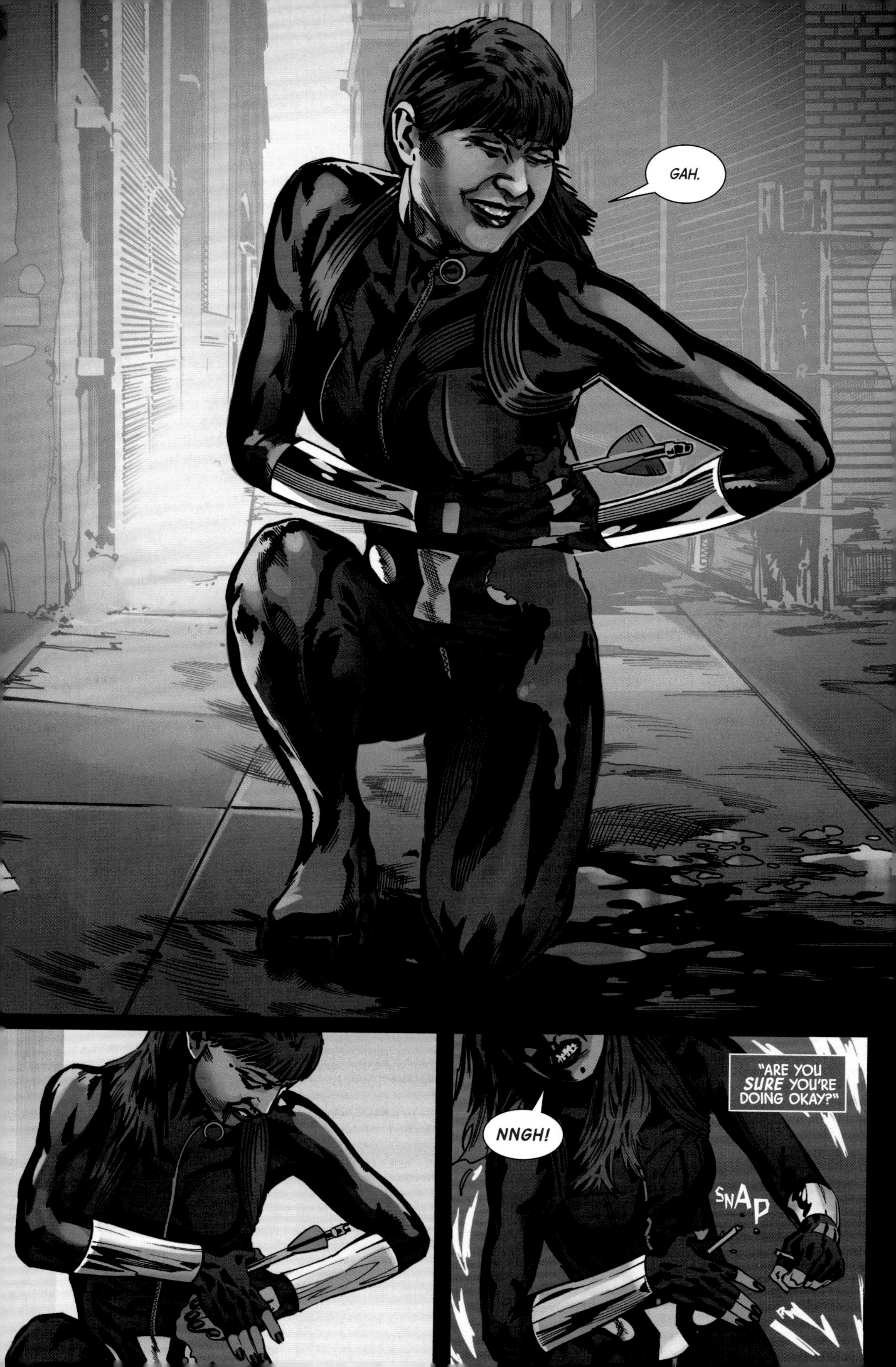
GAH.
"ARE YOU SURE YOU'RE DOING OKAY?"
NNGH!
SNAP

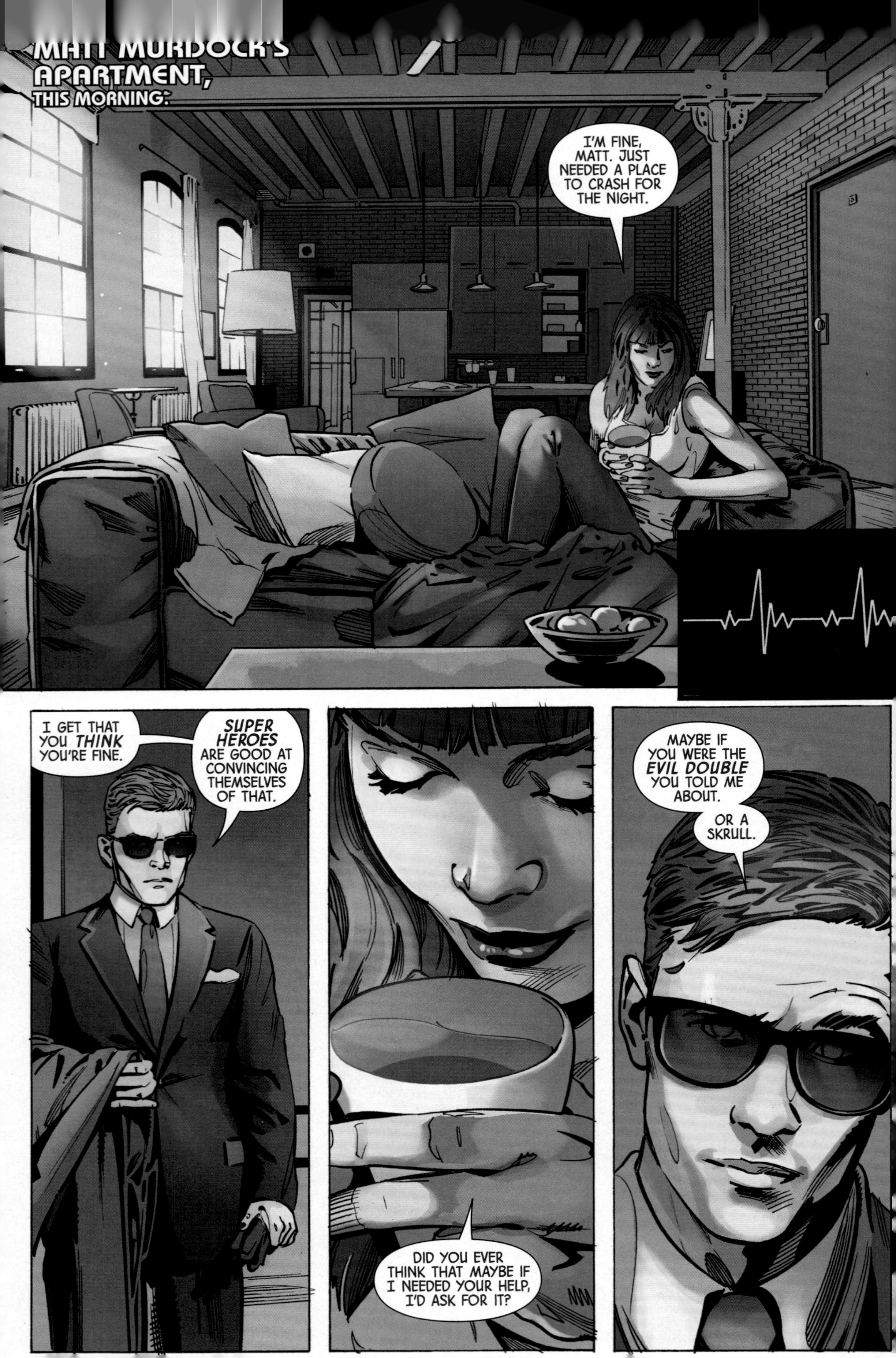
MATT MURDOCK'S APARTMENT, THIS MORNING.
I'M FINE, MATT. JUST NEEDED A PLACE TO CRASH FOR THE NIGHT.
I GET THAT YOU THINK YOU'RE FINE.
SUPER HEROES ARE GOOD AT CONVINCING THEMSELVES OF THAT.
DID YOU EVER THINK THAT MAYBE IF I NEEDED YOUR HELP, I'D ASK FOR IT?
MAYBE IF YOU WERE THE EVIL DOUBLE YOU TOLD ME ABOUT.
OR A SKRULL.

NOPE. MAY BE A NEW BODY, BUT IT'S THE SAME OLD ME.

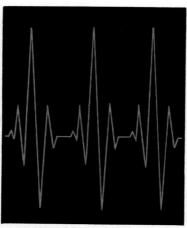

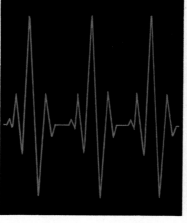

WHAT AREN'T YOU TELLING ME?

NOTHING THAT HAS ANYTHING TO DO WITH YOU. NOTHING YOU CAN FIX.

NATASHA...

YOU'RE GOING TO BE LATE FOR COURT.

I CAN SHOW MYSELF OUT.

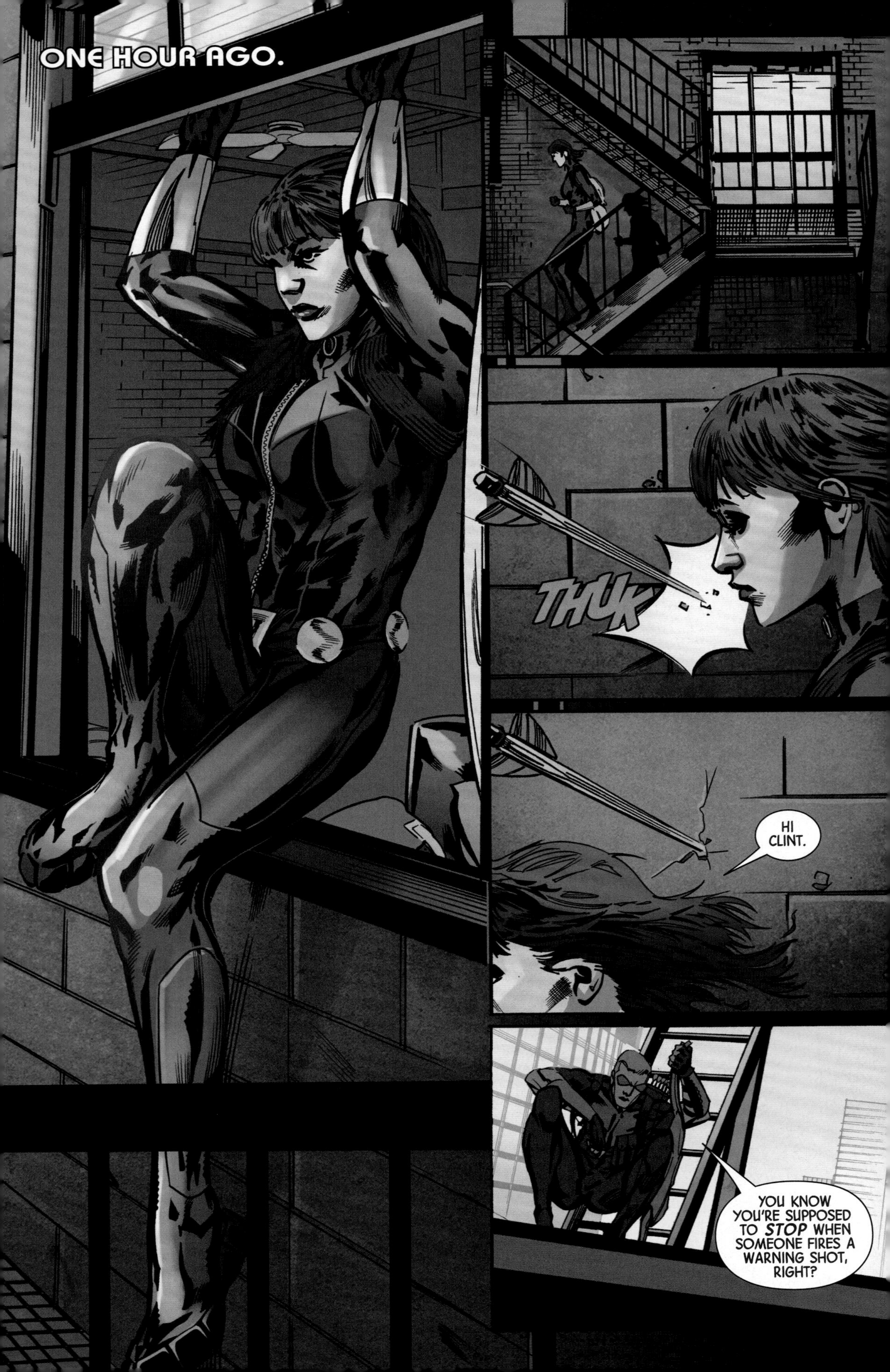
ONE HOUR AGO.
THUK
HI CLINT.
YOU KNOW YOU'RE SUPPOSED TO STOP WHEN SOMEONE FIRES A WARNING SHOT, RIGHT?

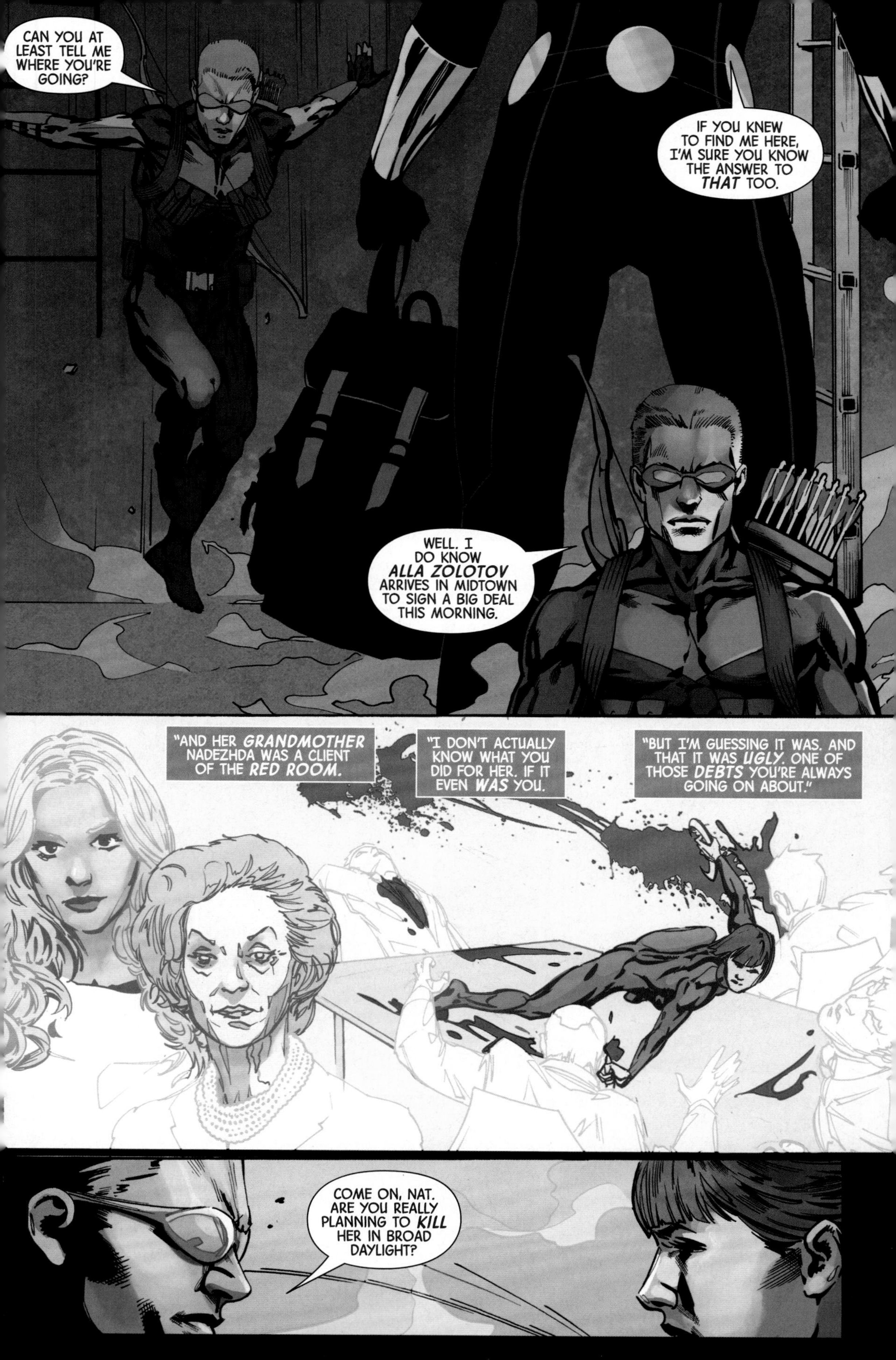
CAN YOU AT LEAST TELL ME WHERE YOU'RE GOING?
IF YOU KNEW TO FIND ME HERE, I'M SURE YOU KNOW THE ANSWER TO *THAT* TOO.
WELL. I DO KNOW *ALLA ZOLOTOV* ARRIVES IN MIDTOWN TO SIGN A BIG DEAL THIS MORNING.
"AND HER *GRANDMOTHER* NADEZHDA WAS A CLIENT OF THE *RED ROOM*.
"I DON'T ACTUALLY KNOW WHAT YOU DID FOR HER. IF IT EVEN *WAS* YOU.
"BUT I'M GUESSING IT WAS. AND THAT IT WAS *UGLY*. ONE OF THOSE *DEBTS* YOU'RE ALWAYS GOING ON ABOUT."
COME ON, NAT. ARE YOU REALLY PLANNING TO *KILL* HER IN BROAD DAYLIGHT?

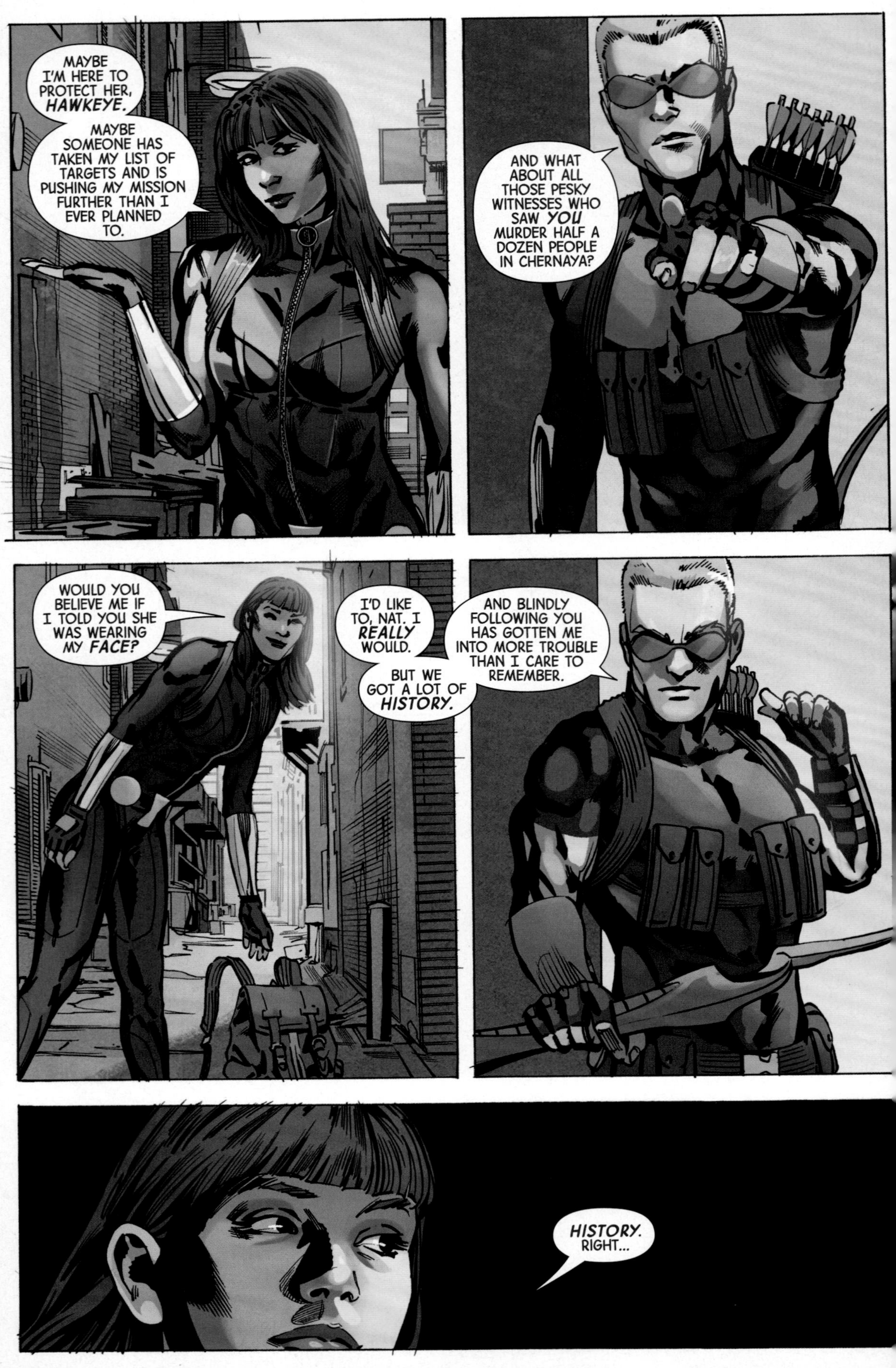
MAYBE I'M HERE TO PROTECT HER, HAWKEYE.
MAYBE SOMEONE HAS TAKEN MY LIST OF TARGETS AND IS PUSHING MY MISSION FURTHER THAN I EVER PLANNED TO.
AND WHAT ABOUT ALL THOSE PESKY WITNESSES WHO SAW YOU MURDER HALF A DOZEN PEOPLE IN CHERNAYA?
WOULD YOU BELIEVE ME IF I TOLD YOU SHE WAS WEARING MY FACE?
I'D LIKE TO, NAT. I REALLY WOULD.
BUT WE GOT A LOT OF HISTORY.
AND BLINDLY FOLLOWING YOU HAS GOTTEN ME INTO MORE TROUBLE THAN I CARE TO REMEMBER.
HISTORY. RIGHT...

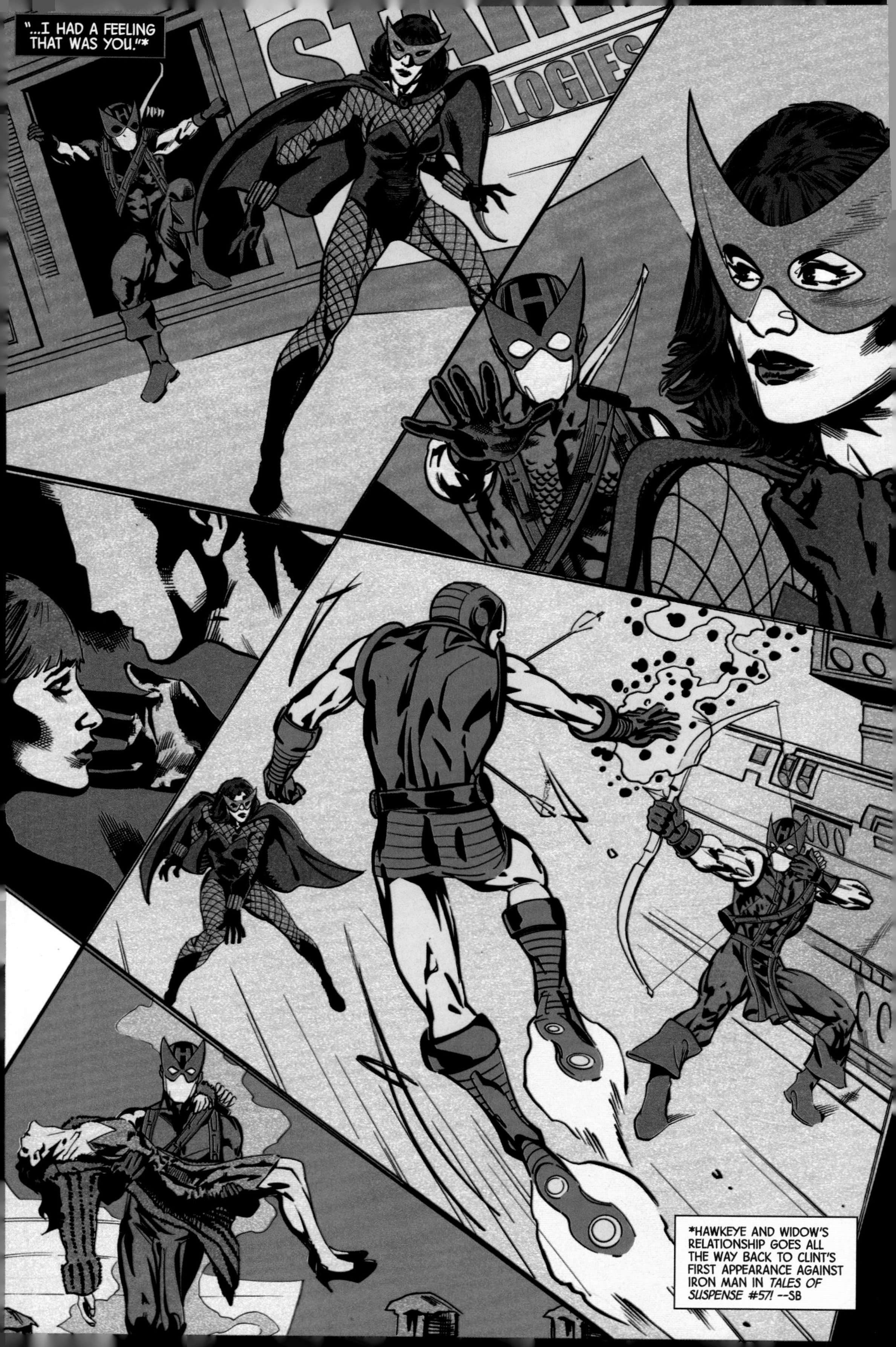
"...I HAD A FEELING THAT WAS YOU."*
LOGIES
*HAWKEYE AND WIDOW'S RELATIONSHIP GOES ALL THE WAY BACK TO CLINT'S FIRST APPEARANCE AGAINST IRON MAN IN *TALES OF SUSPENSE* #57! --SB

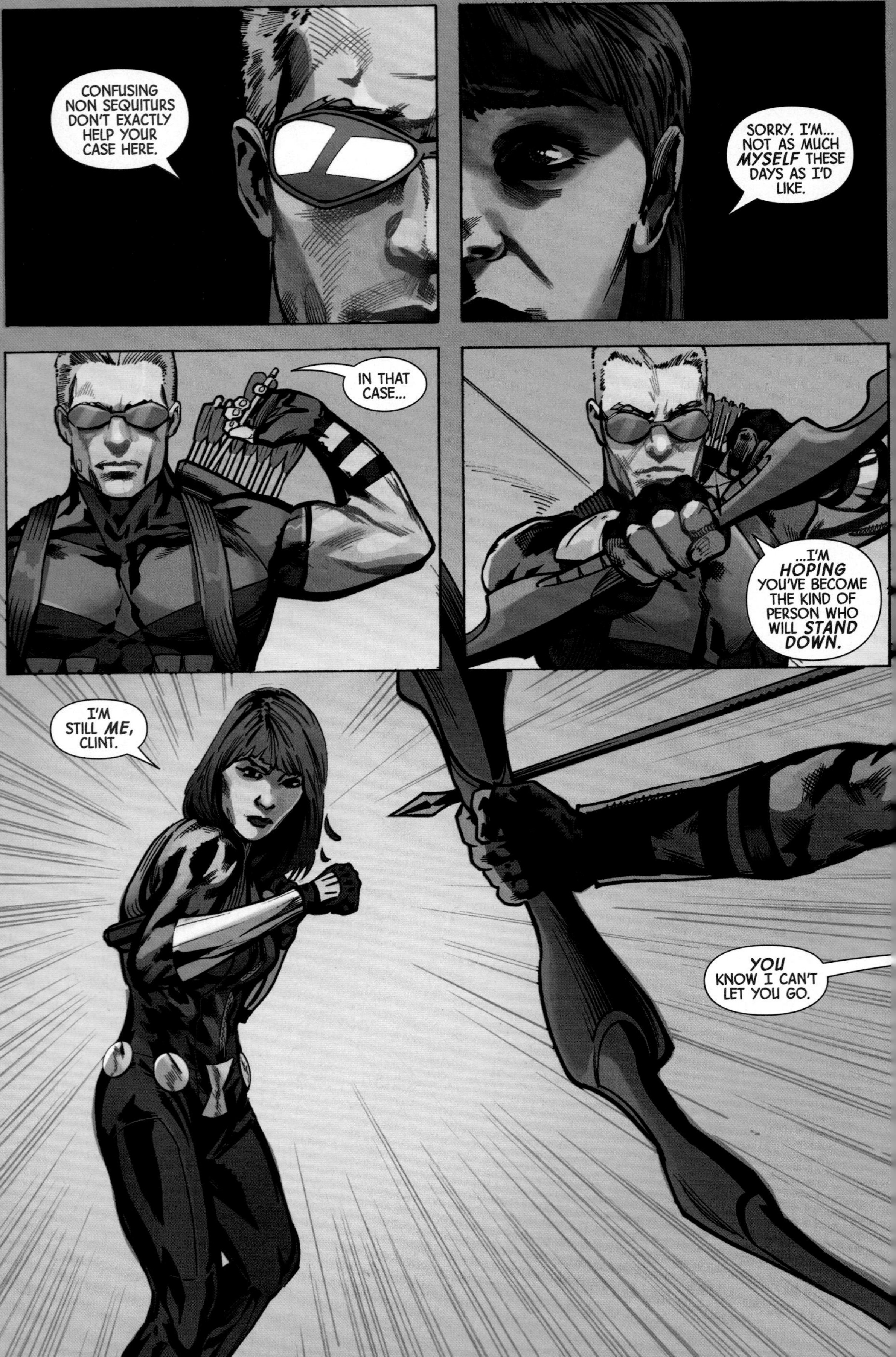
CONFUSING NON SEQUITURS DON'T EXACTLY HELP YOUR CASE HERE.
SORRY. I'M... NOT AS MUCH MYSELF THESE DAYS AS I'D LIKE.
IN THAT CASE...
...I'M HOPING YOU'VE BECOME THE KIND OF PERSON WHO WILL STAND DOWN.
I'M STILL ME, CLINT.
YOU KNOW I CAN'T LET YOU GO.

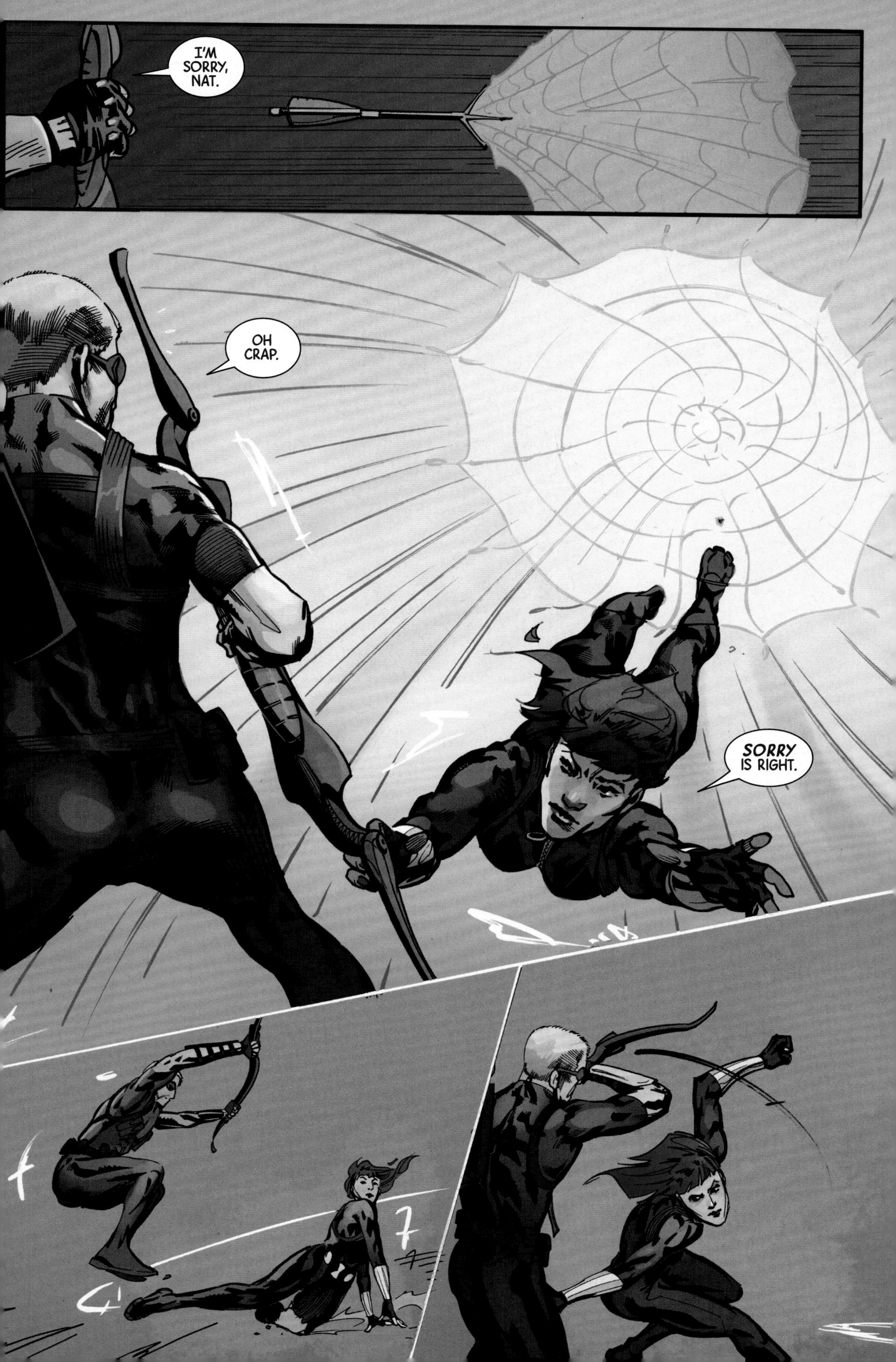
I'M SORRY, NAT.
OH CRAP.
SORRY IS RIGHT.

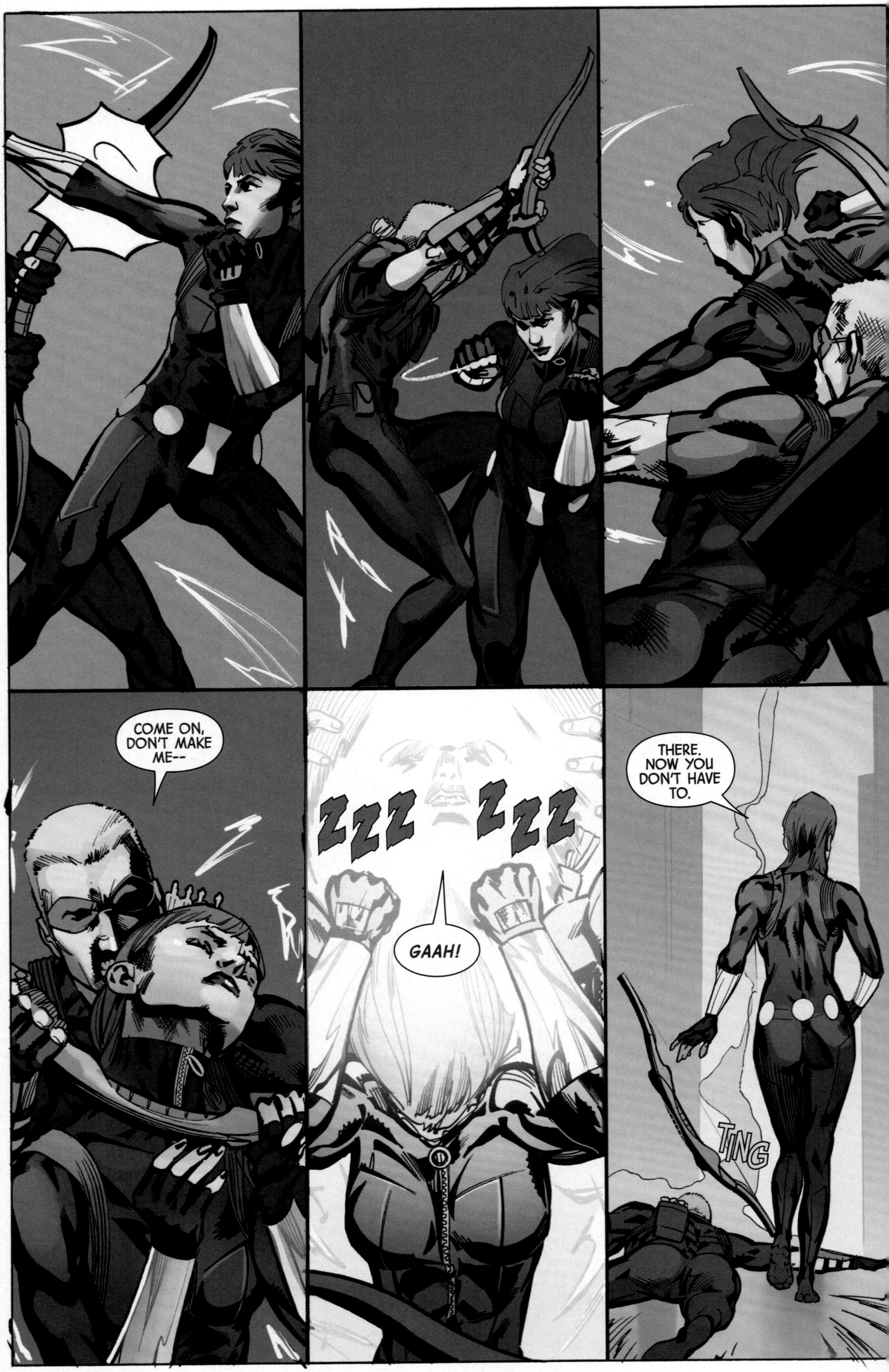
COME ON, DON'T MAKE ME--
ZZZ ZZZ
GAAH!
THERE. NOW YOU DON'T HAVE TO.
TING

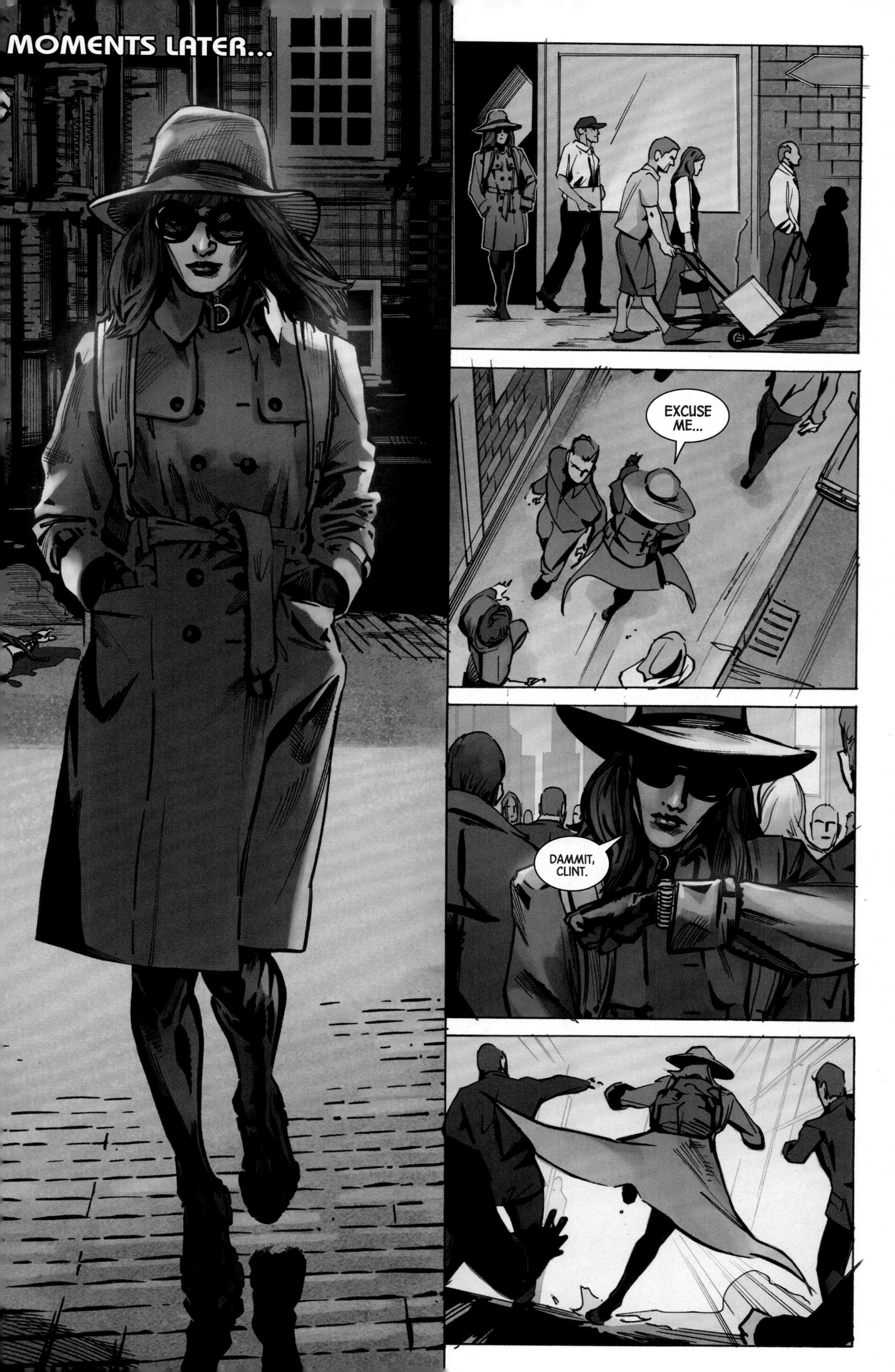
MOMENTS LATER...
EXCUSE ME...
DAMMIT, CLINT.

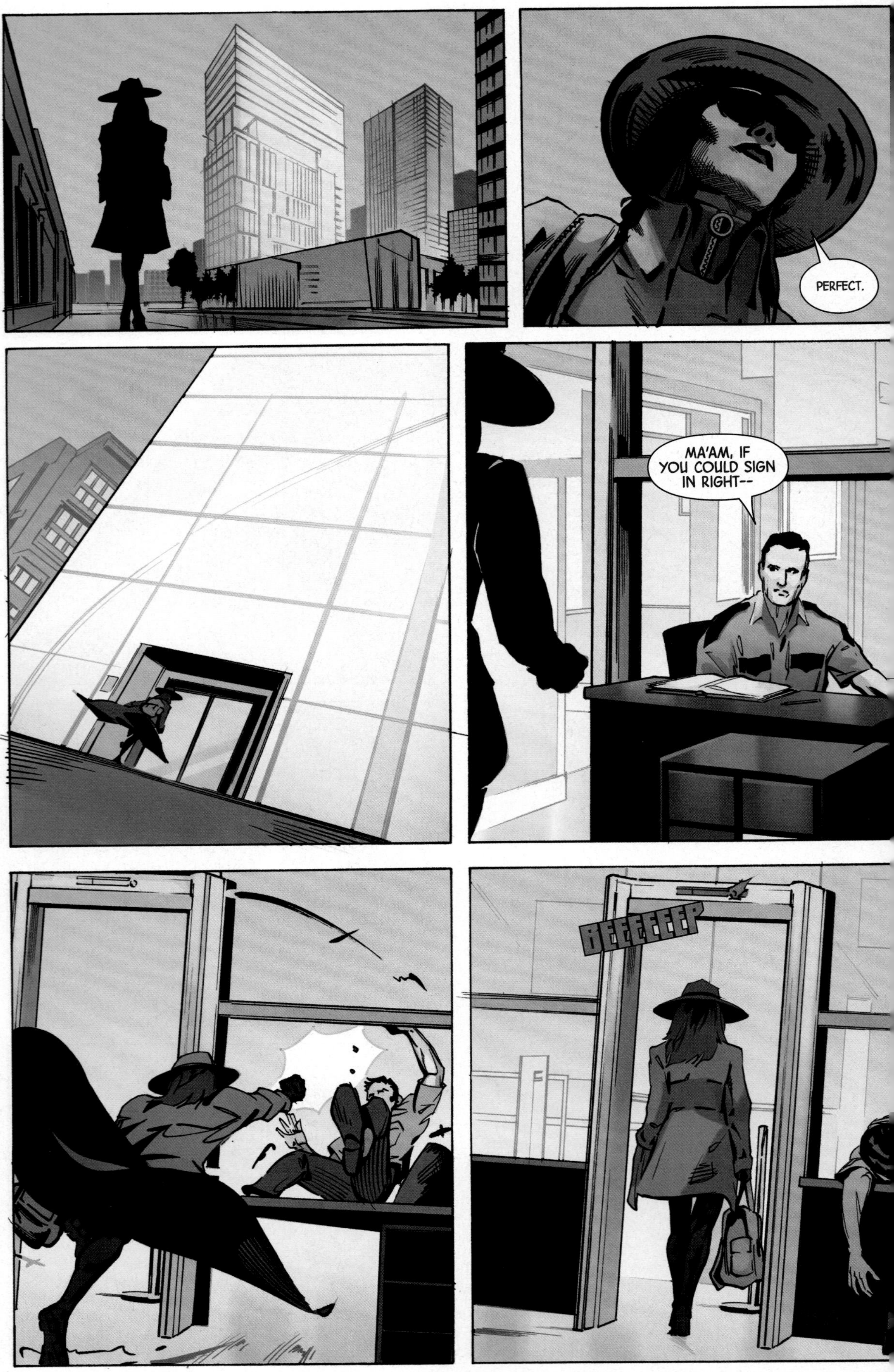
PERFECT.
MA'AM, IF YOU COULD SIGN IN RIGHT--
BEEEEEEP

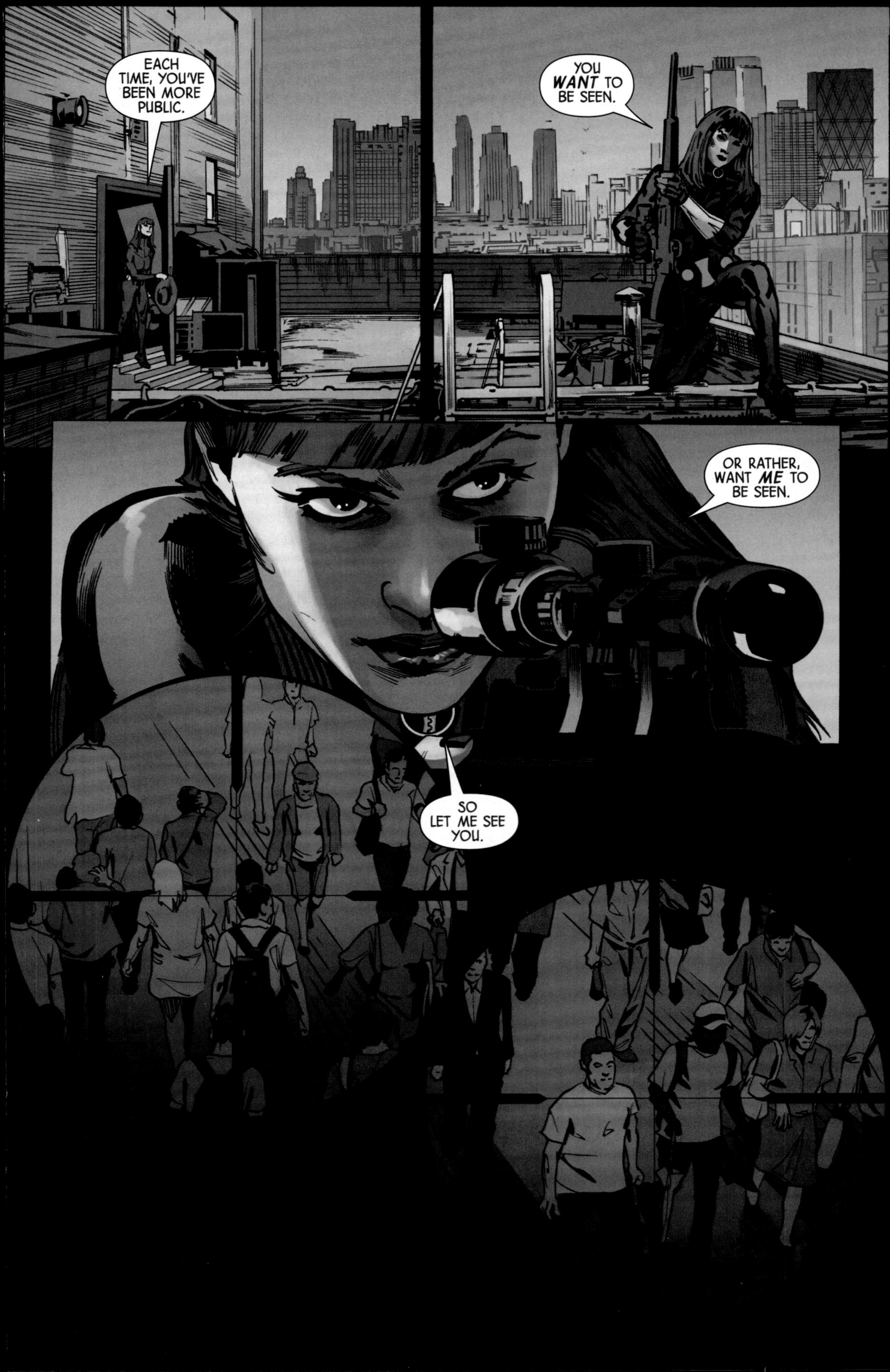
EACH TIME, YOU'VE BEEN MORE PUBLIC.
YOU WANT TO BE SEEN.
OR RATHER, WANT ME TO BE SEEN.
SO LET ME SEE YOU.

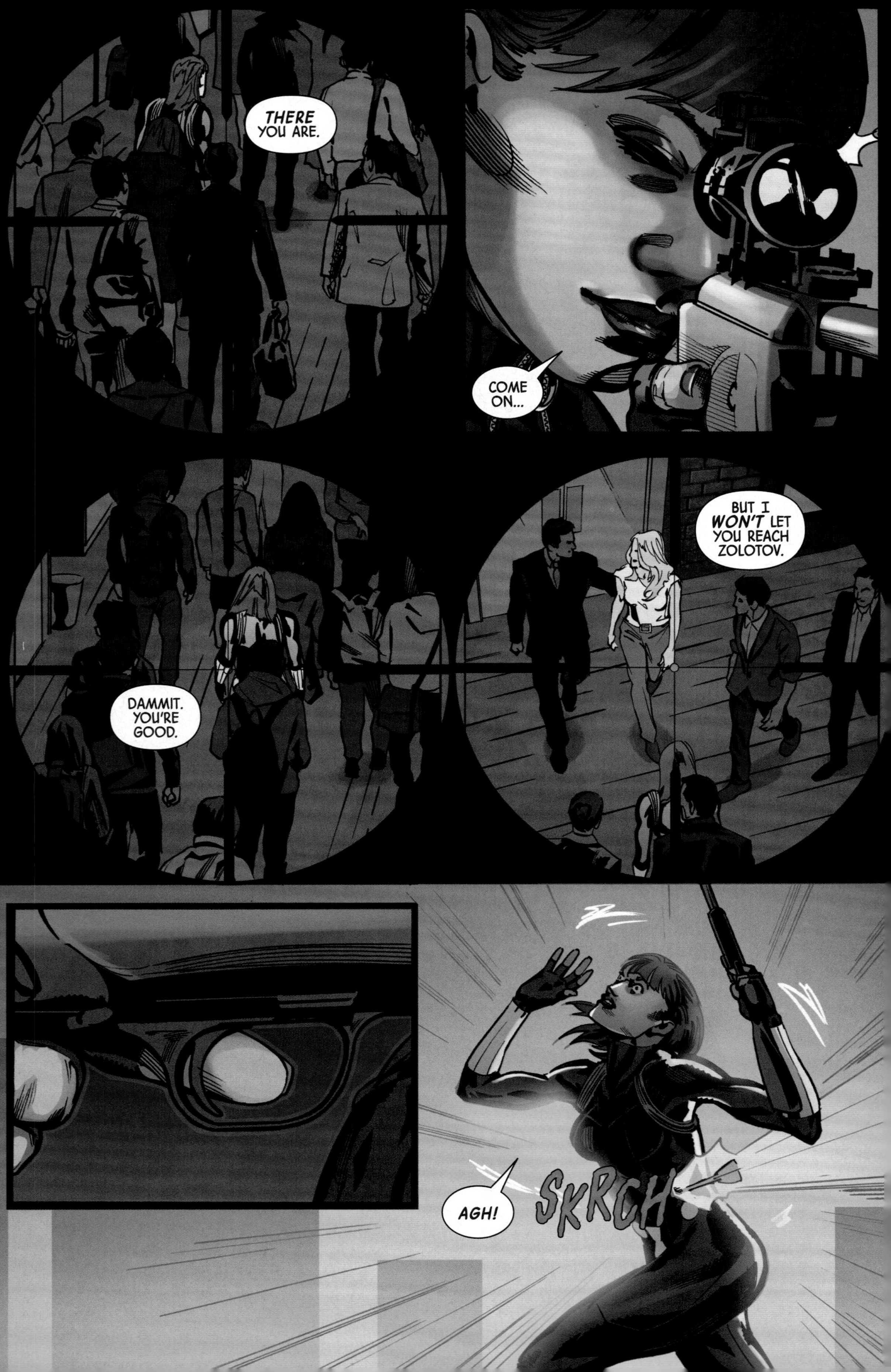
THERE YOU ARE.
COME ON...
DAMMIT. YOU'RE GOOD.
BUT I WON'T LET YOU REACH ZOLOTOV.
AGH!
SKRCH

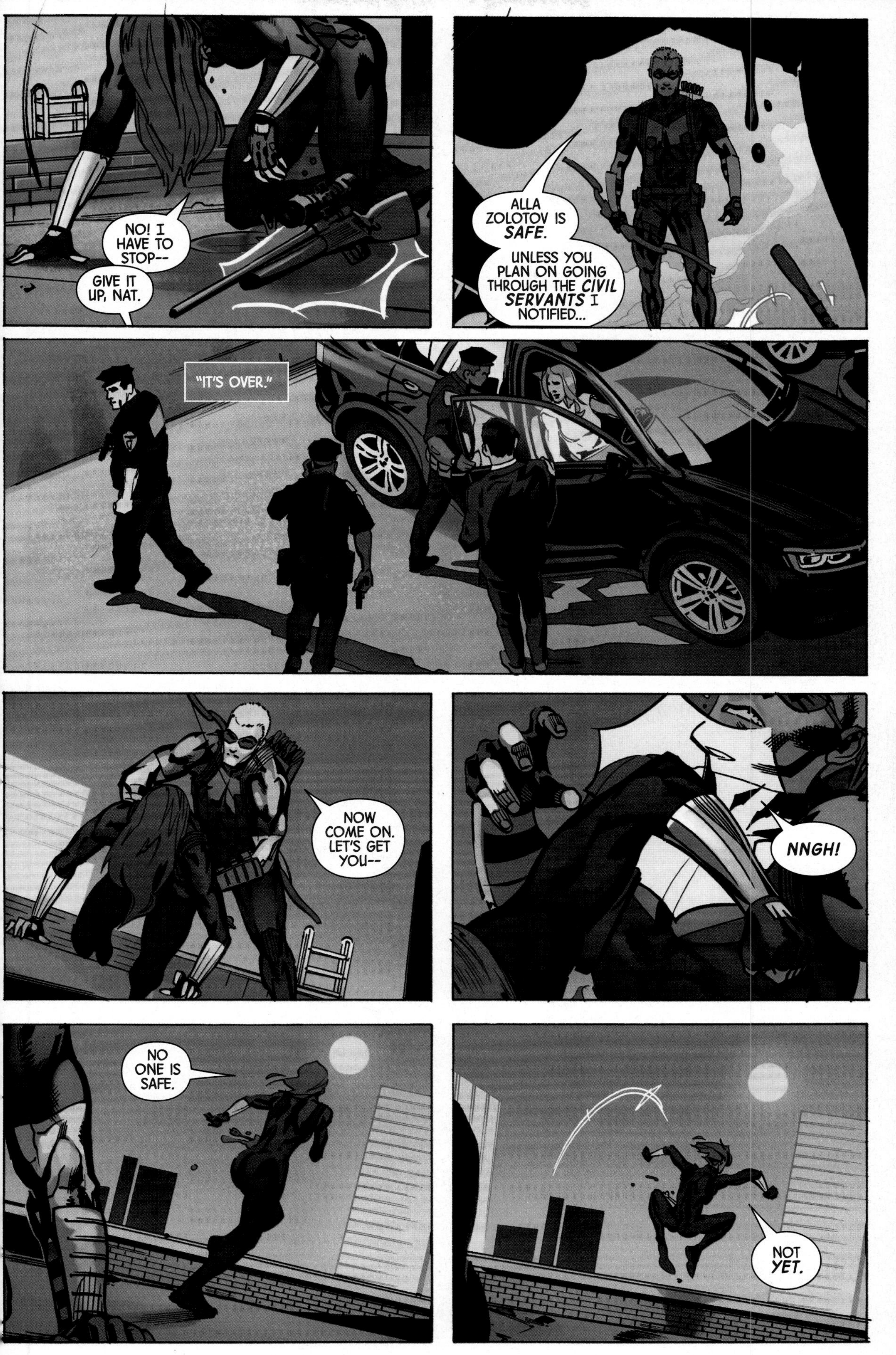
NO! I HAVE TO STOP--
GIVE IT UP, NAT.
ALLA ZOLOTOV IS SAFE.
UNLESS YOU PLAN ON GOING THROUGH THE CIVIL SERVANTS I NOTIFIED...
"IT'S OVER."
NOW COME ON. LET'S GET YOU--
NNGH!
NO ONE IS SAFE.
NOT YET.

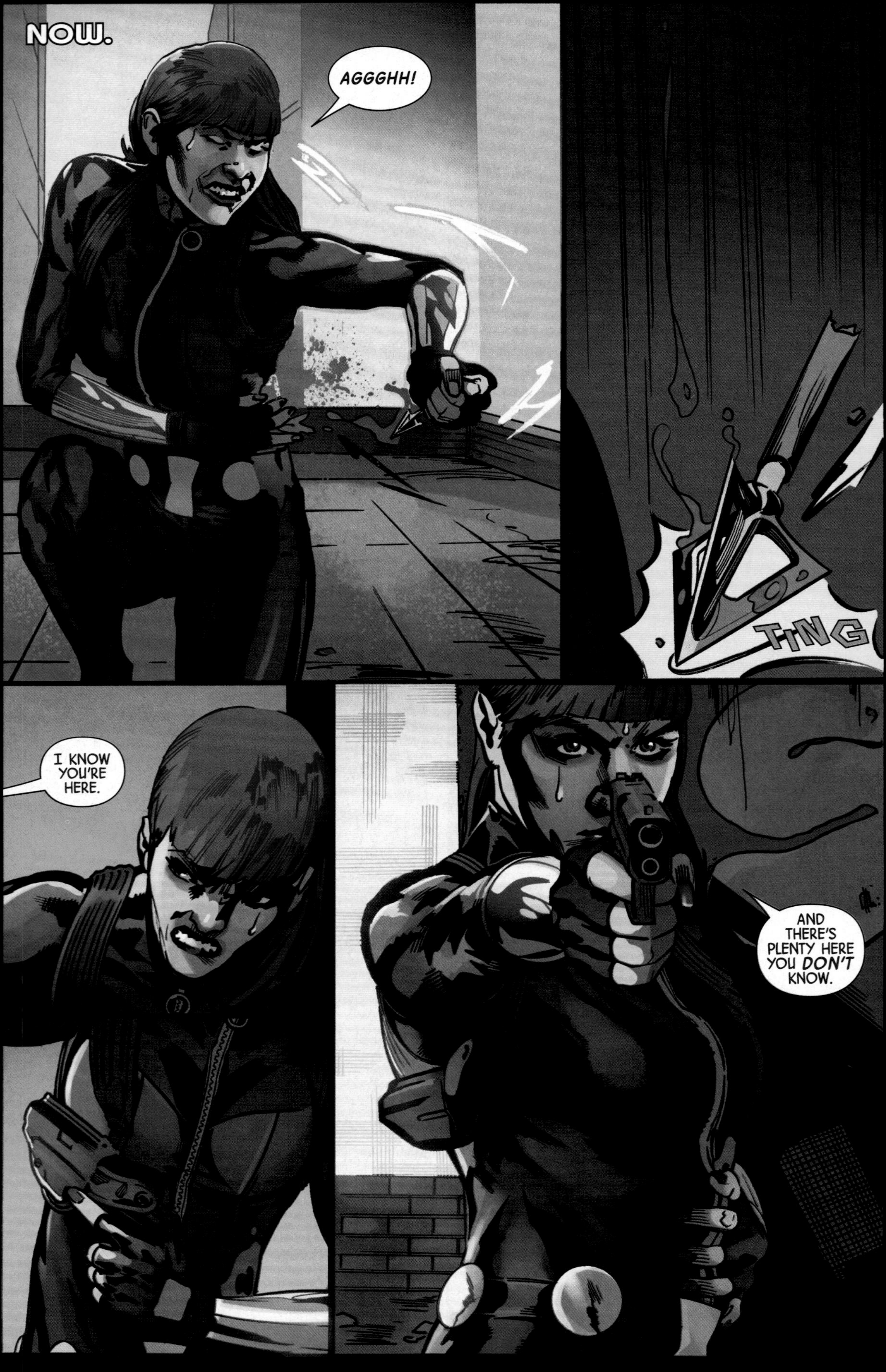
NOW.
AGGGHH!
TING
I KNOW YOU'RE HERE.
AND THERE'S PLENTY HERE YOU *DON'T* KNOW.

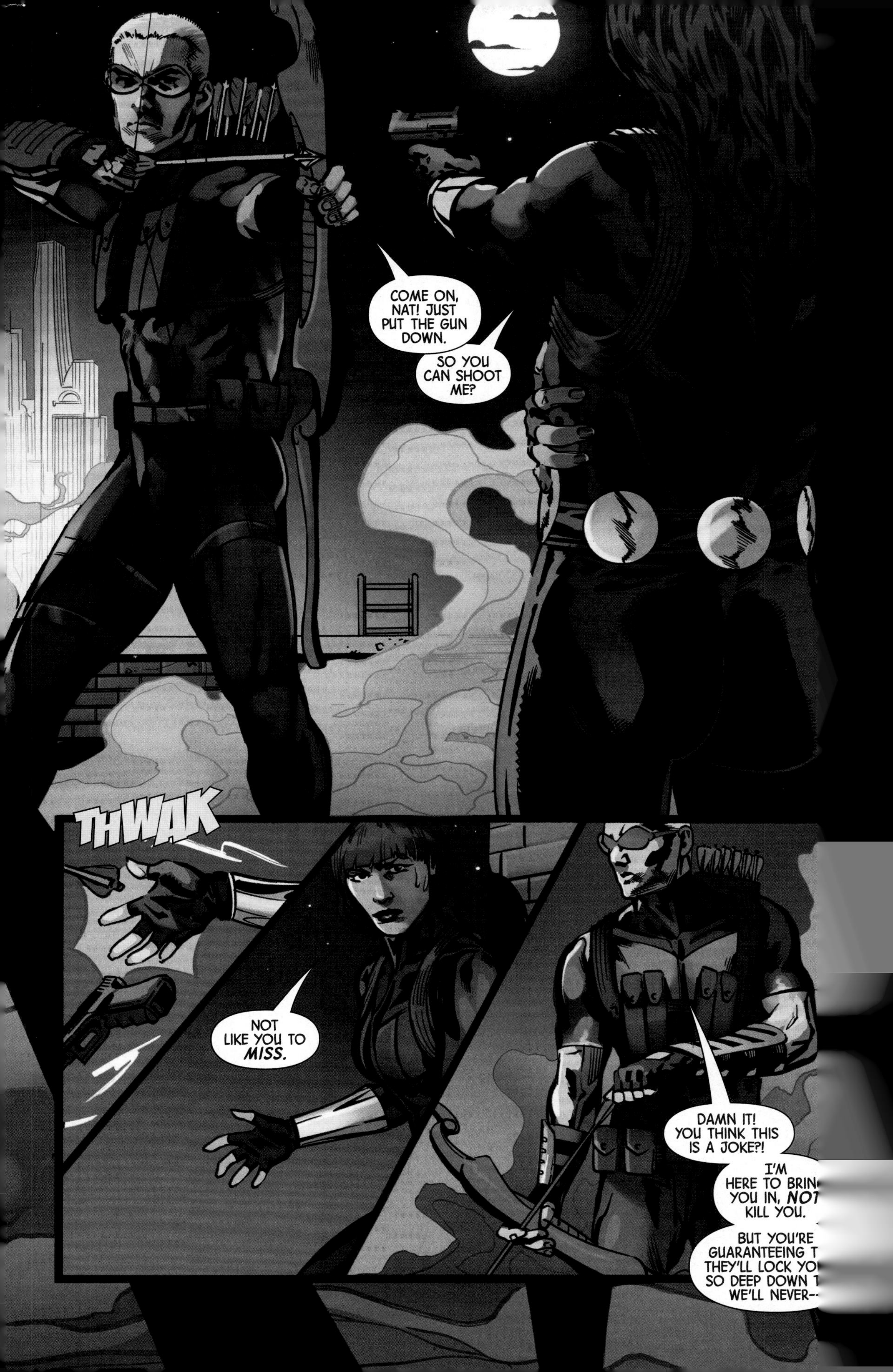
COME ON, NAT! JUST PUT THE GUN DOWN.
SO YOU CAN SHOOT ME?
THWAK
NOT LIKE YOU TO MISS.
DAMN IT! YOU THINK THIS IS A JOKE?!
I'M HERE TO BRIN YOU IN, NOT KILL YOU.
BUT YOU'RE GUARANTEEING T THEY'LL LOCK YO SO DEEP DOWN T WE'LL NEVER--

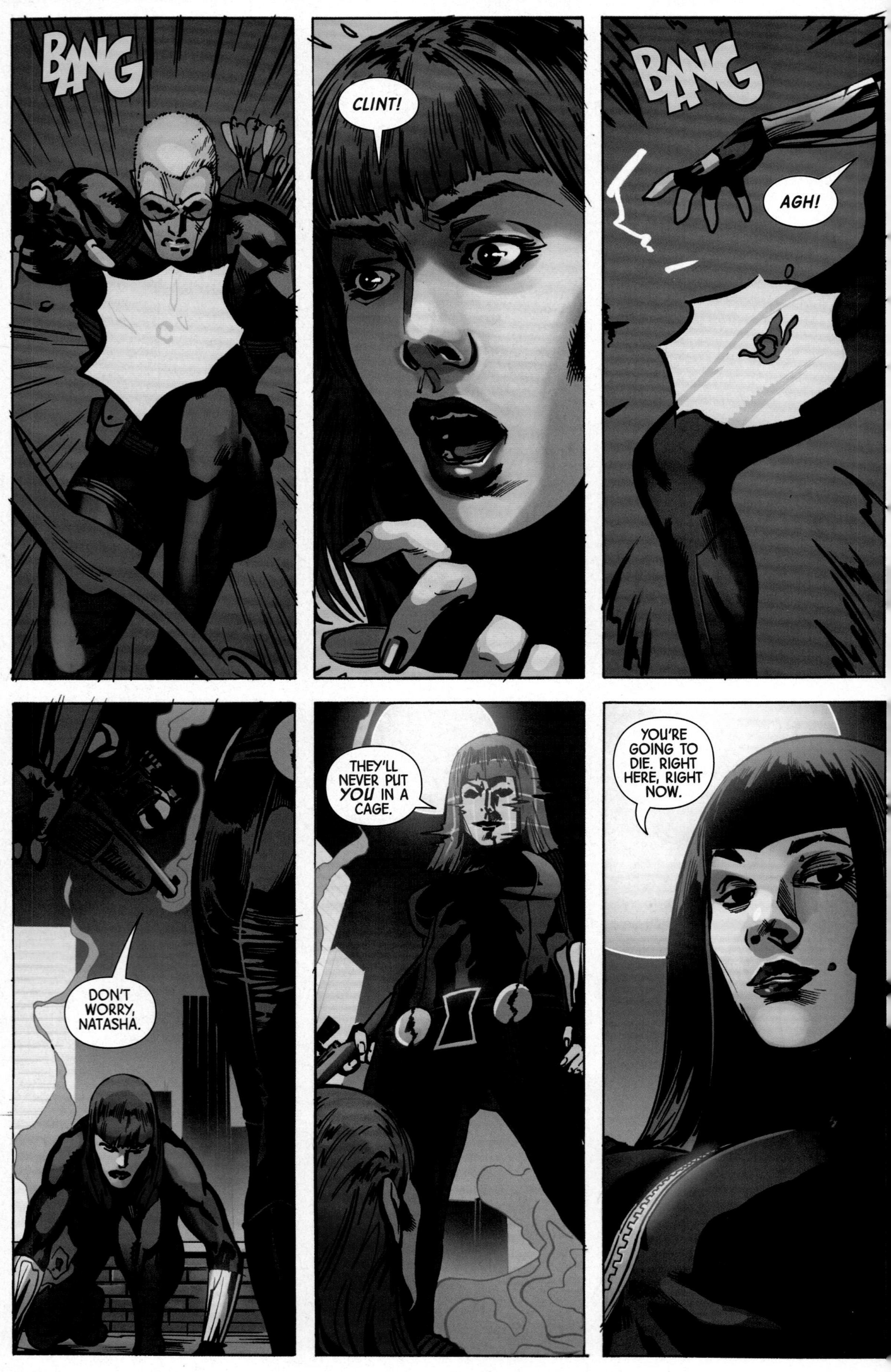
BANG
CLINT!
BANG
AGH!
DON'T WORRY, NATASHA.
THEY'LL NEVER PUT YOU IN A CAGE.
YOU'RE GOING TO DIE. RIGHT HERE, RIGHT NOW.

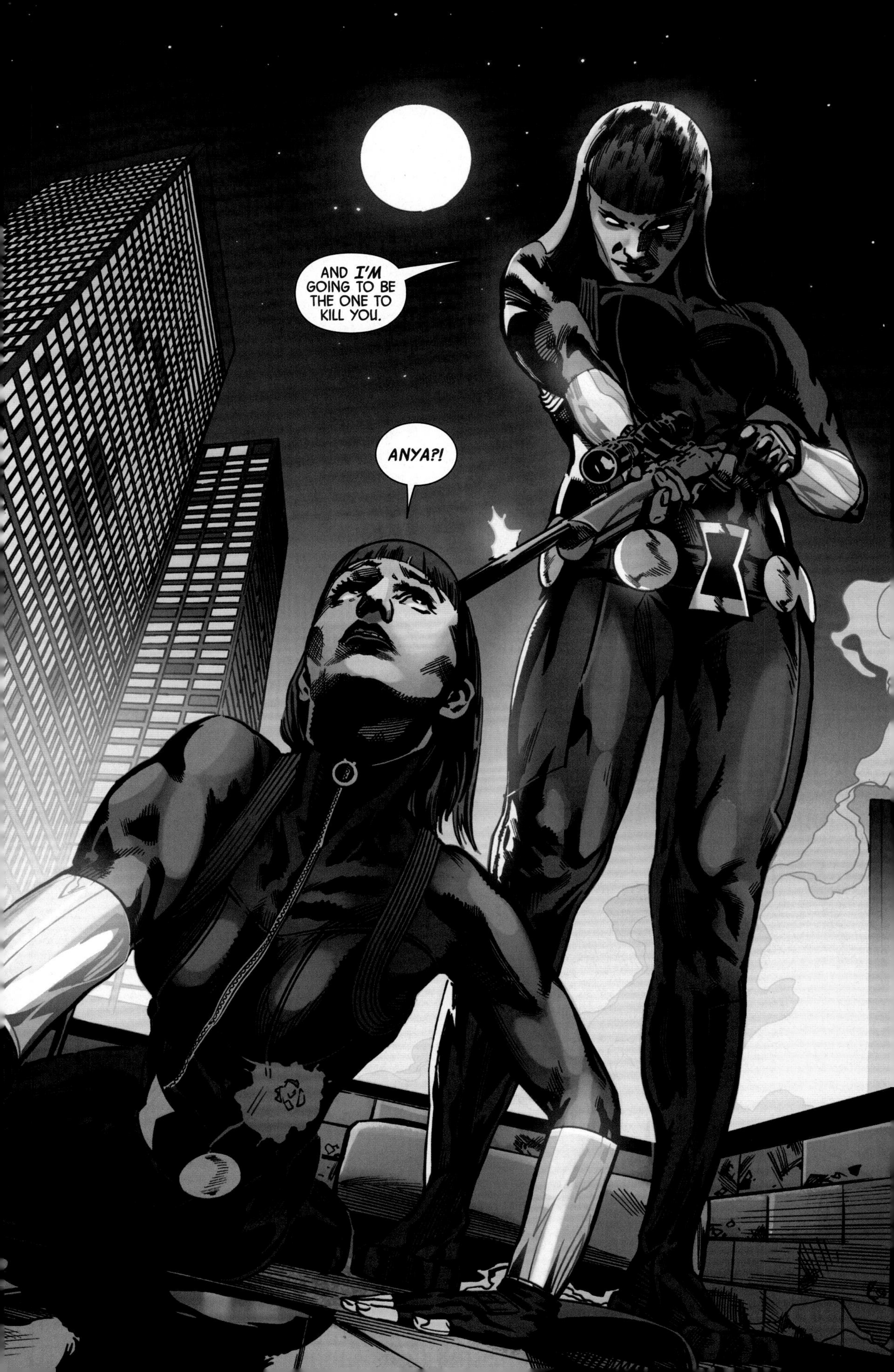
AND I'M GOING TO BE THE ONE TO KILL YOU.
ANYA?!

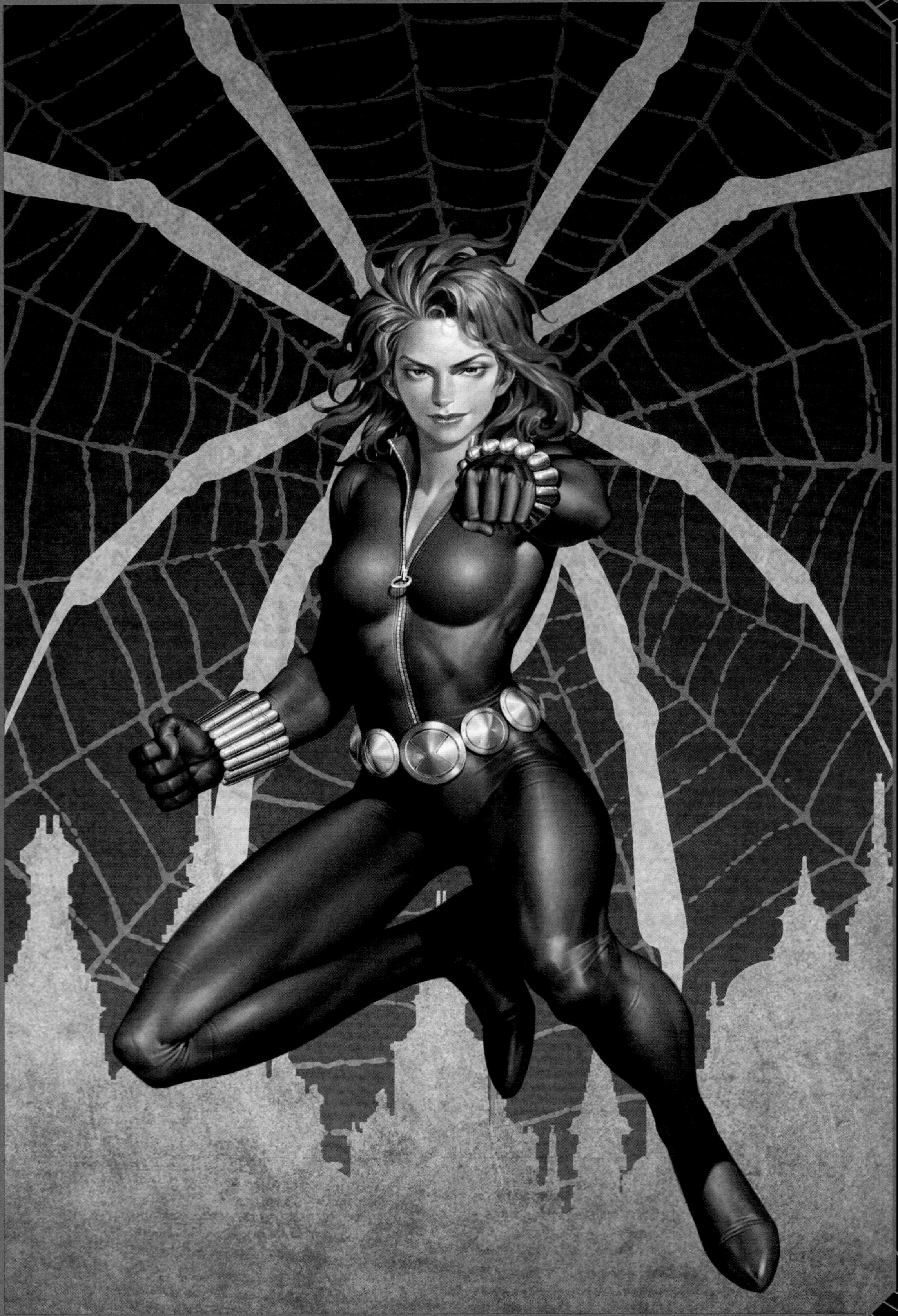

FIVE

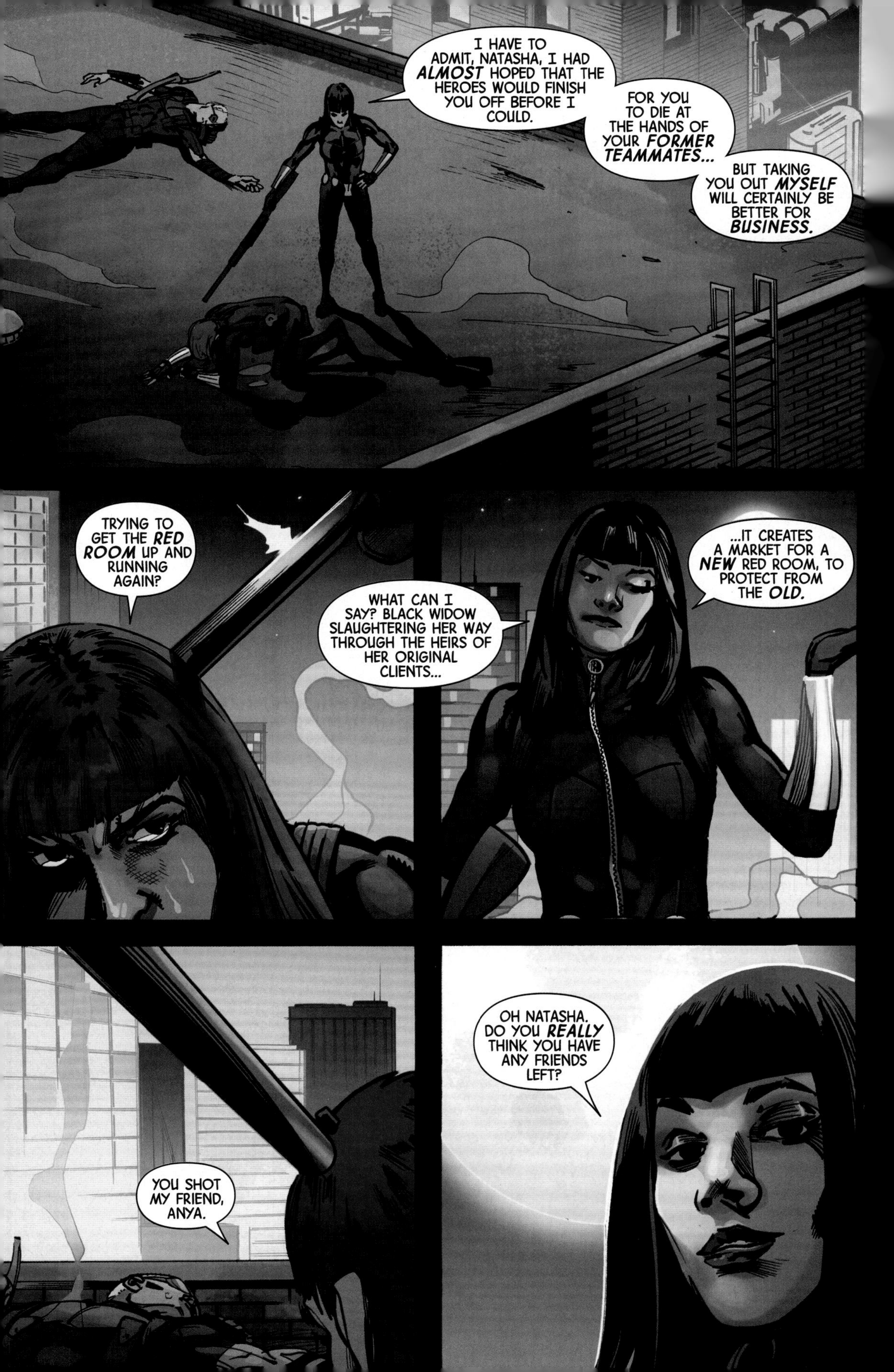
I HAVE TO ADMIT, NATASHA, I HAD ALMOST HOPED THAT THE HEROES WOULD FINISH YOU OFF BEFORE I COULD.
FOR YOU TO DIE AT THE HANDS OF YOUR FORMER TEAMMATES...
BUT TAKING YOU OUT MYSELF WILL CERTAINLY BE BETTER FOR BUSINESS.
TRYING TO GET THE RED ROOM UP AND RUNNING AGAIN?
WHAT CAN I SAY? BLACK WIDOW SLAUGHTERING HER WAY THROUGH THE HEIRS OF HER ORIGINAL CLIENTS...
...IT CREATES A MARKET FOR A NEW RED ROOM, TO PROTECT FROM THE OLD.
YOU SHOT MY FRIEND, ANYA.
OH NATASHA. DO YOU REALLY THINK YOU HAVE ANY FRIENDS LEFT?

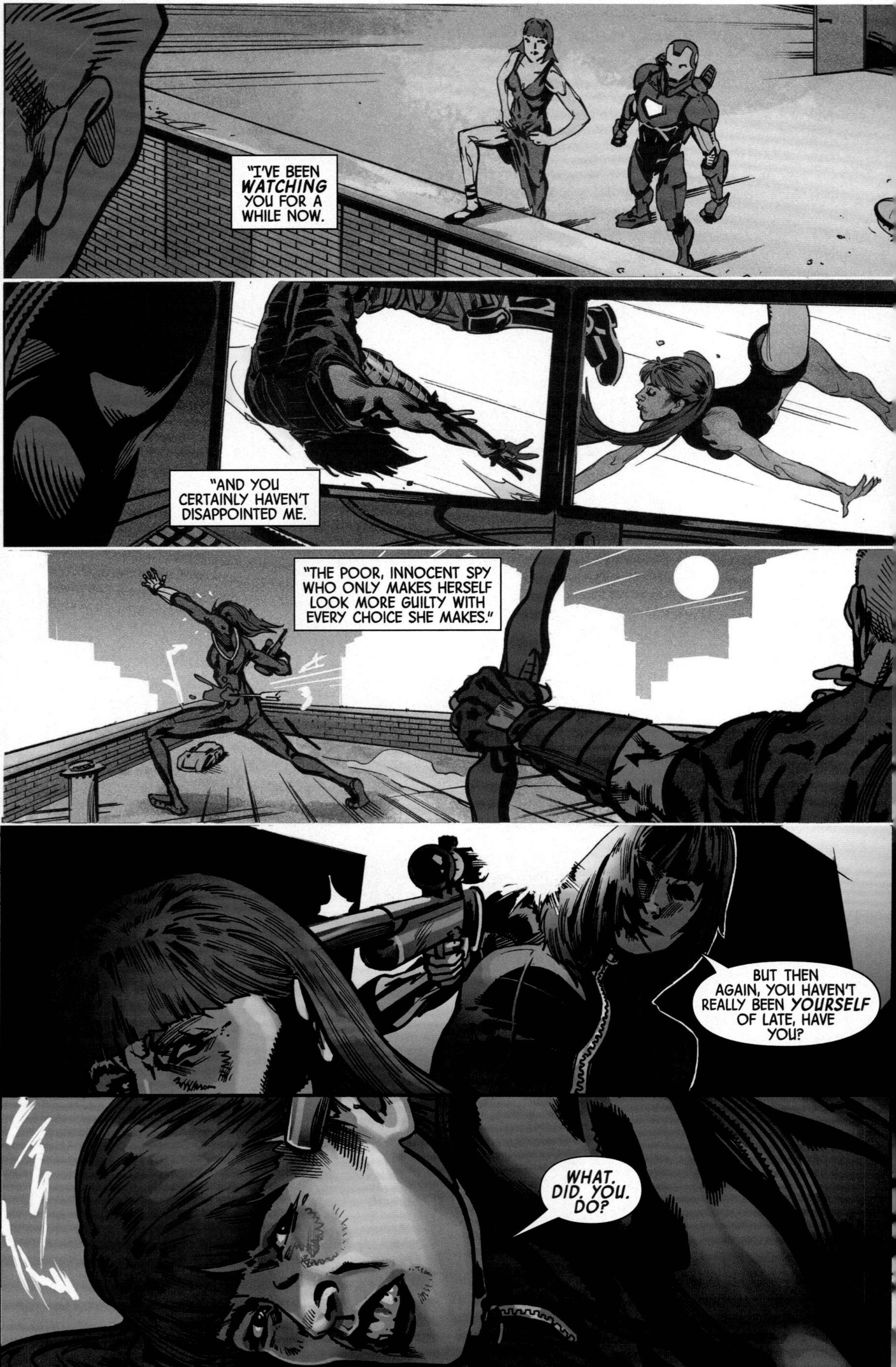
"I'VE BEEN WATCHING YOU FOR A WHILE NOW.
"AND YOU CERTAINLY HAVEN'T DISAPPOINTED ME.
"THE POOR, INNOCENT SPY WHO ONLY MAKES HERSELF LOOK MORE GUILTY WITH EVERY CHOICE SHE MAKES."
BUT THEN AGAIN, YOU HAVEN'T REALLY BEEN YOURSELF OF LATE, HAVE YOU?
WHAT. DID. YOU. DO?

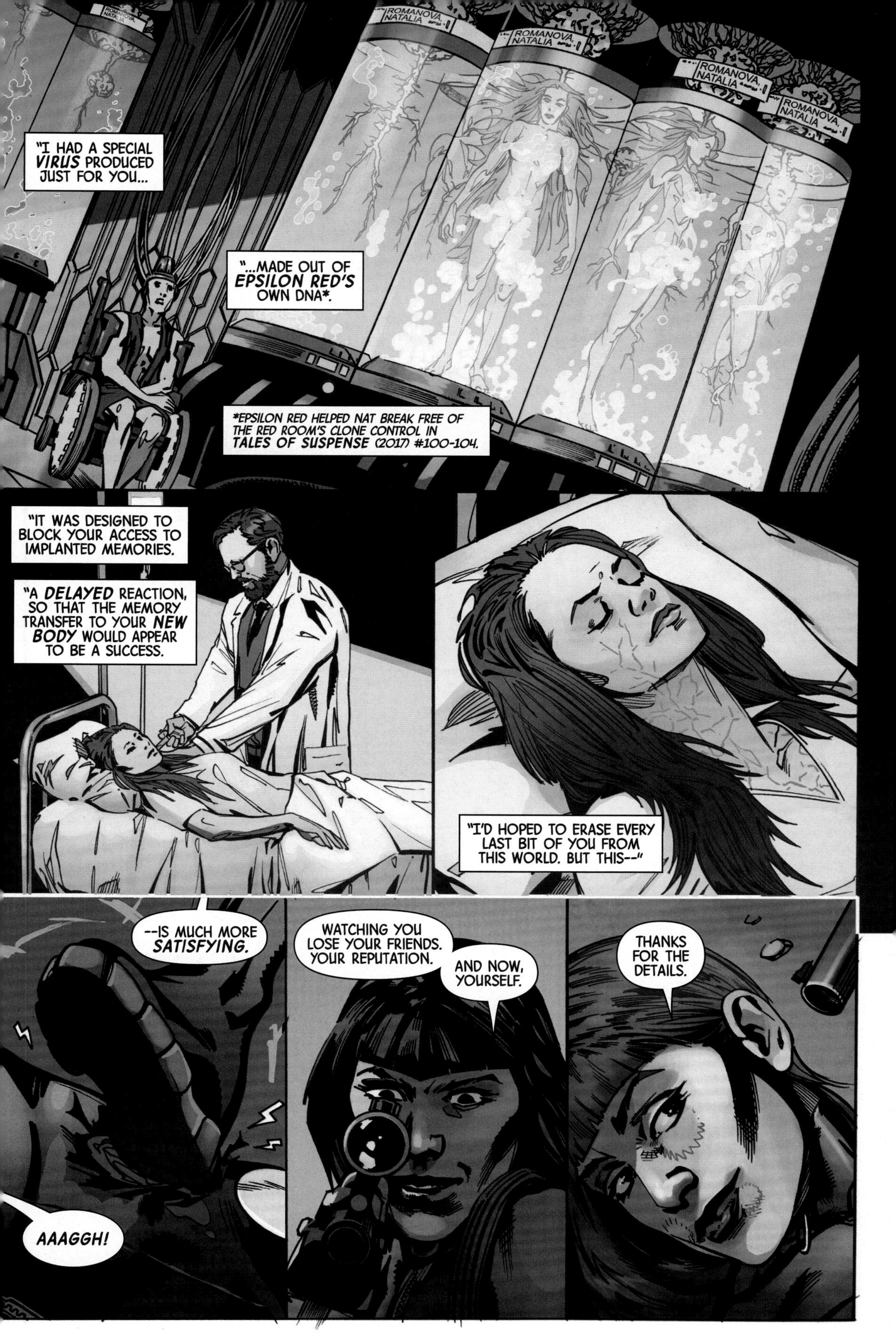

ROMANOVA, NATALIA
ROMANOVA, NATALIA
ROMANOVA, NATALIA
ROMANOVA, NATALIA
ROMANOVA, NATALIA
"I HAD A SPECIAL VIRUS PRODUCED JUST FOR YOU...
"...MADE OUT OF EPSILON RED'S OWN DNA*.
*EPSILON RED HELPED NAT BREAK FREE OF THE RED ROOM'S CLONE CONTROL IN TALES OF SUSPENSE (2017) #100-104.
"IT WAS DESIGNED TO BLOCK YOUR ACCESS TO IMPLANTED MEMORIES.
"A DELAYED REACTION, SO THAT THE MEMORY TRANSFER TO YOUR NEW BODY WOULD APPEAR TO BE A SUCCESS.
"I'D HOPED TO ERASE EVERY LAST BIT OF YOU FROM THIS WORLD. BUT THIS--"
--IS MUCH MORE SATISFYING.
AAAGGH!
WATCHING YOU LOSE YOUR FRIENDS. YOUR REPUTATION.
AND NOW, YOURSELF.
THANKS FOR THE DETAILS.

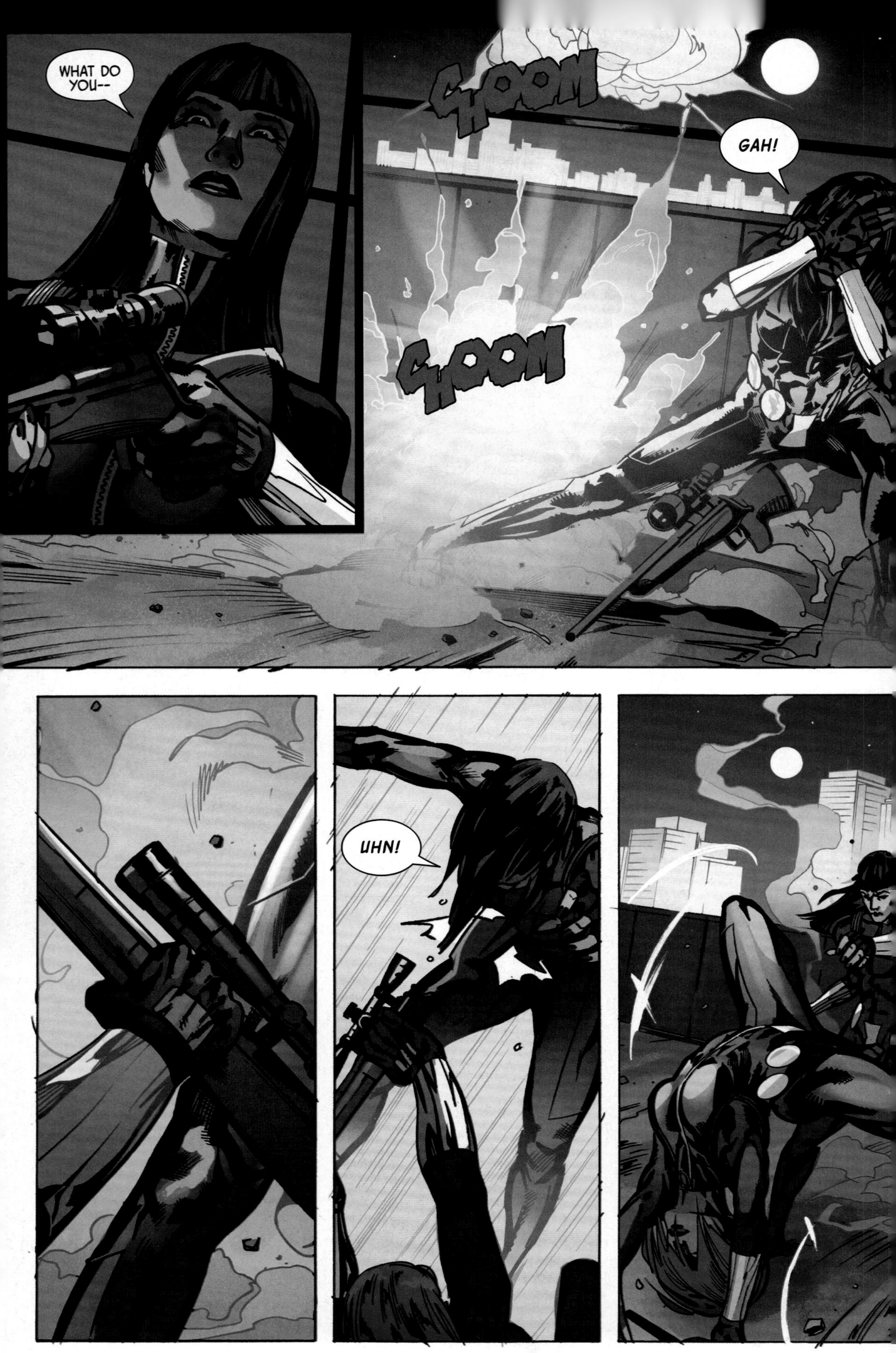
WHAT DO YOU--
CHOOM
GAH!
CHOOM
UHN!

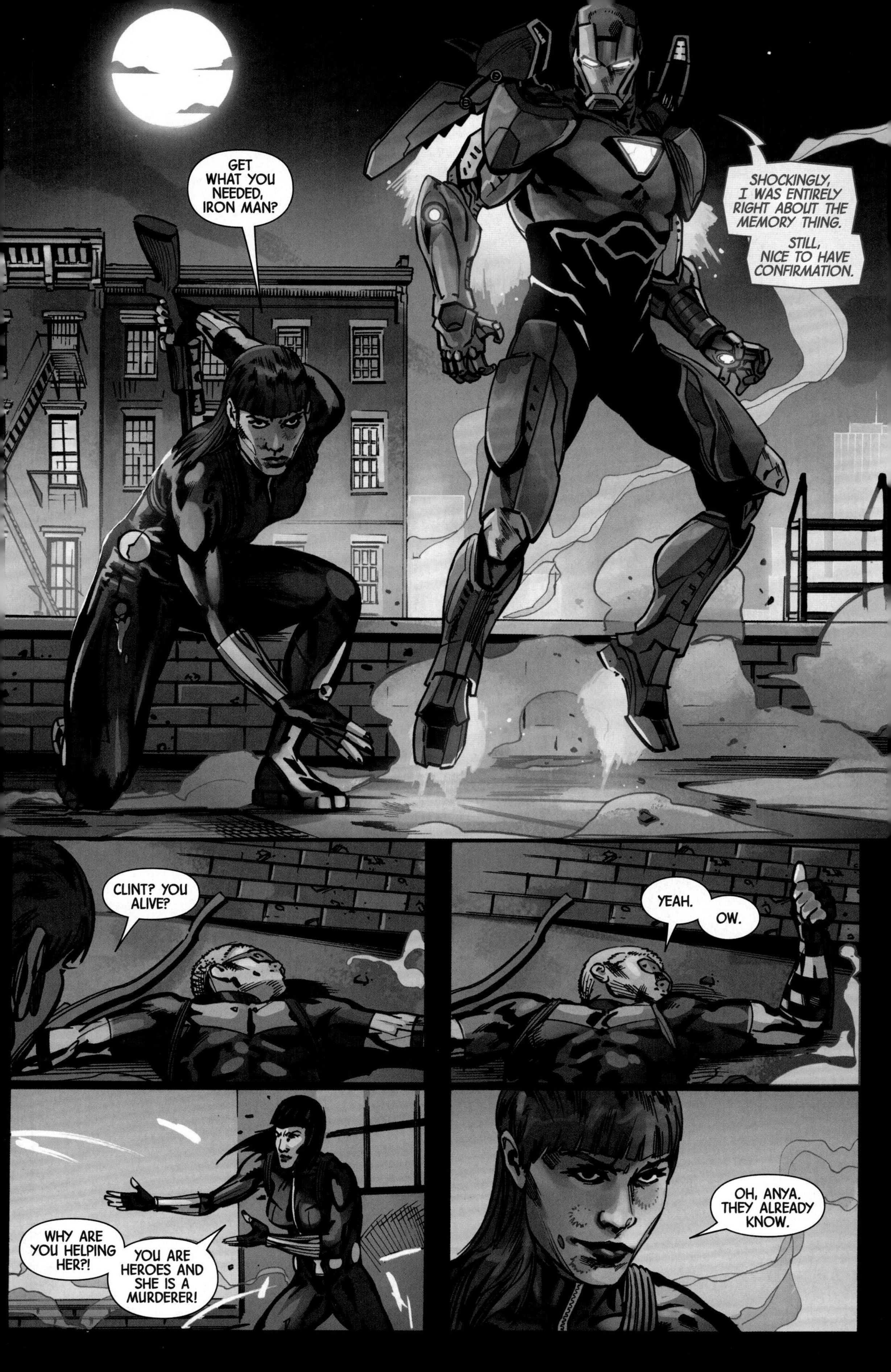
GET WHAT YOU NEEDED, IRON MAN?
SHOCKINGLY, I WAS ENTIRELY RIGHT ABOUT THE MEMORY THING.
STILL, NICE TO HAVE CONFIRMATION.
CLINT? YOU ALIVE?
YEAH.
OW.
WHY ARE YOU HELPING HER?!
YOU ARE HEROES AND SHE IS A MURDERER!
OH, ANYA. THEY ALREADY KNOW.

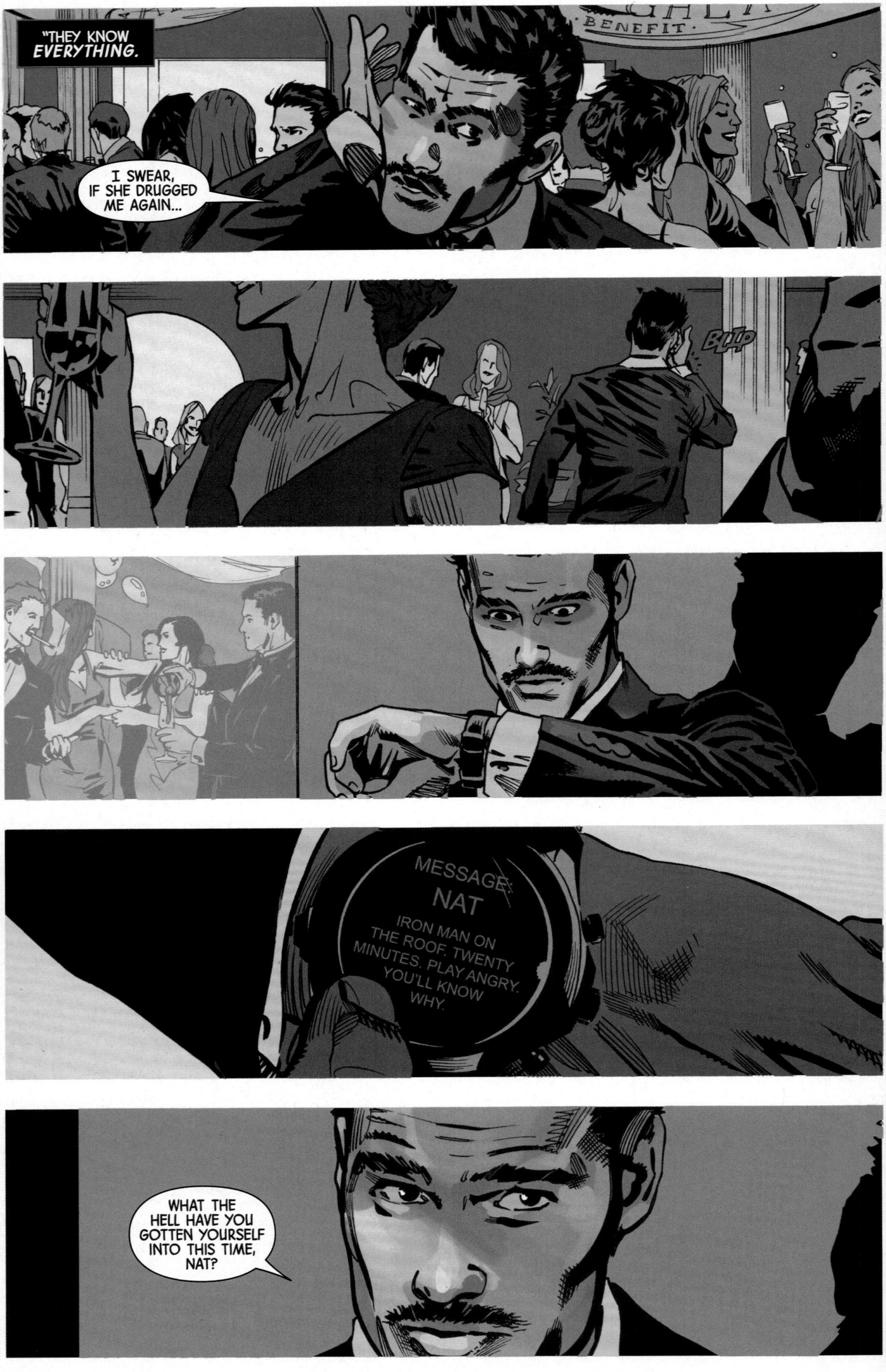
GALA BENEFIT
"THEY KNOW EVERYTHING.
I SWEAR, IF SHE DRUGGED ME AGAIN...
BLIP
MESSAGE: NAT
IRON MAN ON THE ROOF. TWENTY MINUTES. PLAY ANGRY. YOU'LL KNOW WHY.
WHAT THE HELL HAVE YOU GOTTEN YOURSELF INTO THIS TIME, NAT?

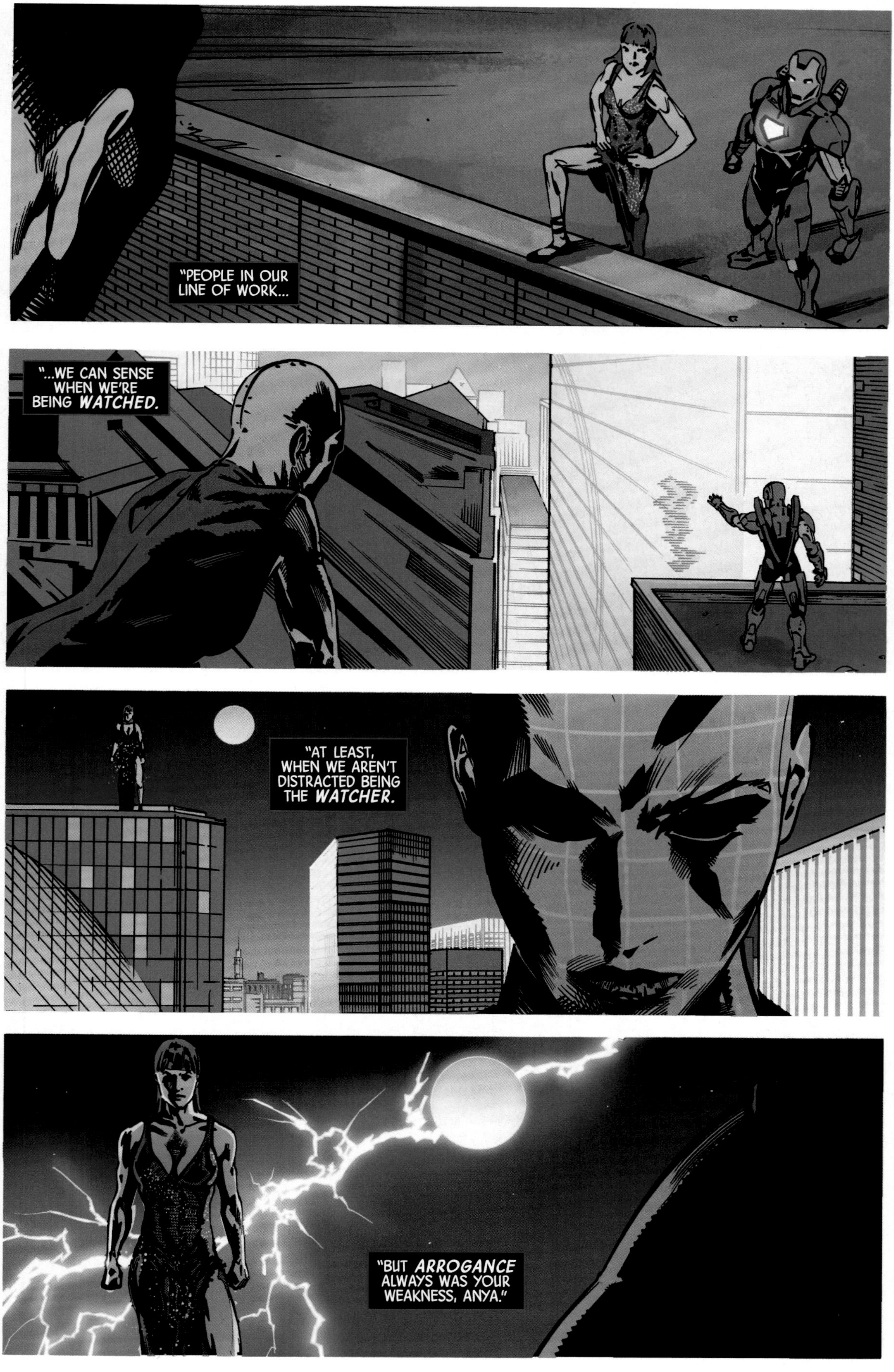
"PEOPLE IN OUR LINE OF WORK...
"...WE CAN SENSE WHEN WE'RE BEING WATCHED.
"AT LEAST, WHEN WE AREN'T DISTRACTED BEING THE WATCHER.
"BUT ARROGANCE ALWAYS WAS YOUR WEAKNESS, ANYA."

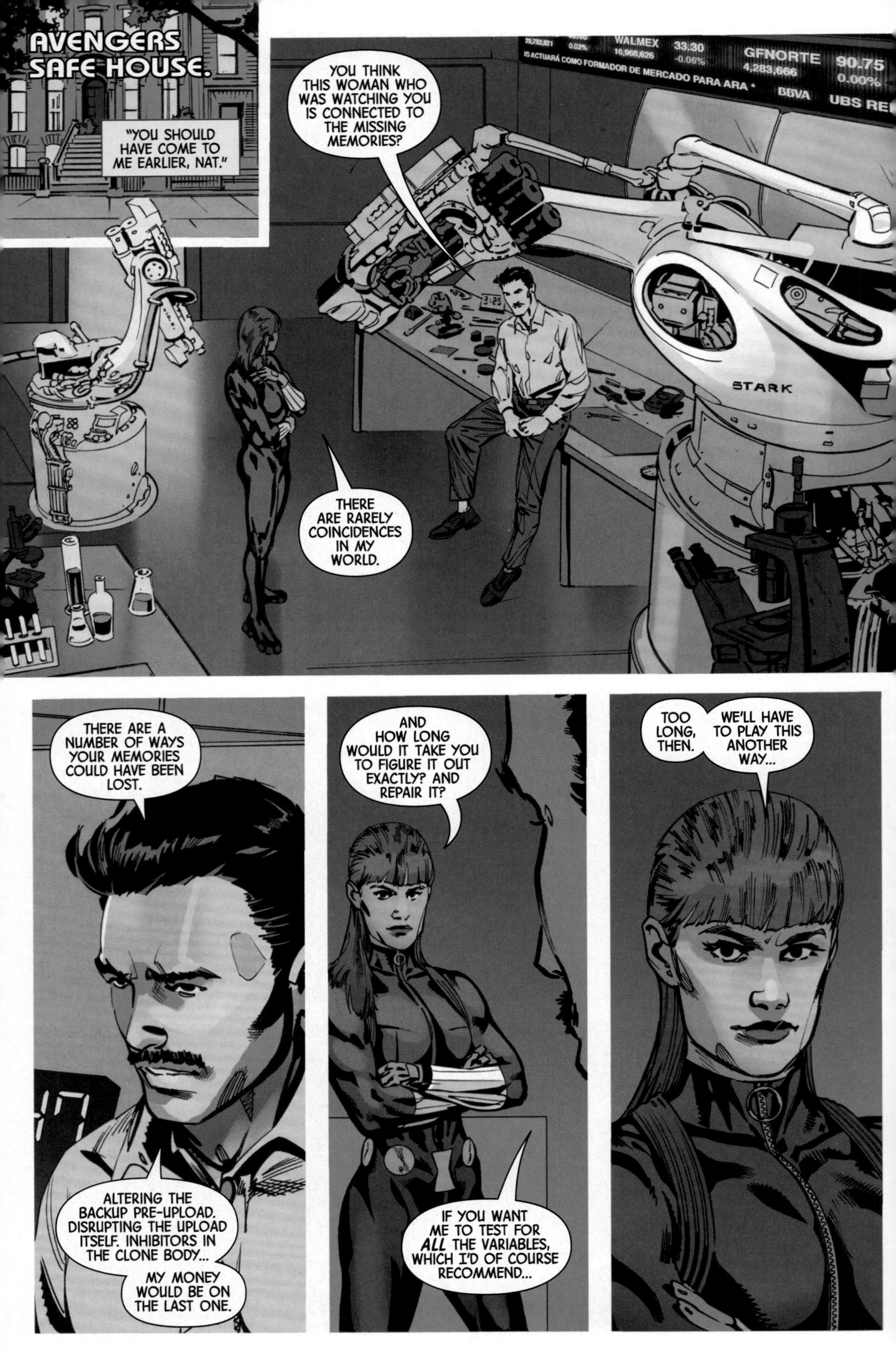
AVENGERS SAFE HOUSE.
"YOU SHOULD HAVE COME TO ME EARLIER, NAT."
YOU THINK THIS WOMAN WHO WAS WATCHING YOU IS CONNECTED TO THE MISSING MEMORIES?
THERE ARE RARELY COINCIDENCES IN MY WORLD.
WALMEX 33.30
GFNORTE 90.75
STARK
THERE ARE A NUMBER OF WAYS YOUR MEMORIES COULD HAVE BEEN LOST.
ALTERING THE BACKUP PRE-UPLOAD. DISRUPTING THE UPLOAD ITSELF. INHIBITORS IN THE CLONE BODY...
MY MONEY WOULD BE ON THE LAST ONE.
AND HOW LONG WOULD IT TAKE YOU TO FIGURE IT OUT EXACTLY? AND REPAIR IT?
IF YOU WANT ME TO TEST FOR *ALL* THE VARIABLES, WHICH I'D OF COURSE RECOMMEND...
TOO LONG, THEN.
WE'LL HAVE TO PLAY THIS ANOTHER WAY...

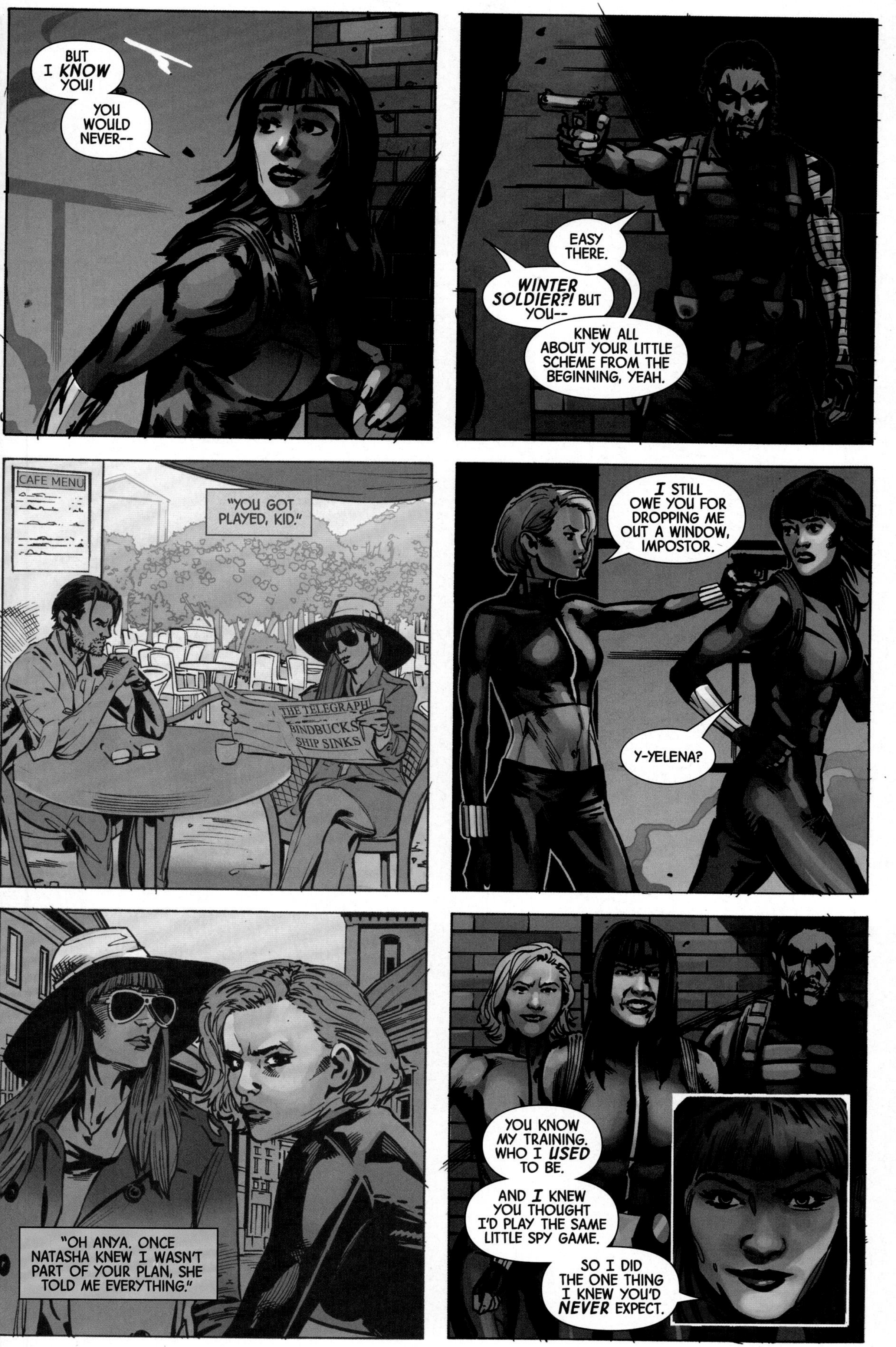
BUT I KNOW YOU!
YOU WOULD NEVER--
EASY THERE.
WINTER SOLDIER?! BUT YOU--
KNEW ALL ABOUT YOUR LITTLE SCHEME FROM THE BEGINNING, YEAH.
CAFE MENU
"YOU GOT PLAYED, KID."
THE TELEGRAPH
BINDBUCKS SHIP SINKS
I STILL OWE YOU FOR DROPPING ME OUT A WINDOW, IMPOSTOR.
Y-YELENA?
"OH ANYA. ONCE NATASHA KNEW I WASN'T PART OF YOUR PLAN, SHE TOLD ME EVERYTHING."
YOU KNOW MY TRAINING. WHO I USED TO BE.
AND I KNEW YOU THOUGHT I'D PLAY THE SAME LITTLE SPY GAME.
SO I DID THE ONE THING I KNEW YOU'D NEVER EXPECT.

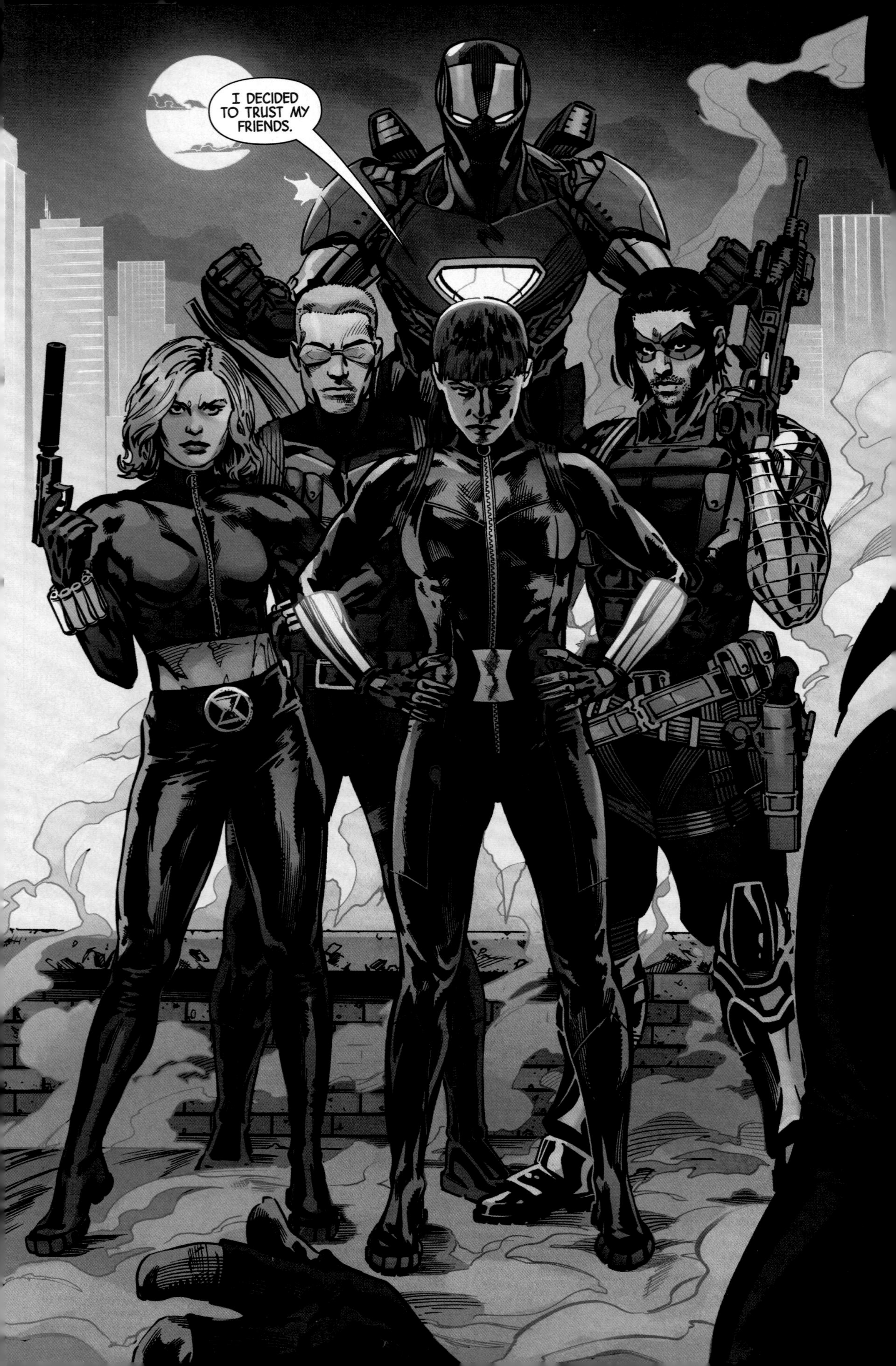
I DECIDED TO TRUST MY FRIENDS.

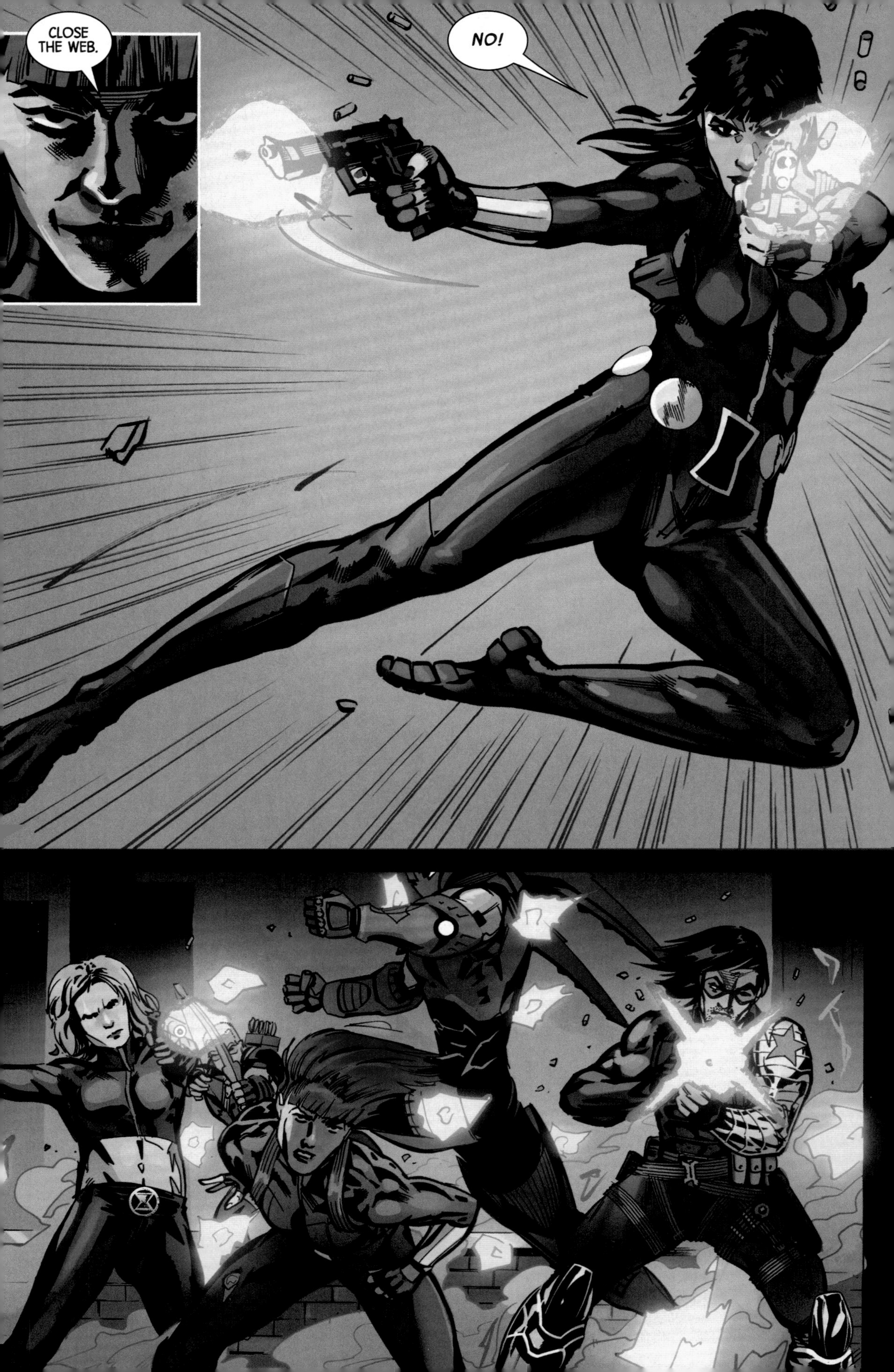
CLOSE THE WEB.
NO!

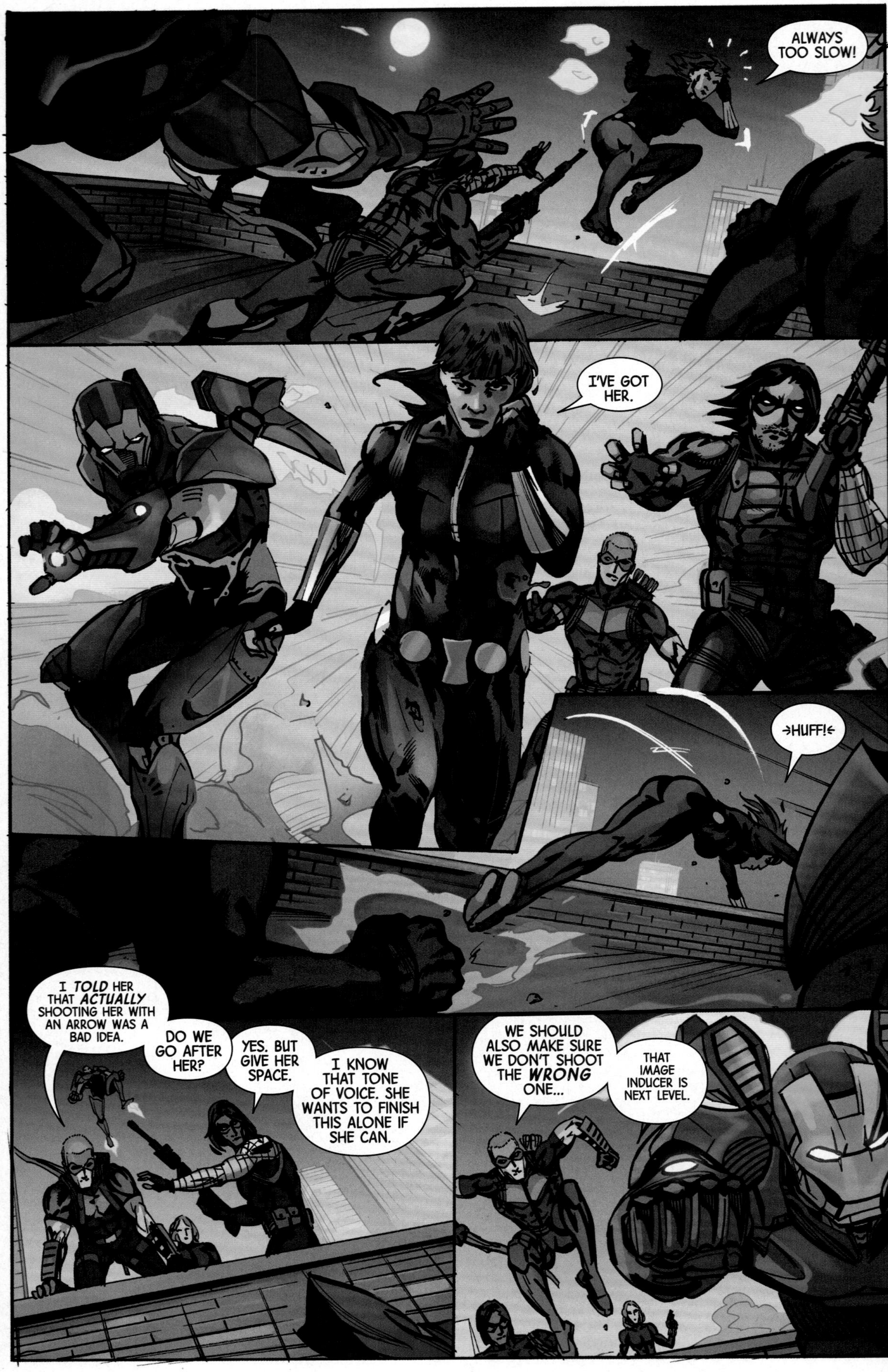
ALWAYS TOO SLOW!
I'VE GOT HER.
HUFF!
I TOLD HER THAT ACTUALLY SHOOTING HER WITH AN ARROW WAS A BAD IDEA.
DO WE GO AFTER HER?
YES. BUT GIVE HER SPACE.
I KNOW THAT TONE OF VOICE. SHE WANTS TO FINISH THIS ALONE IF SHE CAN.
WE SHOULD ALSO MAKE SURE WE DON'T SHOOT THE WRONG ONE...
THAT IMAGE INDUCER IS NEXT LEVEL.

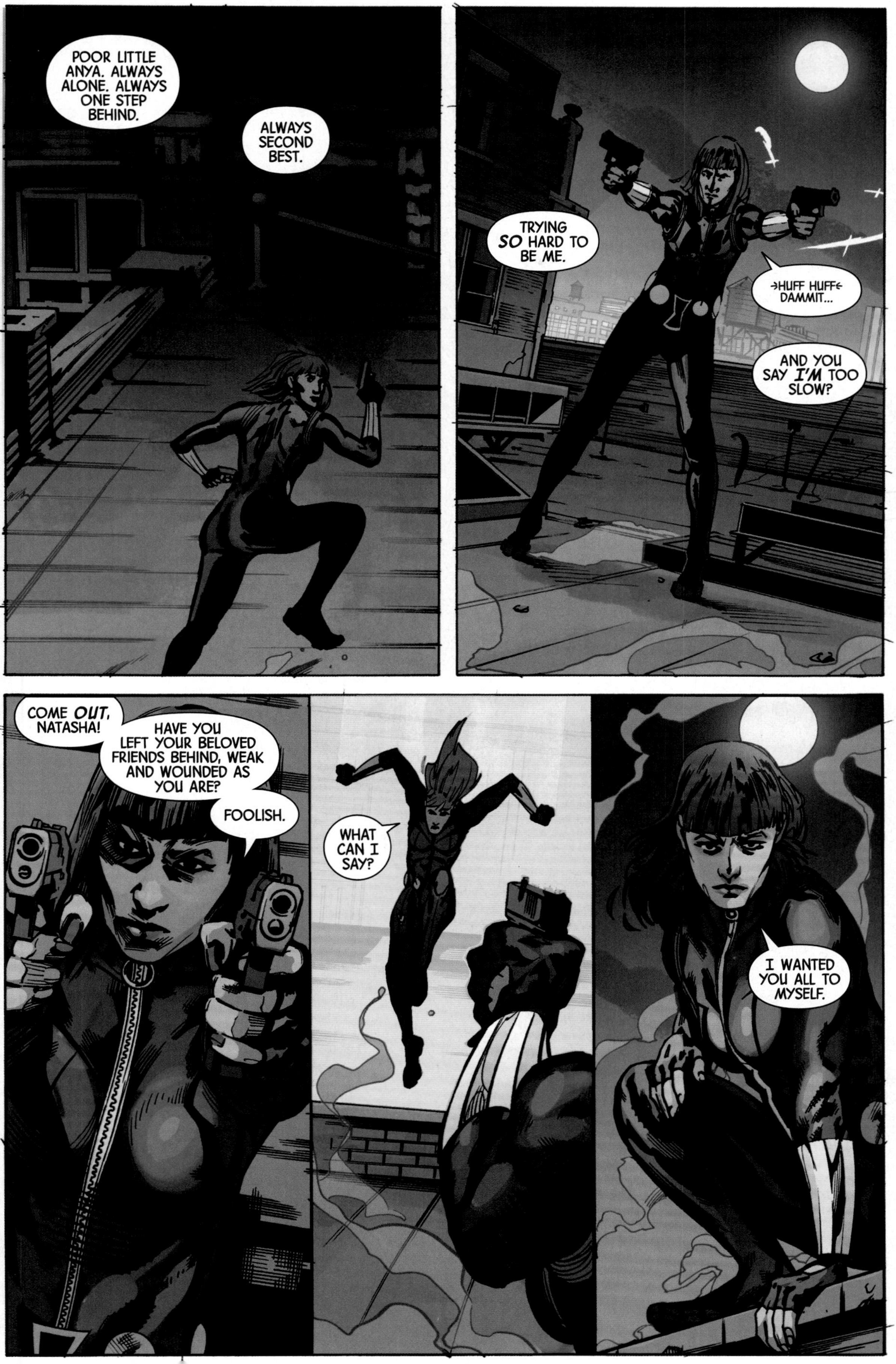
POOR LITTLE ANYA. ALWAYS ALONE. ALWAYS ONE STEP BEHIND.
ALWAYS SECOND BEST.
TRYING SO HARD TO BE ME.
HUFF HUFF DAMMIT...
AND YOU SAY I'M TOO SLOW?
COME OUT, NATASHA!
HAVE YOU LEFT YOUR BELOVED FRIENDS BEHIND, WEAK AND WOUNDED AS YOU ARE?
FOOLISH.
WHAT CAN I SAY?
I WANTED YOU ALL TO MYSELF.

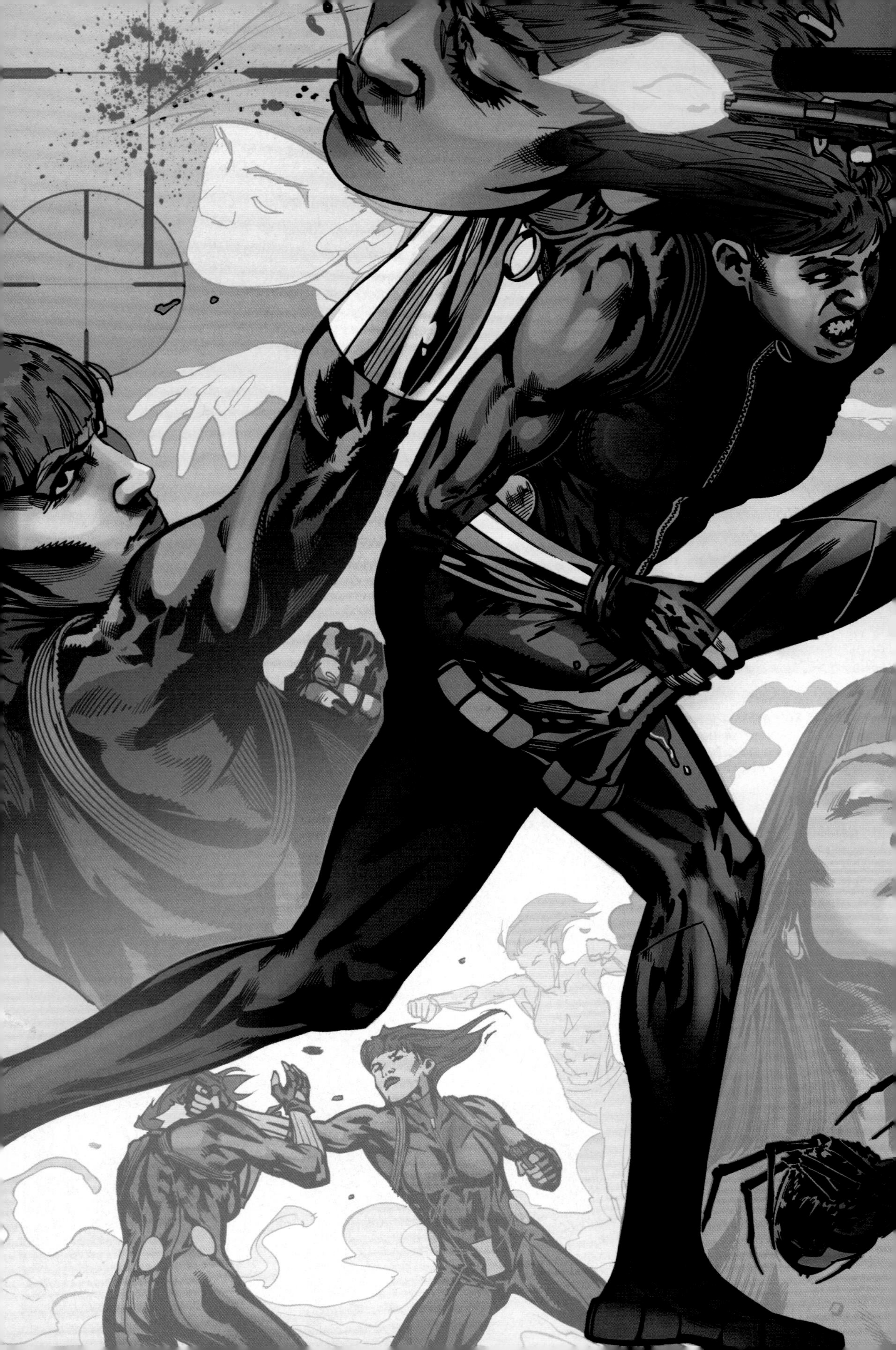

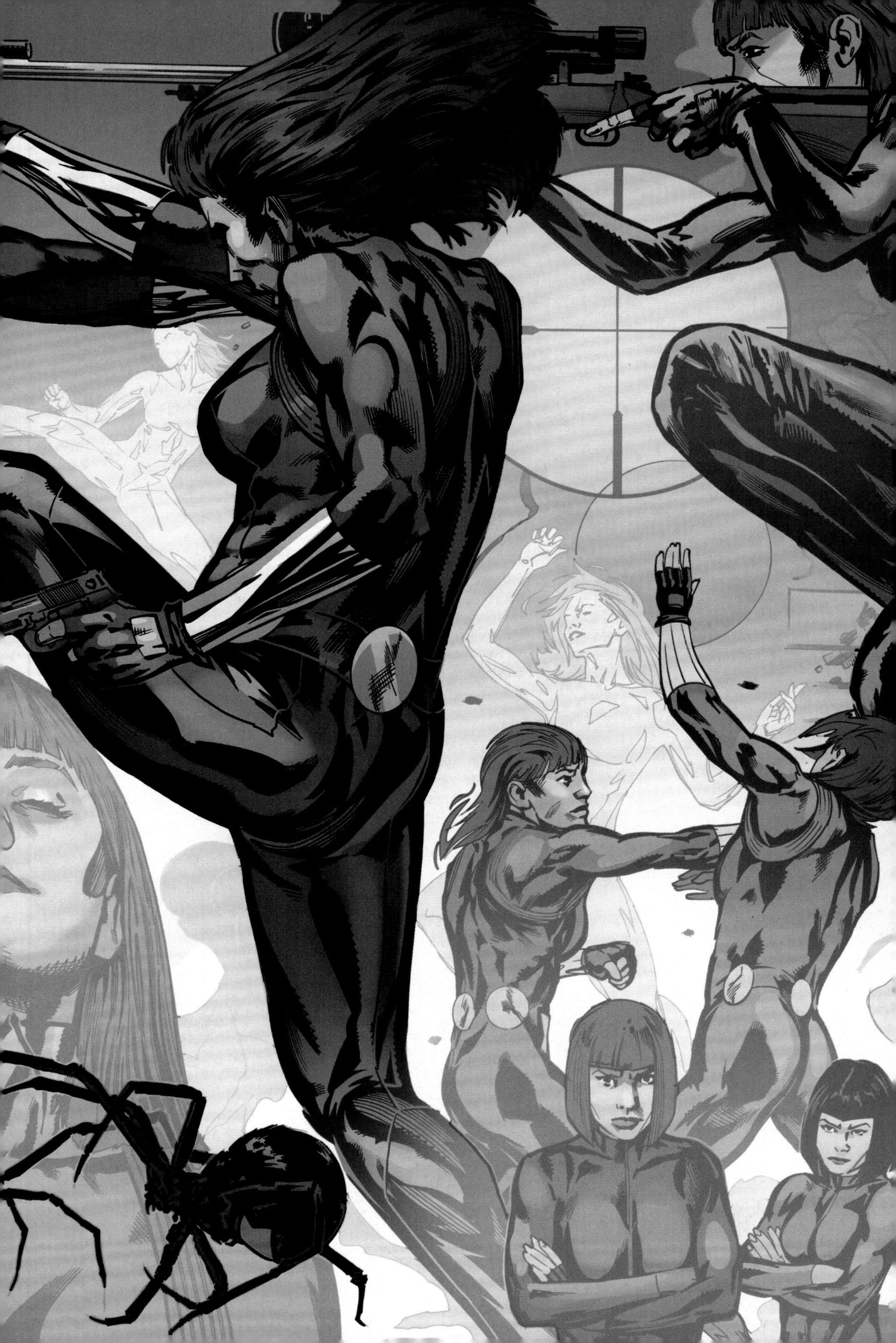

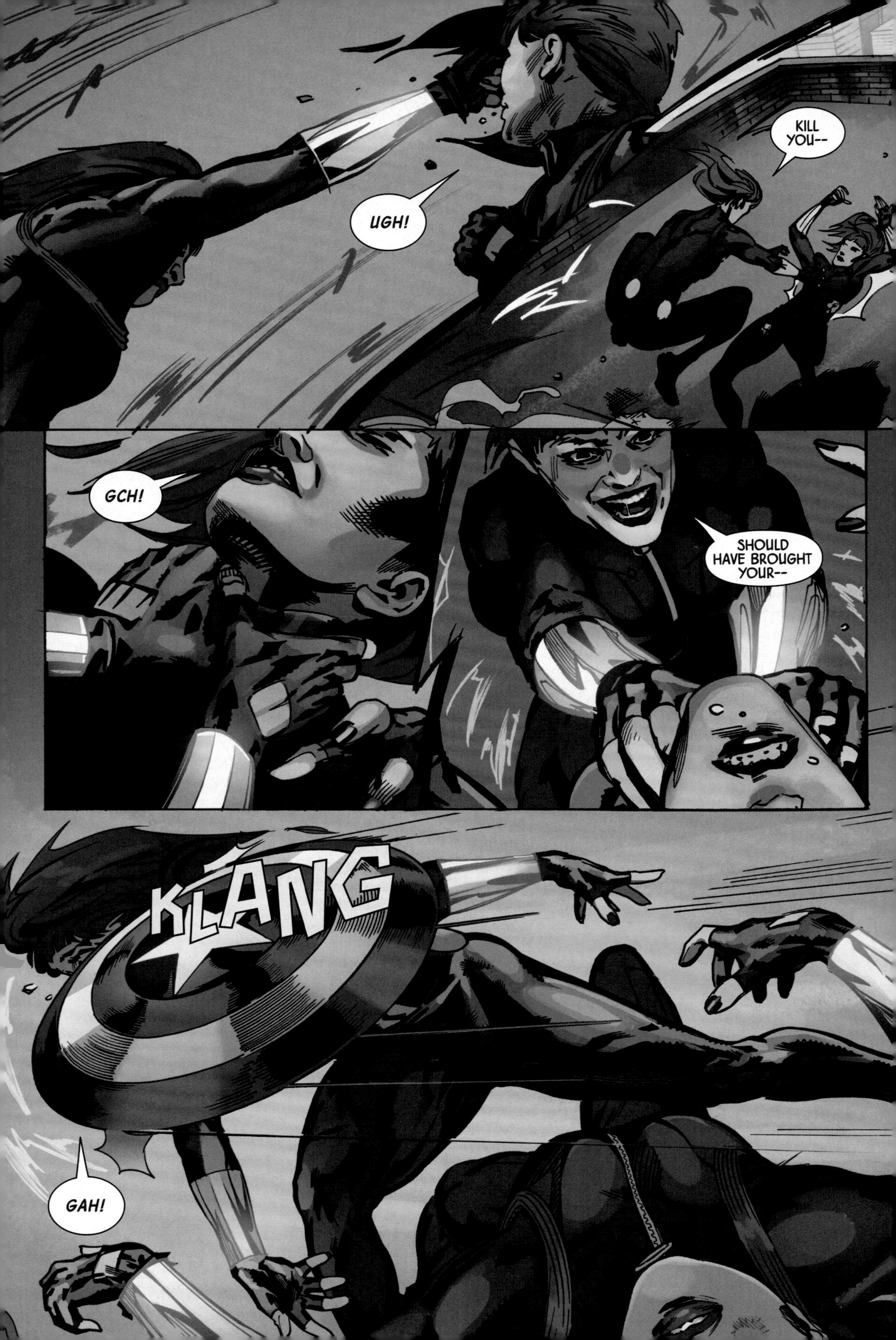
KILL YOU--
UGH!
GCH!
SHOULD HAVE BROUGHT YOUR--
KLANG
GAH!

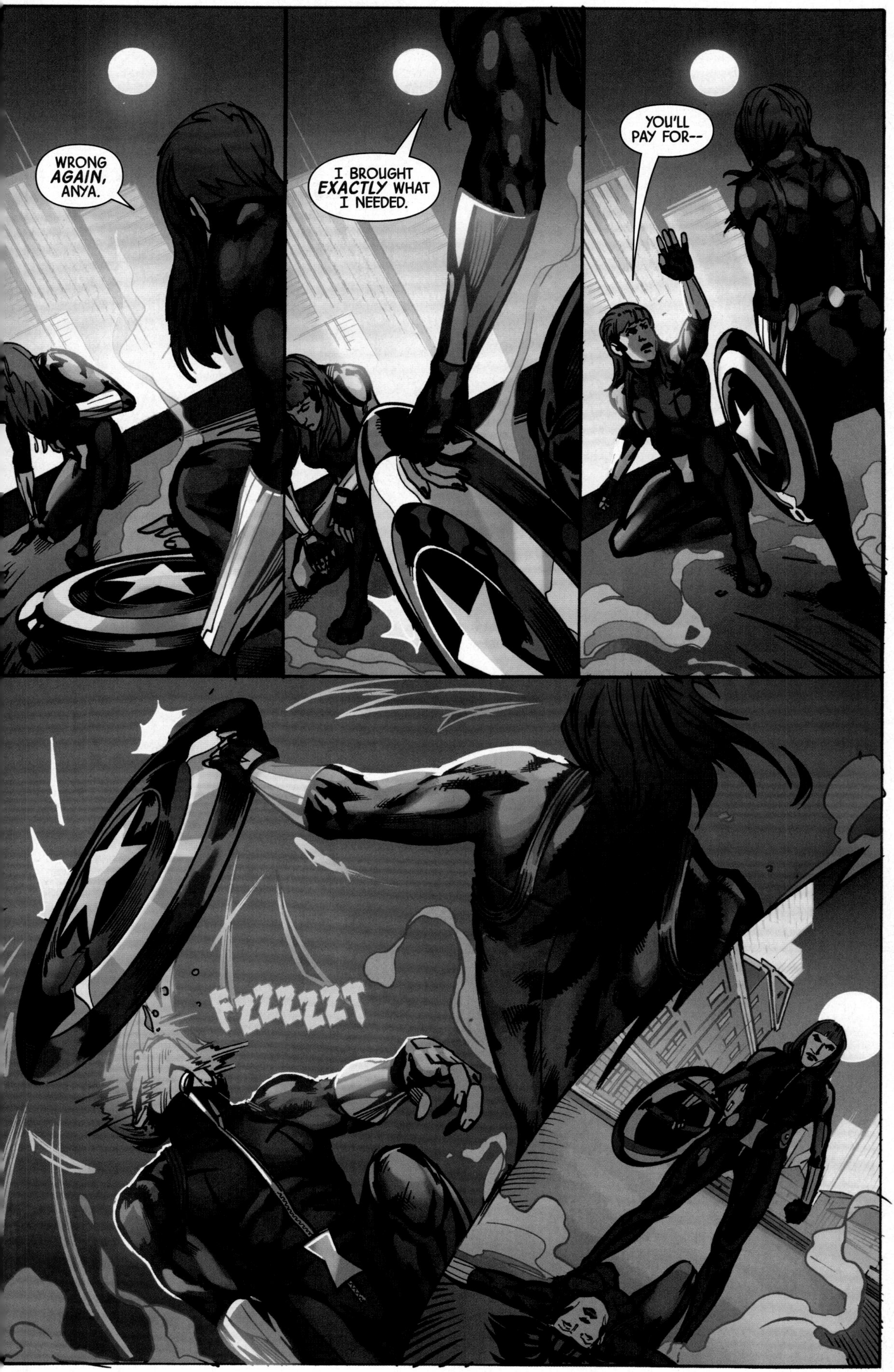
WRONG AGAIN, ANYA.
I BROUGHT EXACTLY WHAT I NEEDED.
YOU'LL PAY FOR--
FZZZZZT

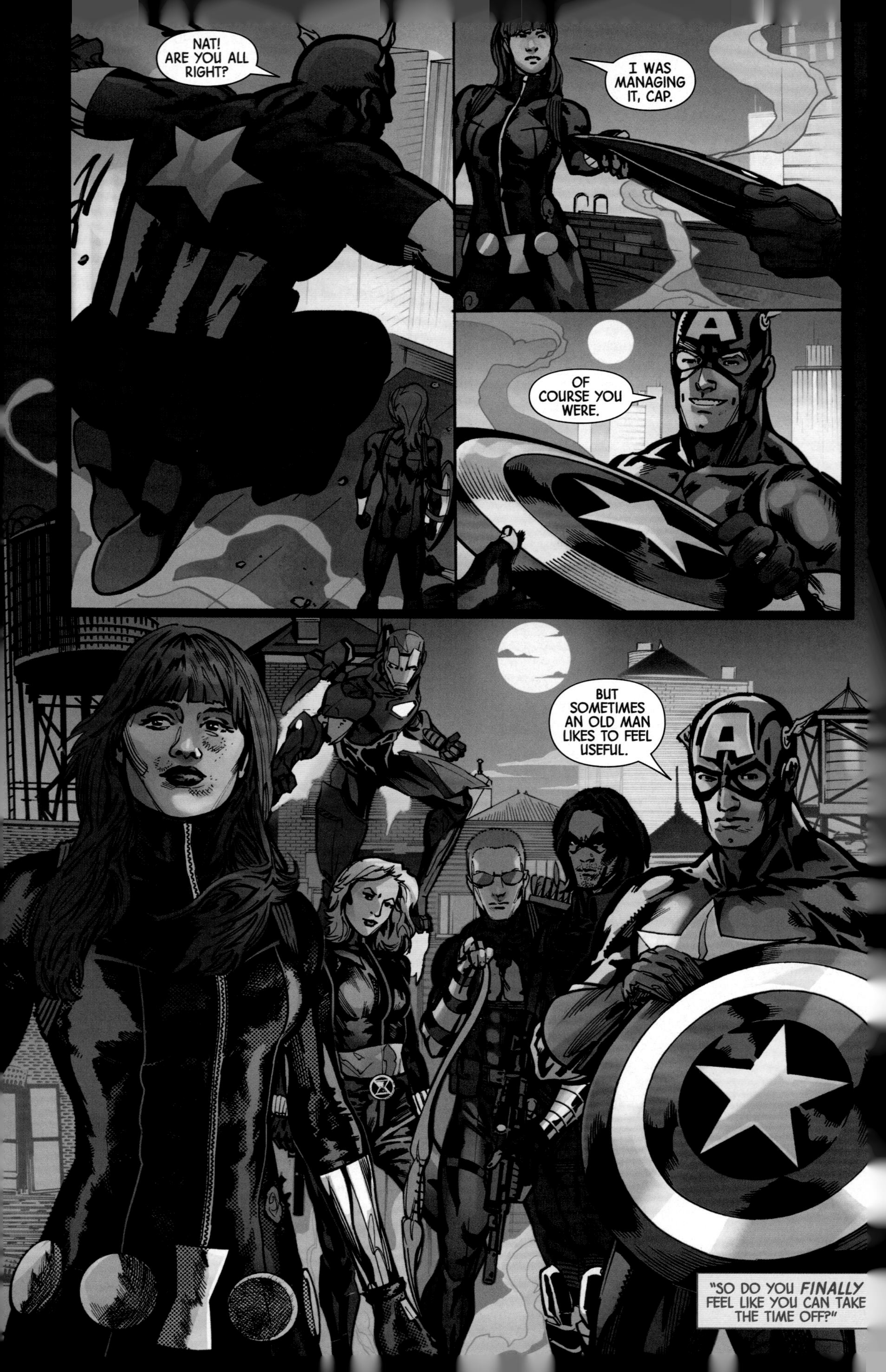
NAT! ARE YOU ALL RIGHT?
I WAS MANAGING IT, CAP.
OF COURSE YOU WERE.
BUT SOMETIMES AN OLD MAN LIKES TO FEEL USEFUL.
"SO DO YOU FINALLY FEEL LIKE YOU CAN TAKE THE TIME OFF?"

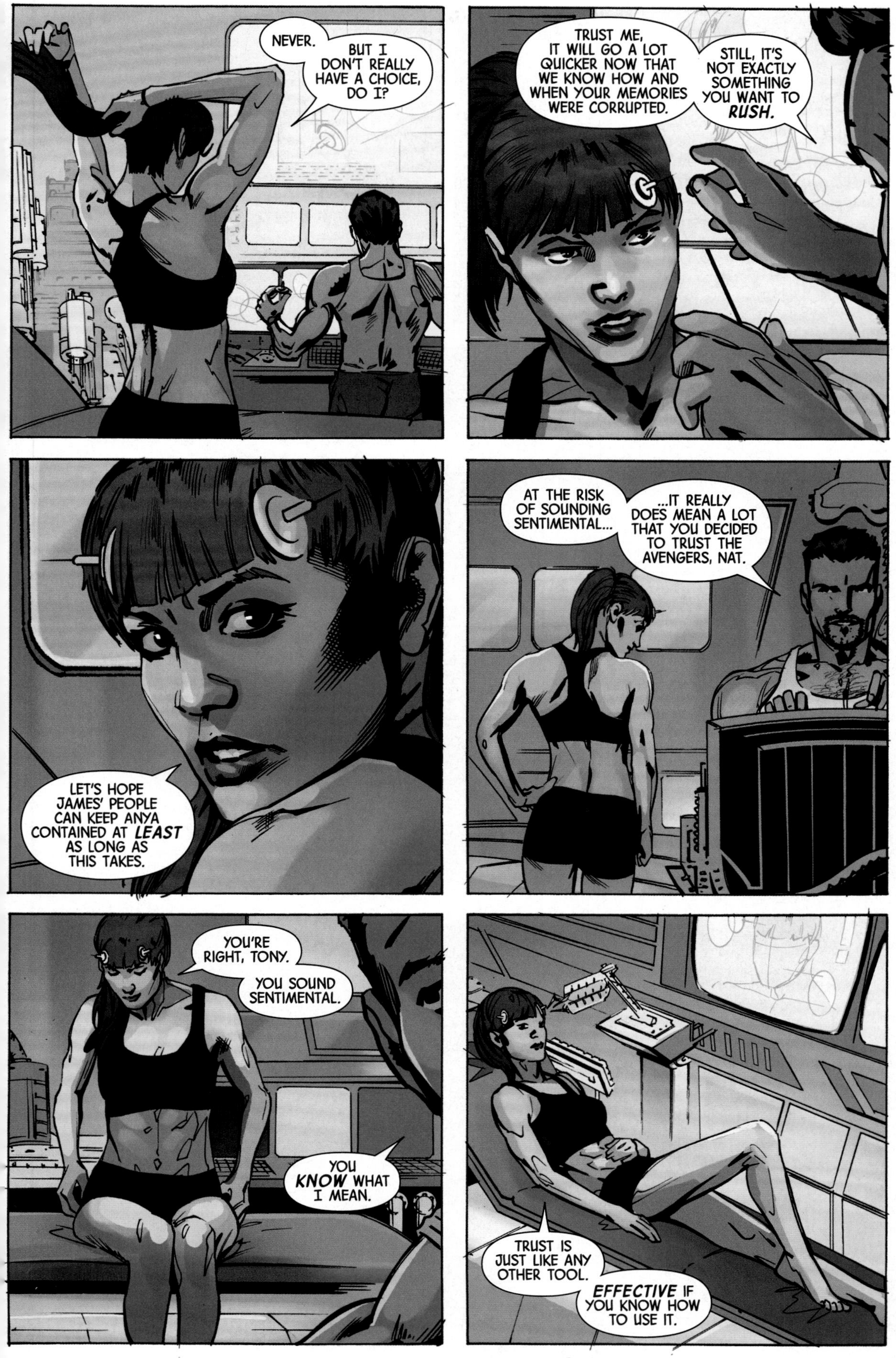
NEVER.
BUT I DON'T REALLY HAVE A CHOICE, DO I?
TRUST ME, IT WILL GO A LOT QUICKER NOW THAT WE KNOW HOW AND WHEN YOUR MEMORIES WERE CORRUPTED.
STILL, IT'S NOT EXACTLY SOMETHING YOU WANT TO RUSH.
LET'S HOPE JAMES' PEOPLE CAN KEEP ANYA CONTAINED AT LEAST AS LONG AS THIS TAKES.
AT THE RISK OF SOUNDING SENTIMENTAL...
...IT REALLY DOES MEAN A LOT THAT YOU DECIDED TO TRUST THE AVENGERS, NAT.
YOU'RE RIGHT, TONY.
YOU SOUND SENTIMENTAL.
YOU KNOW WHAT I MEAN.
TRUST IS JUST LIKE ANY OTHER TOOL.
EFFECTIVE IF YOU KNOW HOW TO USE IT.

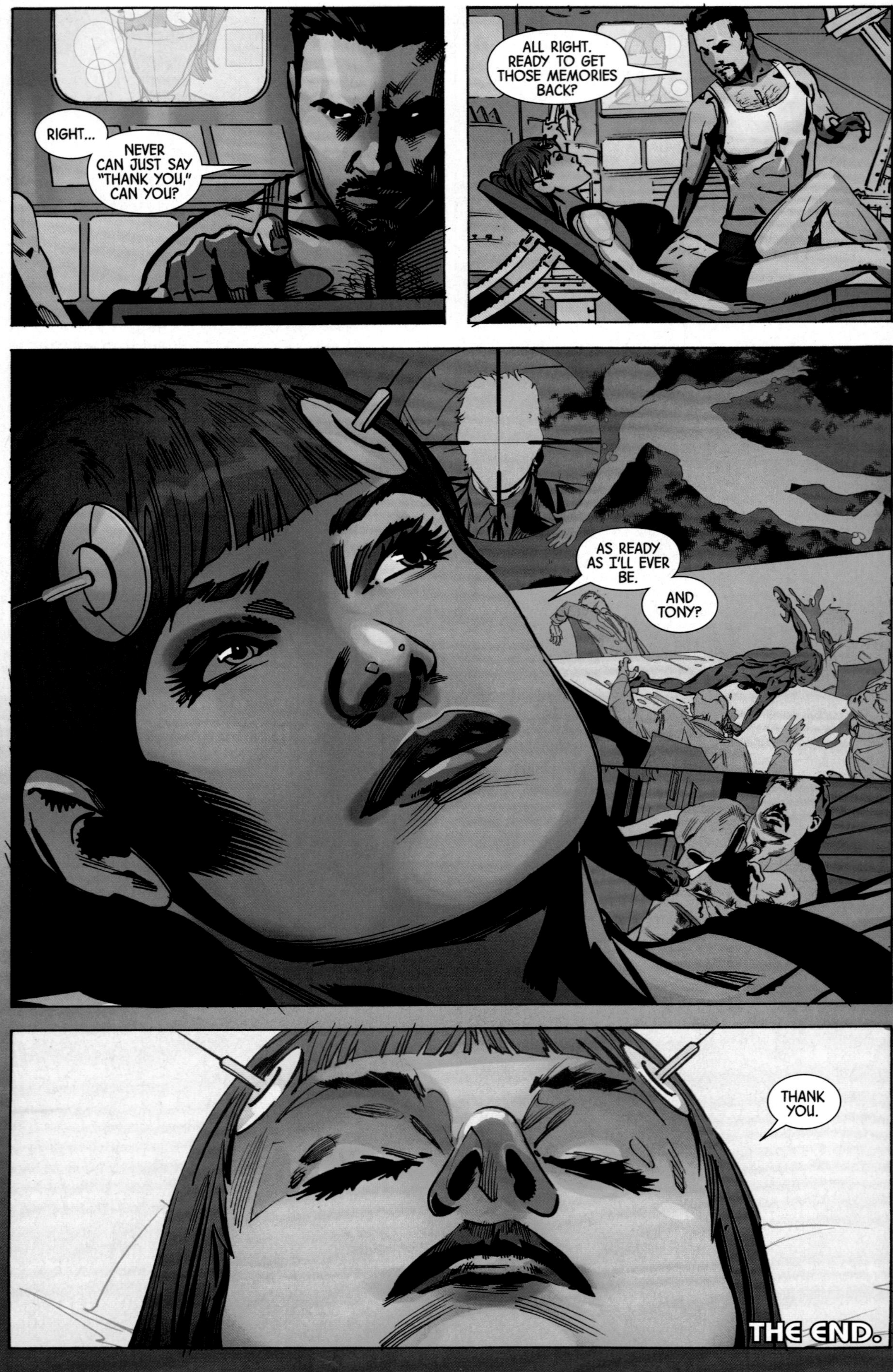
RIGHT...
NEVER CAN JUST SAY "THANK YOU," CAN YOU?
ALL RIGHT. READY TO GET THOSE MEMORIES BACK?
AS READY AS I'LL EVER BE.
AND TONY?
THANK YOU.
THE END.

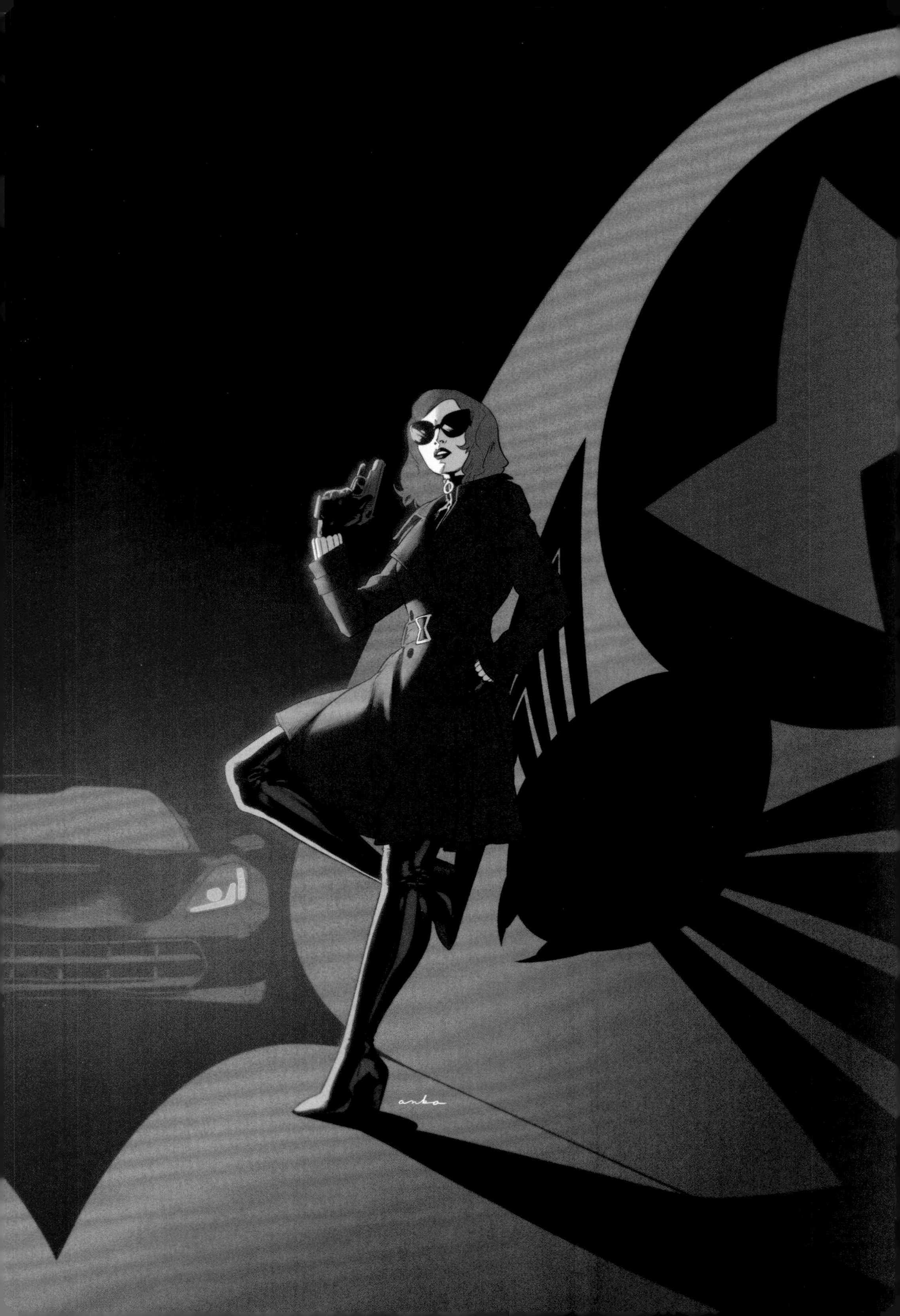
anka

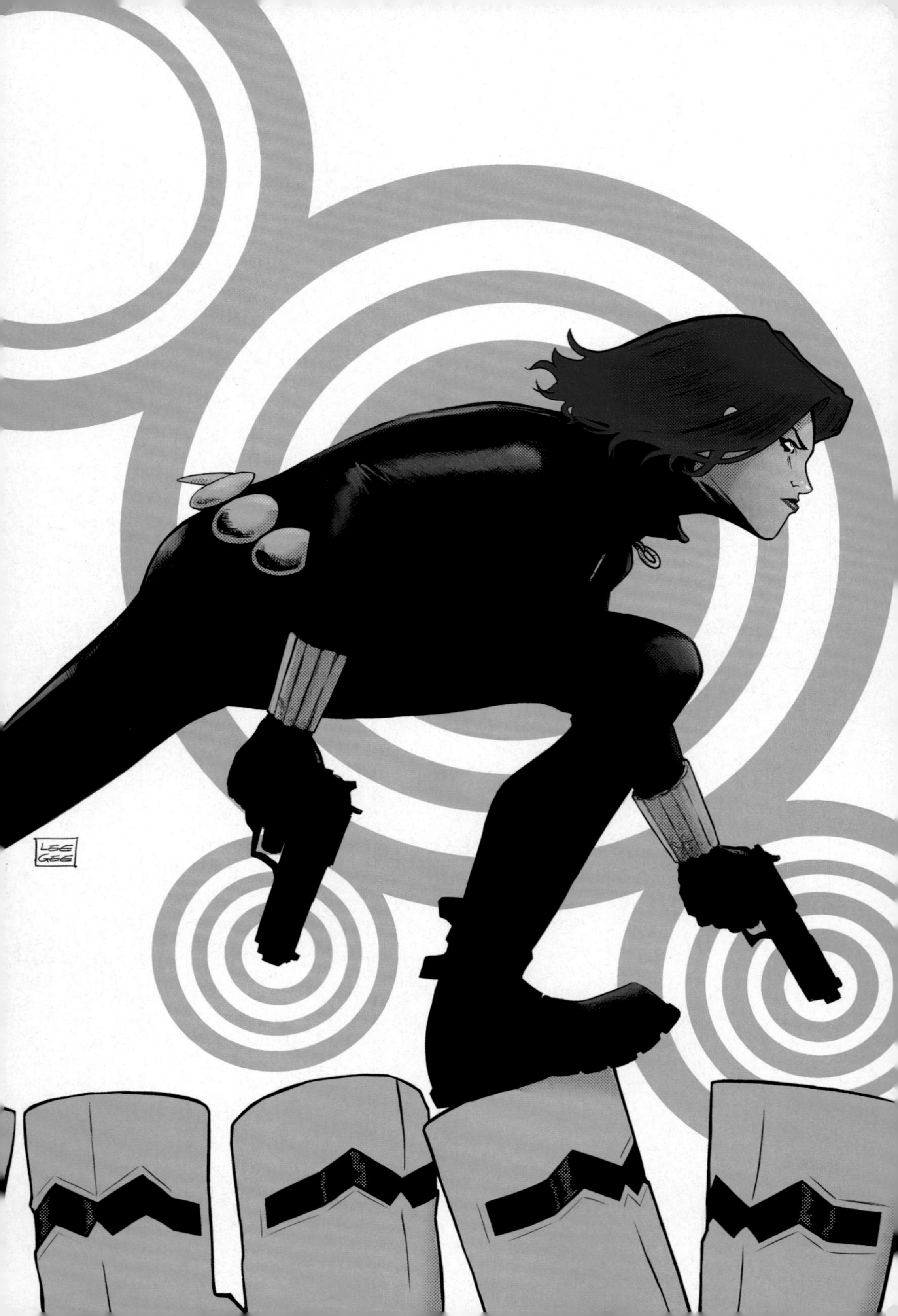

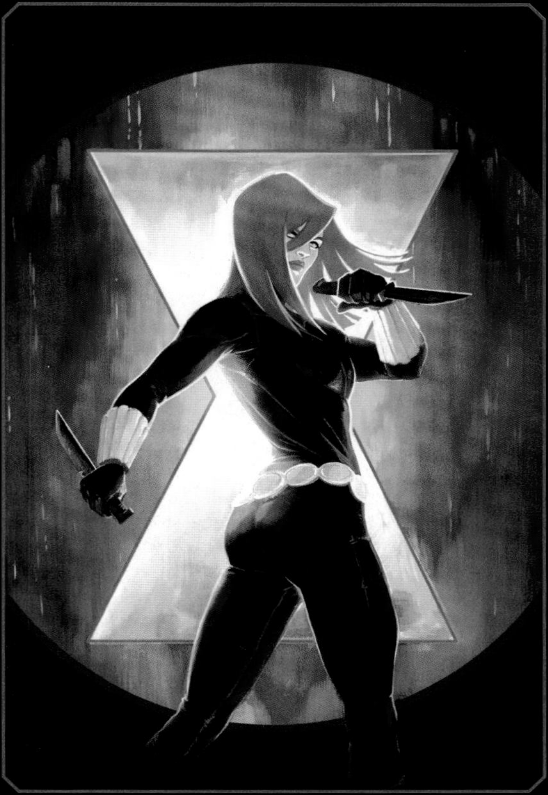

MEGHAN HETRICK
#1 VARIANT

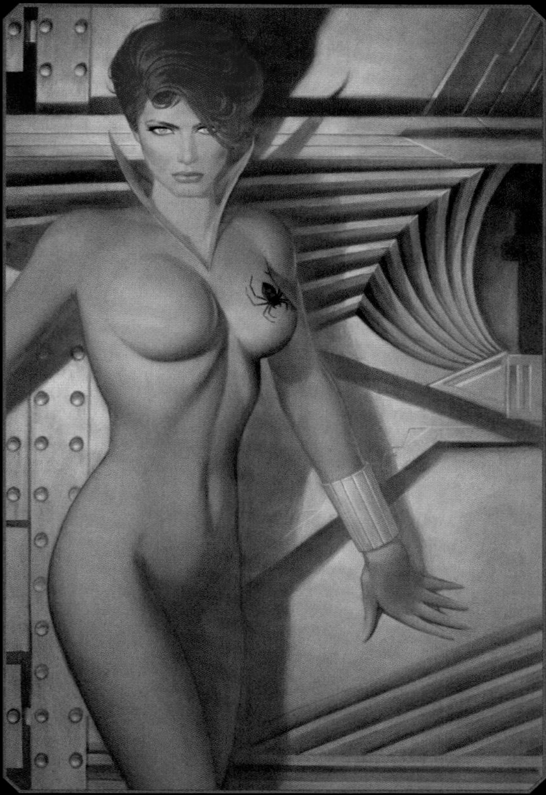

JOE CHIODO
#1 HIDDEN GEM VARIANT

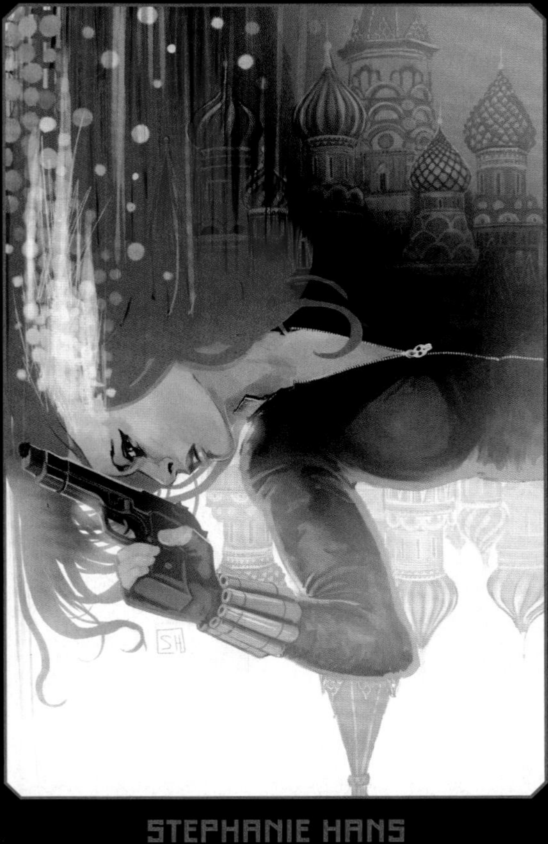

STEPHANIE HANS
#2 VARIANT

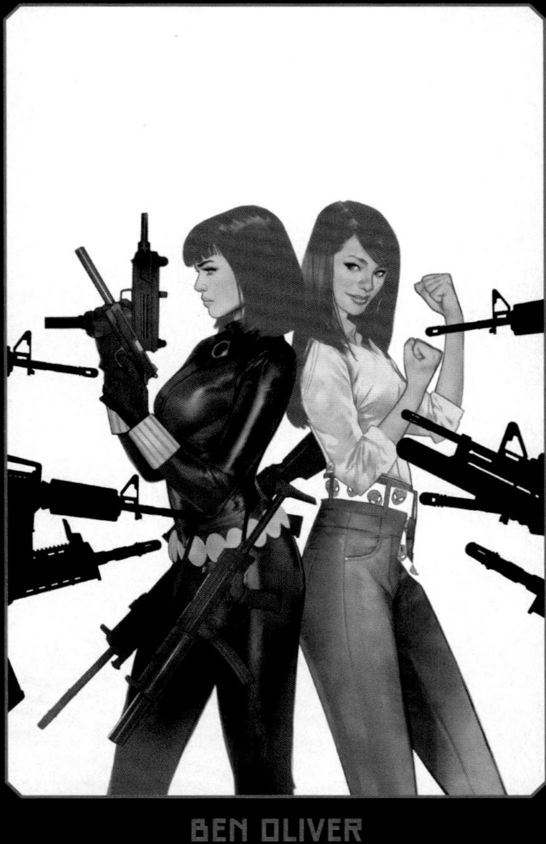

BEN OLIVER
#2 MARY JANE VARIANT

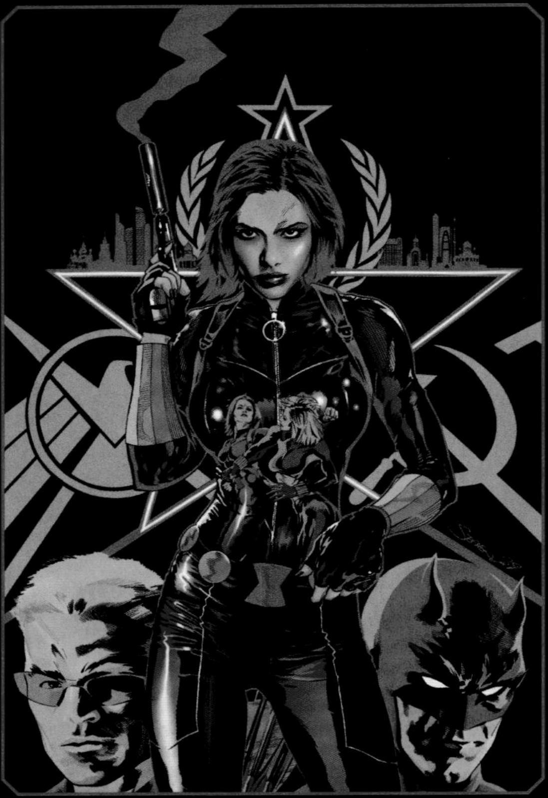

STEPHEN MOONEY
#3 VARIANT

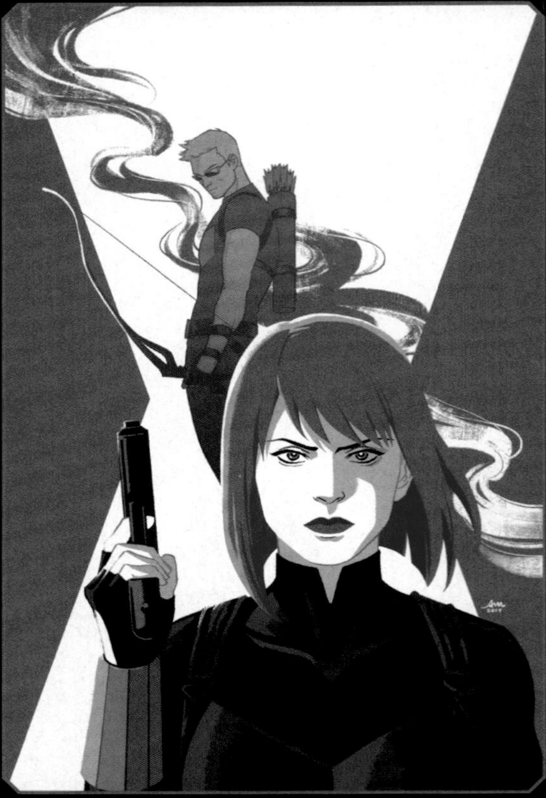

AUDREY MOK
#4 VARIANT

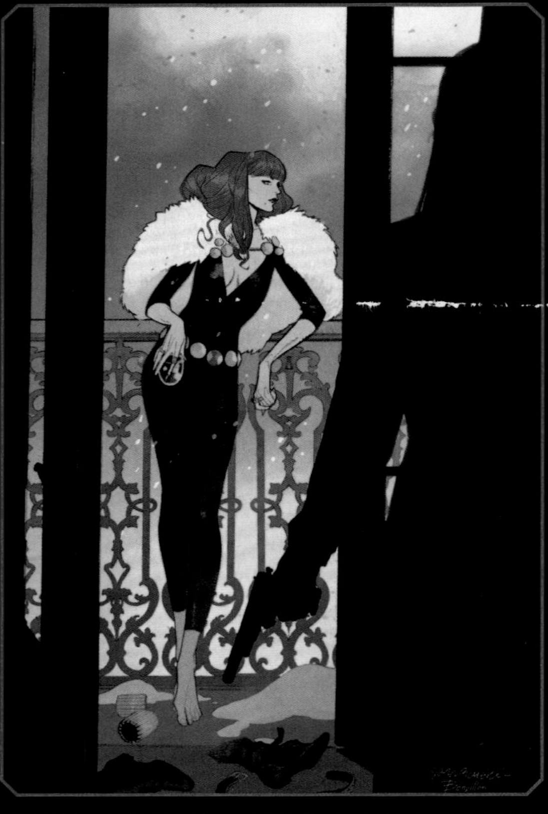

SARA PICHELLI & TAMRA BONVILLAIN
#5 VARIANT

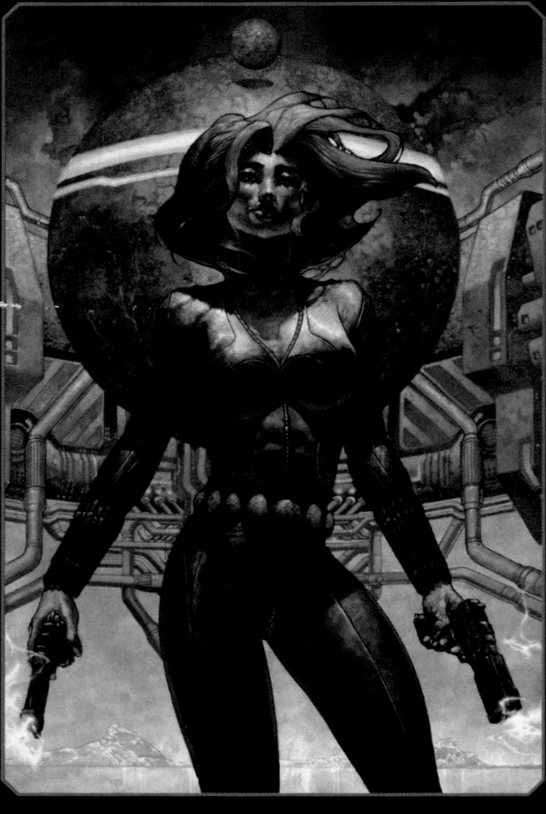

SIMONE BIANCHI
#5 VARIANT